Contested Ground

Contested Ground

HOW TO UNDERSTAND THE LIMITS OF PRESIDENTIAL POWER

Daniel A. Farber

UNIVERSITY OF CALIFORNIA PRESS

University of California Press
Oakland, California

© 2021 by Daniel Farber

Library of Congress Cataloging-in-Publication Data

Names: Farber, Daniel A., 1950- author.
Title: Contested ground : how to understand the limits of presidential
    power / Daniel Farber.
Description: Oakland, California : University of California Press,
    [2021] | Includes bibliographical references and index.
Identifiers: LCCN 2021001867 (print) | LCCN 2021001868 (ebook) |
    ISBN 9780520343948 (cloth) | ISBN 9780520975279 (epub)
Subjects: LCSH: Executive power—United States. | Presidents—
    United States. | Separation of powers—United States. | United
    States. Supreme Court—Decision making.
Classification: LCC KF5053 .F37 2021 (print) | LCC KF5053 (ebook) |
    DDC 342.73/062—dc23
LC record available at https://lccn.loc.gov/2021001867
LC ebook record available at https://lccn.loc.gov/2021001868

Manufactured in the United States of America

30 29 28 27 26 25 24 23 22 21
10 9 8 7 6 5 4 3 2 1

To my grandchildren, Joe Jr., Helene, and Emma

Contents

Preface

When I drafted this preface, we were in the final weeks of the Trump administration. I have since added a few references to the Biden administration to the text, as well as an afterword dealing with President Trump's second impeachment. Throughout his presidency, Trump utilized his executive powers freely in pursuit of his agenda. For some, he was a hero; for others, a threat to democracy. The controversies over his actions have put the spotlight on issues of presidential power.

During most of my adult life, issues of presidential power have been hotly contested. In my first month of law school, a federal grand jury handed down indictments against participants in the Watergate break-in at Democratic Party headquarters. By the time I graduated, the Watergate scandal growing out of that burglary had brought down President Nixon. It had also led to a dramatic ruling by the Supreme Court on executive privilege. Even before Watergate, the Vietnam War had given rise to furious debate over whether the "Imperial Presidency" had gotten out of hand.

Although Nixon and Trump bookend much of my career, conflicts over presidential power have arisen again and again in the intervening years. George W. Bush was accused of going beyond the bounds of the Constitution in the "War on Terror," while Barack

Obama was accused of seizing Congress's lawmaking powers in his efforts to reform immigration policy.

Anyone who lived through those times has strong views about each of these presidents and the legality of their actions. As US politics have become more polarized, the passions surrounding presidential action have risen higher and higher. The views of commentators about presidential power sometimes seem to flip overnight when a new president takes office. It's simply human nature to look kindly on expansive uses of power by the presidents on "our" side and much more skeptically when the president is on the "other" side.

To think clearly about presidential power, we have to break free of this psychology. The nature of power is that it can be used for good and for bad. Actions taken by one president serve as precedents for actions taken by another, even if their politics are opposite. Constitutional rules must cover both the presidents we love and those we disdain.

In this book, I try to get beyond the partisan debates and the issues of the moment. I also try to keep in mind readers who come to the subject with views that are the opposite of mine. I do express my own views on many of the issues, but my main goal is not advocacy. Instead, I want readers, whatever their own viewpoints, to understand the deep conflicts over the proper scope of presidential power that in many cases can be traced back to the framing of the Constitution itself.

Anyone who has followed the news over the past decade knows that issues about presidential power cover a broad range. Can the president withdraw from an international agreement unilaterally? What about the presidential use of force such as drone attacks undertaken without authorization from Congress? Are there any limits on presidential power over other parts of the executive branch? Can the president fire a special prosecutor? And what about presidential decisions to stop enforcing immigration laws against whole categories of people? Or, on the other hand, spending money that Congress refused to appropriate in order to build a wall on the US-Mexico border? The media is full of passionate arguments about these issues, but disinterested analysis is far more rare.

Often, the answers to these questions are anything but cut and dried. The arguments not only come to different conclusions, but often start from different assumptions about how to interpret the Constitution. I try to shed light on all these questions, based on Supreme Court precedent and what we know about the views of the Founding Fathers. My hope is that readers with opposing viewpoints will at least gain insight into the complexities of the debate.

Before closing this preface, I need to acknowledge some debts. The book was prompted by an inquiry from my editor at the University of California Press, Maura Roessner. She had seen a presentation on the subject that I gave on Constitution Day at Berkeley's Free Speech Café and thought it had the germ of a successful book project. I hope the final product will prove her right. My thinking about presidential power has been sharpened by discussions with Mike Paulsen when we were both at the University of Minnesota and John Yoo at Berkeley, both of whom are passionate advocates of the unitary executive theory. My colleague Amanda Tyler helped clarify my thinking about individual rights and executive powers. I also benefited from discussions with Neil Siegel on presidential power, in connection with our book, *United States Constitutional Law*. My biggest debt, however, is to my wife, Dianne. She carefully edited each chapter, tirelessly streamlining the prose, clearing up ambiguities, and weeding out legal jargon. To the extent that the book is understandable to a general audience, she deserves the bulk of the credit.

Beyond these individuals, there is the much larger group of scholars in the field from whom I have learned. Space prohibits naming them all or even citing all their work in the notes on sources and further reading. I remain grateful to them, even where I disagree, for having done so much to illuminate the subject.

Introduction

Here is a quick multiple choice exam:

1. Barack Obama . . .
   (a) was a wise leader who faithfully observed constitutional limits.
   (b) abused his powers and violated the Constitution.
2. Donald Trump . . .
   (a) was a wise leader who faithfully observed constitutional limits.
   (b) abused his powers and violated the Constitution.

It is unlikely that many of us chose the same option for both questions. Such disputes over the constitutionality of presidential actions are nothing new. Many Americans, not just in the South but also in the North, denounced Abraham Lincoln as a dictator wielding unconstitutional authority. Over the past forty years, Presidents Ronald Reagan, George W. Bush, Barack Obama, and Donald Trump stand out as lightning rods for claims of unconstitutional usurpation of power. Two presidents during those four decades were impeached by the House of Representatives (one of them twice), though they both escaped conviction in the Senate.

We need to keep in mind that the same constitutional powers are held by the presidents we revere and those we detest. There's a powerful temptation to celebrate presidential powers when exercised by the presidents we admire, forgetting that those powers can also be used badly by other presidents. I felt this temptation when writing a book about Lincoln and the Constitution. I constantly had to remind myself that other presidents had used those same powers with less judgment and compassion and sometimes toward bad ends. The great American historian Arthur Schlesinger Jr. fell into this trap while celebrating Franklin D. Roosevelt's use of the war power, only to realize during the Vietnam War that he had overlooked the dark side of that power.

Our tendency to tailor our view of presidential power to the current political situation makes the constitutional issues even harder to understand. Regardless of who is in the White House these days, there has been a fiery debate over whether that particular president has stepped over the constitutional line. The debate features spirited claims of constitutional usurpation on one side and the need for strong leadership on the other. Someone is sure to say there's a constitutional crisis. All of which must leave many people wondering: What constitutional powers does the president have? And why, after more than two centuries, are the boundaries of those powers so unclear?

I wish I could give definitive answers to those questions. But even among scholars, many of the issues are hotly contested. Not everything is up for grabs, and this book is partly about what constitutional law *does* tell us about presidential power and its limits. But it is also about the gaps and uncertainties. I cannot always provide answers, but I can explain what the debate is about so you can judge for yourself.

Ultimately, there are two reasons for the gaps in established law. One is simply that from the beginning, Americans have found it difficult to strike the right balance between limiting abuse of power and authorizing its exercise when needed. The other reason, however, is that the process of resolving conflicts over presidential power is as much political as legal. Many disputes take place outside the courts, so there is no neutral party to decide when the president has transgressed congressional mandates or whether those mandates themselves are constitutional. Without a neutral arbitrator, we end up with a tug-of-war between presidents and Congress with no definitive answer in sight.

Presidential powers can provide sorely needed national leadership, especially in times of crisis. Those powers also come at a price. Centralizing control of the executive branch in the White House can lead to more coherent, decisive federal policies. Centralized power also allows presidents to force the executive branch into actions that may be unconstitutional or violate a federal statute. A president may act for personal gain or to reward campaign contributors. Giving the president broad authority over foreign policy and the military can be crucial in a dangerous world, but it creates dangers of its own if those powers are misused.

My political views are no secret. A quick look online will reveal my opposition to President Trump. But this is not a book about the Trump presidency. There are already plenty of books attacking or defending the constitutionality of his actions. That's an important debate but not one this book aims to join. Pitched disputes about the scope of presidential power existed long before he became president and will long outlast him. For me, Trump is a reminder of the need to balance the dangers of executive power against its benefits. If you disagree about Trump, I'm sure you can find another recent president whose actions you consider an abuse of power.

Like virtually everyone else in America, I have strong views about Trump and other recent presidents. But this is not a book about the terrible transgressions of President X or Y, or the unjust accusations of abuse of power by President Z, or even the glorious achievements of A, B, or C. It can be really hard to think about the constitutional issues in isolation from our strong feelings about the person who currently inhabits the White House. Rules that give power to good presidents also give power to bad ones; and rules that prevent presidents from doing bad things will also sometimes prevent them from doing good things. This is true whatever your personal opinion about which presidents are good and what presidential actions are bad. That's why rules have to strike a balance between empowering presidents and constraining them—an extremely difficult balancing act.

This book is not intended as an argument, much less a polemic, about any particular president. It's not even an advocacy piece for a narrow or broad reading of presidential powers. But it is very much an advocacy piece in another sense. It advocates for something simple, something we all used to take for granted: the need to carefully consider arguments that we disagree with, along with the need to apply the same legal standards to the leaders we like and those we hate. Maybe that seems like a trite perspective. Yet a quick look at current public discourse makes it dramatically clear just how endangered that perspective is. I feel strongly that our health as a democracy and the preservation of the rule of law depend on strengthening that perspective. It may seem strange to say that I am passionately devoted to the ideal of reasoned debate. Yet that *is* what I believe, and it is the perspective I mean to advocate.

If there has never been full consensus about what the Constitution intended for the presidency, that may well be because the Framers did not have a very clear sense of the office they were creating, or at least not one that was sufficiently explicit and clear to drive a consensus in later years. After the Constitution was ratified, conflicts almost immediately arose about the role of the president among some of the Constitution's leading supporters.

Many issues that arose in the early years continue to percolate today. One such issue involves the degree of presidential control over the executive branch: What positions does the president get to fill, when do those appointments need Senate approval, and can the president remove government officials at will, including special prosecutors? The Supreme Court has been especially active in this area recently. Other major disputes concern the president's power on issues relating to foreign affairs and national security. These include the power to recognize foreign governments, make executive agreements (rather than treaties), and withdraw from treaties. Especially fraught issues involve the president and the war power: the decision to use force, Congress's power to declare war, the commander in chief power, and the delegation of power from Congress. And cutting across these categories is the power of presidents to take emergency action without express authority from Congress or sometimes even contrary to congressional dictates.

Of course, there are many informal forces that can keep a president in check, including public opinion, the desire for reelection, and resistance from other parts of the executive branch. But constitutional law also limits presidential power in several ways. Courts may intervene either to prevent the president from invading the powers of other branches of government or to enforce the restrictions that the Bill of Rights places on all governmental powers. The clash between presidential powers and individual rights has led to some dramatic Supreme Court decisions, the War on Terror and Donald Trump's travel ban being recent examples. Judicial efforts to limit presidential powers encounter constitutional issues of their own, involving matters such as executive privilege, presidential immunity from damages, and possible limits on criminal prosecution of a president. Congress also has the ability to impose checks on the president, using the power of the purse, congressional investigations, and ultimately the power of impeachment. These also raise constitutional issues.

I would like this book to be useful for everyone, regardless of political stance or viewpoint on executive power. My focus is not on proposing a new theory for resolving disputes about the constitutionality of presidential power. I try to distinguish as clearly as I can between my descriptions of the history and state of the law and the parts of the discussion where I am giving my own views. In general, my own view is that the presidency is best seen as an evolving institution, heavily shaped by the course of our history. Many disputes about presidential power are resolved through the political process, but when courts intervene, they need to maintain a balance between the need for vigorous presidential authority and the necessity of restraints against autocracy.

To set the stage for the discussion, I begin with some general background about the institution of the presidency and the Constitution's relatively brief discussion of presidential powers. Then I give a preview of the main issues involving presidential power.

The American Presidency

Questions about presidential power are not unique to the United States. Some other countries have followed our approach to executive power. But this is far from universal. Americans are so focused on the presidency that many would be surprised to learn that our presidential form of government is in the minority among democratic systems internationally.

Most democracies have a parliamentary system in which the head of government, usually called the prime minister, is chosen by the legislature (or sometimes one house of the legislature). Thus, the British parliamentary system has actually turned out to be more popular than our system. Some nations with prime ministers have a separate figure, often called the president, who serves a largely ceremonial function as head of state. In the British setting, parliamentary government generally guarantees that the executive and the House of Commons represent the same political party, minimizing conflict between the two branches. Divided government of the kind we see in the United States is unlikely to occur in Britain, and normally the prime minister and the House of Commons are in full agreement. But such conflicts do sometimes arise. During Brexit, the British Parliament demanded a role in decision making, even though foreign affairs issues have always been considered the province of the Crown (meaning, in practice, the prime minister). In contrast, our own system of government is actually designed to produce tension between the executive and legislative branches, in the name of "checks and balances."

Commentators are divided about the merits of presidential and parliamentary systems. Critics of the presidential system argue that it invites impasses between the executive and the legislature, often tempting the executive to take unilateral action. They also argue that our system leads to a "cult of personality" surrounding the president that lends itself to populist politics rather than reasoned public debate. Moreover, second-term presidents are not eligible to run for a third term, so they are lame ducks from the time they take office. Supporters of presidential government argue that it has many compensating virtues. They argue that it provides more unified administration and greater electoral accountability because the president provides a focal point for voters and greater stability because Congress and the president generally have to agree to any change in law. Supporters of the presidential system also point to flaws in the parliamentary system, such as the possibility that party control will leave the prime minister unchecked and unaccountable.

Both systems have strengths and weaknesses. Our system of government is clearly committed to the presidential model. Yet the critics are right about some of the weaknesses of this system. Alongside the formal constitutional rules, informal norms have evolved that can sometimes counter those weaknesses. Those norms aren't "law," but they can have real power to restrain presidents. Donald Trump was as uninhibited by norms as any president in history, but even so, he found it necessary to give way to them on more than one occasion.

For instance, Trump clearly had the legal authority to halt an investigation by a special counsel into possible cooperation between the Trump campaign and the Russian government. Doing so would have required some roundabout action. He clearly had the authority to fire the attorney general and install an acting attorney general who would carry out his wishes. The attorney general could have rescinded the regulation authorizing the appointment of special prosecutors and then fired Robert Mueller. If necessary, Trump could have repeated the process as often as needed until he got an acting attorney general who would do what he wanted. That is essentially what Richard Nixon did during the "Saturday Night Massacre" when he tried to halt the Watergate investigation.

Although Trump did eventually fire Attorney General Jeff Sessions, none of the rest of this process occurred. It would have been legal for Trump to fire Mueller, but even his congressional advisers told him that doing so would provoke a crisis that would imperil his presidency. Sometimes norms are stronger than law: Trump did not have the practical power to do what he clearly had the legal power to do.

The constitutional text provides a barebones sketch of presidential power. The first sections of the Constitution deal with Congress (Article I), the president (Article II), and the courts (Article III). Article II of the Constitution, which defines the presidency, is relatively brief—much shorter than Article I's coverage of Congress and its powers. And the language specifically relating to presidential powers is even shorter. Maybe that's because everyone already understood what those powers would be. Or maybe it was because no one was really sure, so they left the issue for later development.

Article II begins with the statement, "The executive Power shall be vested in a President of the United States of America." As we will see, this vesting clause can be read either as a grant of authority or as merely descriptive of the president's role vis-à-vis the other branches of government. One of the great fracture lines in constitutional debates over presidential power is what to make of this language. For some, it means everything; for others, it means almost nothing.

Section 1 then provides a lengthy description of election procedures. This was the result of much labored debate at the Constitutional Convention. The delegates to the convention had a hard time figuring out who should elect the president, how long the president should serve, and whether the president should be term limited. Section 1 concludes with the presidential oath clause, prescribing a special oath for this office, in which the new president swears to "faithfully execute the Office of President of the United States, and to the best of my Ability, preserve, protect, and defend the Constitution of the United States."

Sections 2 and 3 of Article II describe certain presidential powers. In terms of national security and foreign affairs, the president is made commander in chief of the military, given the power to make treaties (subject to Senate approval), and given the authority to receive ambassadors. In terms of the internal operations of the government, the president can request written opinions from "principal officers," can appoint government officials including ambassadors and judges, can issue pardons for "Offenses against the United States," can propose legislation, and is more generally directed "to take Care that the Laws be faithfully executed." By its language, the take care clause imposes a duty on the president; there is debate about whether by implication it gives the president additional powers to carry out this duty.

There are some powers that are not specifically described: the power to begin military hostilities, the power to recognize (or refuse to recognize) foreign governments, the power to remove federal officials, the power to order lower-level officials to take specific actions or refrain from those actions, and the power to withhold information from Congress or the courts. The vesting clause might give the president some or all of these powers, or perhaps they can be implied from some of the specific grants of power. Or maybe the president does not have these powers at all, except to the extent that Congress chooses to give them. Constitutional issues about presidential powers are not cut and dried.

After prescribing how to pick a president and what the president's powers are, Article II describes how to get rid of a president. Section 4 states that the president and all other civil officers "shall be removed from Office on Impeachment for, and Conviction of, Treason, Bribery, or other high Crimes and Misdemeanors." The courts have never defined the scope of the grounds for impeachment, such as whether impeachment is limited to activities that violate criminal laws. (Most commentators believe that impeachment is not so limited.) Three presidents (Andrew Johnson, Bill Clinton, and Donald Trump) have been impeached by the House, but none has been convicted by the constitutionally required two-thirds of the Senate. It is generally thought, however, that Richard Nixon would have been impeached and convicted if he had not resigned first.

What presidents do today is far more sweeping than Article II's list of powers might suggest. Domestically, the Office of the President rests atop a giant bureaucracy administering laws on subjects from immigration to environmental protection. Internationally, the president controls ambassadors, as well as the State Department, the Central Intelligence Agency (CIA), the National Security Agency (NSA), and other agencies of the world's most powerful country. The president is commander in chief of the world's strongest military, with everything from navy SEALs to nuclear weapons at the ready. Presidential responsibilities have become so large that the Office of the President now has several thousand employees.

As we will see, the modern president's powers are robust, to say the least, but they are not unlimited. Every recent president has been accused of usurpation of power by the political opposition. Courts have intervened when they have concluded that the president has transgressed legal limits. Congress, too, has attempted to curb the powers of the president, sometimes in ways that the Supreme Court has held unconstitutional.

One reason that the scope of presidential power remains contested may be that the people who drafted, adopted, and put into effect the Constitution failed to achieve a clear consensus. At the Philadelphia convention, the Framers spent most of their time debating the structure of the office (one president or several), the length of the term and method of selection, and allocation of some specific powers between branches. Originalists, who believe that the Constitution's meaning was fixed in place when it was adopted, argue that the term "executive power" had a clear meaning at the time. They have to rely largely on inference rather than an indication that the people who voted to ratify the Constitution explicitly articulated a specific vision. These originalists' inferences might well be warranted, but constitutional interpretation would certainly be easier if the Framers of the Constitution had spelled out presidential powers in more detail or if the Constitutional Convention and ratifiers had spent more time discussing the exact nature of those powers.

No sooner had the new government formed than disputes began about presidential power. James Madison and Alexander Hamilton took sharply opposed positions, with Thomas Jefferson allied with Madison. Congress was divided on the issue. It does not appear that the first generation implementing the new Constitution fully agreed about its meaning. Rather, during this period, we can see the early roots of disputes that have continued to today. These disputes also play out within a debate over how to interpret the Constitution—in particular, the divide between believers in originalism and supporters of a living constitution. Some of the disputes are no longer ongoing. They have now been settled by Supreme Court rulings or by shared understandings between presidents and Congresses. Other issues, such as when a president can use military force, remain heatedly debated.

Major Areas of Dispute

By common agreement, presidential power is at its peak in the area of foreign affairs. But Congress, too, has foreign affairs powers: the Senate's treaty authority and the congressional power to regulate international trade. Over time, however, presidents have expanded their own power at the expense of Congress. The modern Supreme Court has generally stayed out of these interbranch disputes but occasionally has intervened on behalf of the president.

Despite the acknowledgment of the president's primary role, there are some important areas of dispute. One issue is whether Congress can use funding conditions or other tools to force the president to adopt its view of foreign policy. Another issue relates to agreements with foreign powers. Presidents have acquired the power to enter into many legal agreements with foreign countries without the Senate consent required for treaties. But what are the limits of that power? For instance, did the Paris Agreement on climate change require Senate approval? And when the Senate has approved a treaty, can the president simply withdraw from the treaty at will, or is some congressional involvement required?

Closely connected with the president's role in foreign affairs is the president's command over the military. Many of the hottest disputes over presidential power have involved the decision to go to war. There are a large number of articles debating what the Framers intended about the president's power to use armed force. This is another area that the courts have shied away from, at least in modern times. But the overall trend has been the steady accretion of presidential control of the decision to use force. Still, Congress often pushes back, and recent presidents have felt the need to get congressional approval before major military actions like the Gulf War and the Iraq War. There is no consensus on the constitutional issues.

The president is not only commander in chief but also bureaucrat in chief, in charge of running an enormous government bureaucracy. There has been ongoing conflict over the extent of the president's power over the bureaucracy. This issue arose during the First Congress, resulted in the impeachment of a president after the Civil War, and then escalated during the modern period with the rise of the administrative state. Current law is clear on some points but is under attack from conservatives; on other issues, the Supreme Court has steadily expanded presidential control. But legal power doesn't always translate into effective political control, as shown by Trump's inhibitions about firing the special counsel who was investigating him.

One of the most bitterly contested issues involves the inherent power of the president to take action during emergencies. At least since Lincoln, presidents have laid claim to such a power. The Supreme Court has taken up the issue several times, trying to accommodate the need for presidential flexibility with the need to limit the potential for arbitrary abuse. History has acted as a tie-breaker: presidents are given more leeway in areas where Congress has been willing to allow maneuvering room, less where actions are unprecedented or have been the subject of congressional pushback. Line drawing is difficult given the need to accommodate the realities of modern government while preserving checks and balances. For that reason, this is an area where the tug-of-war between Congress and the president is especially important in setting boundaries. But those boundaries always seem to be contested. Emergency powers are necessary but easily abused, so the stakes are high in these disputes.

Short of the ballot box—which is not an available remedy for second-term presidents—the most effective checks on the president come from Congress. In areas subject to its control, Congress can legislate to limit presidential powers, but the presidential veto power means that this strategy works best far in advance of any specific presidential action. Congress is not left without other recourse, however. It can refuse to fund activities that it disagrees with and drag executive officials before investigating committees. The scope of congressional power to investigate the executive branch, however, remains in dispute. The ultimate—but rarely used—tool is impeachment, a method of control that is subject to large unsettled constitutional issues. In particular, as we saw during the two impeachments and trials of President Trump, there are heated disputes over what constitutes an impeachable offense.

None of Congress's tools is effective in the absence of congressional will to use them, meaning that these limits on the presidency are inevitably intertwined with politics. But even in political decisions constitutional concerns are not wholly absent, as shown by the number of Republican senators who were willing to vote against President Trump's declaration of a national emergency on the US-Mexico border.

At one level, disputes about presidential power are about boundaries between two branches of government. But they are also about checks and balances that protect individual liberty. One key issue has involved judicial review of presidential action. To what extent will the courts either step aside or defer so strongly to the president that judicial review is meaningless? That issue goes back at least to Lincoln but has been highlighted with the expanding power of presidents since Franklin Roosevelt. The Court has taken an unsteady path, sometimes deferring strongly (as with the Japanese internment cases and the Trump ban on travel from certain majority Muslim countries), sometimes intervening on behalf of individual rights (as with detention under the War on Terror). Courts face a difficult task: giving presidents scope to respond to true emergencies while also protecting the rule of law and civil liberties.

Even if the president has violated the law, getting judicial redress can be difficult. Often, executive officers other than the president are subject to litigation, but the president is sometimes at the receiving end of a lawsuit. Can the president be required to testify or submit documents? Can the president be sued for damages? Can the president be prosecuted for criminal activity? Courts insist that the president is not above the law, but they are also worried about possibly exposing the president to harassment and interference with official duties. They have struck a balance that largely but not entirely favors the president. Some key issues, such as whether a sitting president can be sued in state court, are yet to be decided.

Because the arguments of debaters so often rely on what they claim is the original understanding of the Constitution, we need to begin with a little history. Although it may have evolved since then, the presidency was brought into being at a specific moment in time. We need to understand that time, the disputes over the presidency, and the areas of consensus.

If the goal is to understand what the language of the Constitution meant when it was drafted, evidence from that period is obviously crucial. Originalists believe that the primary (perhaps exclusive) driver of constitutional law should be historical meaning. For them, the materials I am about to discuss are central to resolving disputes about constitutional interpretation. Non-originalists don't think the clock stopped when the required nine states ratified the Constitution. They give greater weight to the way the presidency has evolved over time, taking into account the fundamental values underlying the Constitution. But for virtually all non-originalists, the views of the Framers remain important though not decisive.

Either way, the history of the 1780s and 1790s carries special weight in analyzing issues about the presidency. Besides, there is relatively little Supreme Court precedent regarding many issues, so evidence of the original understanding is especially valuable as a guide. Let's turn now to that history.

1 Creating the Presidency

In the midst of the coronavirus outbreak, President Trump announced his view of presidential power: "When someone is president of the United States, the authority is total." In reading this chapter, consider how it might bear on that statement.

To understand the creation of the presidency, we need to understand how Americans thought about the executive branch at the time. Obviously, there was no "President of the United States" before there was a United States. Before American independence, colonists were legally subject to the English king and his appointed governors. It was only after independence that Americans had to worry about how to design the executive branch. In the immediate aftermath of independence, they created a joint government with no executive head at all. All authority over the thirteen colonies, to the extent there actually was such authority, resided in the Continental Congress. In the first state constitutions, governors were given severely limited powers. Judging by most of their initial blueprints for government, Americans did not see much need for executive power. Yet little more than a decade later, the Constitution created a powerful new chief executive.

This chapter tells the story of that development. The story begins after independence, with the state constitutions, then moves to the

Constitutional Convention, where the delegates struggled to define the office, and to the ratification debates. Even then, much was unclear about the meaning of the Constitution, and important aspects of the presidency only started to come into focus in the early years of the Republic.

In thinking about the creation and early implementation of the Constitution, keep in mind that the United States was a far different place when the Constitution was framed and first put into effect. Only five cities had more than 10,000 people. New York City, the largest, had a population of 30,000, about the same as Fairbanks, Alaska, today. Washington, DC, did not exist. Virginia, the state with the largest population, had approximately as many people as El Paso, Texas, has today. In some ways, the closest analogy to the United States of that time is present-day New Zealand, which is heavily agrarian, like 1790s America, and has a population a bit bigger than the United States had then. Like New Zealand today, the America of 1789 was far from the main centers of global power. Britain and France were the great world powers, and Spain still had significant clout. A large chunk of what is now the United States remained under Spanish control. It was not until fourteen years after George Washington took the oath of office that the United States extended past the Mississippi.

American governments were also different in earlier times. After independence, Americans seem to have developed an allergy to strong executives. The early state constitutions generally gave state legislatures effective control over weak governors. State legislatures were considered the heart of democratic government, directly representing the sovereign people. In contrast, the executive branch was considered a dangerous staging point for potential tyrants.

But the Framers of the Constitution chose not to follow those early state constitutions. Like some of the revised constitutions more recently adopted by some states, they created a more powerful chief executive who was less dependent on the legislature. There is considerable dispute about just how much stronger and more independent they intended to make the president, but there is general agreement that they did plan for a stronger executive. That vision was fleshed out in the early years of the new Republic under the first presidents. To understand the modern presidency, we must begin with this formative period.

The creation of the presidency was part of the larger project of designing a government strong enough to deal with nationwide problems, yet not so strong as to threaten individual liberty (or at least, the liberty of white people). During the writing of the Constitution, much of the discussion revolved around federalism, the relationship between the states and the Union. That is not surprising, since the fundamental goal of the Constitution was to transform that relationship, giving the federal government far more power at the expense of the states. Connected with this was the question of how the new government would connect with the people themselves and, more broadly, how to make it strong enough to accomplish its mission without becoming a threat to liberty.

Creating the executive branch involved its own set of issues. There was a general desire to give the executive branch some degree of independence from the legislature and of course to ensure that it was able to perform its role effectively. How to do so was more puzzling, and it took considerable time to settle this and to determine the division of authority between the president and the Senate. The early drafts of the Constitution entrusted the Senate with special authority, much of which was shifted in whole or in part to the president in the final version.

When the new government finally took office in 1789, Congress and the president both had to do additional work to figure out how to make the constitutional scheme operational. It is enlightening to see that much that we take for granted about the role of the presidency did not seem obvious when the Constitutional Convention met or even in the early years of the government. Some of those issues were settled at the convention or in the government's start-up phase; others remain fiercely debated even today.

Although this history might seem irrelevant to current events, it remains very much a part of modern debates. Every facet of the history I am about to discuss has been pored over by lawyers and scholars ever since, looking for clues about the meaning of the Constitution.

As with any story, the beginning point is a bit arbitrary. In designing and launching the government, the Framers were heirs to ideas and practices that were rooted in history. Even the British monarchy, the national executive that was most familiar to Americans, had evolved over centuries as a result of constant back and forth with Parliament while meanwhile creating a substantial administrative apparatus. This evolution may have been assisted by the fact that Britain has never had a written constitution. And the Framers themselves looked back even further, frequently to the ancient Roman Republic. The age requirements for various federal offices track those of ancient Rome, and the use of the term "Senate" also harkens back to Roman times. But rather than begin two thousand years ago, let's start with the run-up to the Constitutional Convention.

The Tangled Drafting Process

The Philadelphia convention that produced our Constitution was the outgrowth of a decade of discontent with the existing framework of government. The year after declaring independence, the Continental Congress produced the Articles of Confederation. As the name indicated, the Articles envisioned a federation of states rather than a true national government. Under the Articles, Congress had control of foreign affairs and waging war. Its domestic powers, however, were very weak, and its only way of obtaining money or enforcing its directives was through the states. There was no executive branch. Congress was unable to repay money borrowed to finance the war for independence or soldiers' pensions, and trade suffered from barriers enacted by individual states. There was also considerable discontent with state governments. Many people—in particular, those with property—worried that populist state laws threatened their existing rights.

These problems created a sense of crisis. Some historians contend that the actual circumstances facing the country did not actually constitute a crisis. The economy was not doing badly; the country was at peace; and more or less the same people as before were leading state governments. The feeling of crisis was nevertheless widespread. It may have been due in part to foreboding over whether the government was strong enough to deal with future issues. But it owed even more to the failure of "republican" state governments to live up to the high expectations of the Revolutionary War period. The states were run by legislatures that were directly responsive to the public, yet the results were disappointing and too often economically destabilizing. And under the Articles of Confederation, the congress of state representatives was stymied by the need for unanimity and the absence of any way of obtaining its own financing and implementing its own laws. It had to rely on the states both for funding and for enforcement of its dictates.

Along with what some considered irresponsible legislatures, the state governments tended to have very weak governors, in reaction to the excesses of the royal governors under the British regime. Most were elected by the state legislatures and had limited powers, required to consult executive councils before acting. New York was a major exception. The New York governor held office for three years, unlike the shorter terms elsewhere, was not saddled with the duty of consulting a council except in appointing judges, and was elected by the public rather than the legislature. He belonged to a council of revision that had the power to overturn legislative enactments. The New York model proved influential elsewhere, such as in the 1784 Constitution adopted in Massachusetts. Opponents of the strong-governor model considered it undemocratic and a threat to liberty.

In 1786, delegates of five states met in Annapolis and called for a convention to consider changes in the Articles of Confederation, which Congress then called. All the states sent delegates except Rhode Island (often called "Rogue Island" by critics). That convention convened in Philadelphia on May 14, 1787. Although one often hears about the "long hot summer" during which the delegates met, the weather was actually fairly mild.

The discussion of the presidency at the Constitutional Convention was primarily focused on structural issues: whether to have a single head of the executive branch or divided control by several leaders; and if the former, how and by whom the president would be chosen and how the president could be removed. The convention's perplexity over these issues can be seen in the number of inconclusive discussions and votes before delegates finally came to a resolution. More time was spent on these matters than on precisely delineating the powers of the office.

One of the convention's difficulties was working out the relationship between the president and Congress, particularly the Senate. The Framers tended to think of the Senate as a council of community leaders and wise men, as opposed to the more populist House of Representatives. It was no easy matter to make the executive branch powerful and independent enough to be effective without making it powerful enough to threaten tyranny. When the convention began, delegates already had strong views about the relationship between state and national governments, which was the convention's central focus. In contrast, they did not generally seem to have come to Philadelphia with any clear vision of the executive branch.

Because the primary task facing the country was strengthening the union between states, James Madison prepared for the convention by researching past and contemporary confederacies, including their executive officers (if any). But Madison didn't concern himself with the executive branch of government when he wrote about the defects of American government that required fixing. Prior to the convention, he remained undecided about the executive branch. In an April 1787 letter, speaking of the executive branch, he wrote, "A National Executive will also be necessary. I have scarcely ventured to form my own opinion yet either of the manner in which it ought to be constituted or of the authorities with which it ought [to be] cloathed."

If Americans had had a more sophisticated understanding of developments in England, they might have considered something like a prime minister system in the United States. Their understanding of English political developments, however, was filtered through their knowledge of the conflicts between the Court and Country factions earlier in the century and of the earlier disputes leading to the Glorious Revolution of 1688. Thus, where we might see the emergence of modern English parties and parliamentary government in the late 1700s, they saw a conflict between a corrupt, monarchical faction and the advocates of virtuous, public-spirited government. Although the actual power of the English king was fading, Americans still saw the king as the central power in English government. That was not a model they wanted to emulate.

The Articles of Confederation provided another possible model but not a successful one. The Articles had not provided for an executive branch. Instead, all power was reposed in the Congress. In practice, this didn't work very well since it was impossible for Congress as a whole to keep track of all the details of governing or to engage in day-to-day decision making. Congress ultimately created four offices to implement policy. The heads of two of these offices were particularly vigorous. Robert Morris, superintendent of the office of finance, got into trouble when he attempted to manipulate government finances in order to force Congress to adopt his policies. John Jay, head of the office of foreign affairs, got pushback from southern states for his proposal that the Congress agree to a commercial treaty with Spain without demanding navigation rights on the Mississippi.

Apart from these models, good or bad, there had also been some well-regarded theoretical discussions of the separation of powers in the writings of the political philosophers John Locke and Charles-Louis de Secondat, Baron de La Brède et de Montesquieu, better known as Montesquieu. The extent to which their theories were embraced by the drafters remains controversial. Some scholars see their definitions of executive power as crucial to understanding the Constitution; others see them as peripheral. I have more to say about these political philosophers later.

When the Constitutional Convention assembled, the picture of the future national executive remained blurry. At the beginning of the convention, Madison and other Virginians presented a blueprint that provided the starting point for later discussions. It called for selection of the president by Congress for a fixed term. The president would have "general authority to execute the National laws" and would have "the Executive rights vested in Congress by the Confederation," whatever those might be. The president would also be part of a council of revision having the power to veto laws passed by Congress. This brief description of the presidency seems to have been in the nature of a placeholder, requiring substantial fleshing out.

When the subject of executive power came up at the convention, there were concerns about the extent of the president's powers in the Virginia blueprint. One delegate feared that the president's powers "might extend to peace & war & c., which would render the Executive a Monarchy, of the worst kind, to wit, an elective one." There was a motion to make the executive a single person, which was attacked as "the foetus of monarchy" and an imitation of British royalty. The response was to distinguish the king's role as an executive implementing laws enacted by Parliament from the king's "prerogatives," a set of powers giving the king independent authority in a number of areas, including treaties and war making. The convention then endorsed the idea of election by Congress of a single executive. The

Council of Revision was rejected, largely because it would include judges, and delegates were worried that this would compromise the independence of the courts.

In July, the discussion again turned to the executive branch. The delegates went around in circles. Various methods of electing the president, such as direct popular vote and the electoral college, came up for discussion. Direct popular vote had two major defects: few people were likely to be well known across the whole country, so voters would be ill informed, and a popular vote would give too much power to the populous North, as opposed to the South. There were also doubts about the ability of voters to judge the character of presidential candidates. One delegate said that it would be "as unnatural to refer the choice of a proper character for Chief Magistrate to the people, as it would, to refer a trial of colours to a blind man." There was also great debate about the president's term of office and eligibility for reelection. The Council of Revision idea was again debated and again rejected.

When the Committee on Detail was appointed to put together a comprehensive draft of the Constitution based on all the discussions, the Senate was given the power to make treaties, appoint ambassadors and judges, and decide disputes between states over boundaries. The first two functions ultimately went to the president, subject to Senate approval, while disputes between states ultimately were assigned to the Supreme Court. Later in the convention, rather than Congress having the power to "make" war, it was given the power to "declare" war. Many trees have been felled by arguments over the meaning of the few short lines about this decision in Madison's notes of the proceedings, which are presented in chapter 3.

In late August, a committee was appointed to deal with the unresolved questions before the convention. It came out in favor of giving the power to select the president to the electoral college, with the Senate to decide between the top candidates if no one had a majority of electoral votes. This was soon switched to the House rather than the Senate, for fear that the Senate's role in selecting the president, combined with its power over appointments and treaties, would give it too much power. The committee also recommended that appointments of government officers be made by the president with the advice and consent of the Senate.

Several things stand out from the debates over the presidency. First, there was little discussion of some key issues we would like answered today. No one explicitly addressed the line between the president's power as commander in chief and Congress's power to declare war. No one addressed the extent of the president's role in foreign policy outside of treaties and the appointment of ambassadors. It would have been nice, for instance, if they had added language to the Constitution saying exactly when (if ever) the president could order the use of armed force without prior congressional authorization. There was some discussion but no clear-cut resolution of other issues, such as exactly what "high Crimes and Misdemeanors" meant. So we are left to puzzle over the meaning of a handful of remarks on these issues as we search for enlightenment.

If we were able to ask them, perhaps the Framers would have said that the answers to some of these questions were too obvious to require discussion. Or perhaps they would have said that they had enough trouble agreeing on a framework for government without trying to settle every future issue. In any event, there was enough uncertainty about many of these issues to fuel another two centuries of debate.

Second, it was plain that the delegates to the convention did not foresee that the election of the president would become the fulcrum of American politics. They worried greatly that a president might carry out a coup in order to establish a monarchy or that senators might form a cabal to take over the operation of the government. They generally failed to realize how much ability the president would have to seize the initiative and set the national agenda, instead worrying endlessly about how to protect the executive branch from being pulled into the "vortex" of legislative power. This reflected their experience under the post-independence state governments, where the legislatures often seemed to monopolize power.

The most notorious failure of political foresight was the Framers' failure to imagine the rise of organized political parties providing the machinery for electoral politics and national governance. In fairness, the process had not really begun in America yet. It actually *had* begun in England, but it wasn't well understood until later. What was not yet clear was that parties would become a permanent, institutional feature of government rather than loose, divisive factions. Thus, many of the institutional design decisions by the Framers were made under mistaken assumptions. It did not occur to them that presidents, members of Congress, and state governments might all line up on the same side regardless of the merits of an issue, simply because they were part of the same political party. And if the Framers *had* known, they probably would have been horrified.

The Framers were obviously familiar with political conflicts between different groups, but they thought of them much differently than we think of political parties today. Rather than legitimate parts of democratic government, the Framers considered them "factions" whose political influence needed to be eliminated. They saw factions as interest groups seeking personal gain rather than the public interest. When disputes arose between one group headed by Jefferson and Madison and another headed by Hamilton, the inability to conceive of a legitimate "loyal opposition" led members of each group to conclude that their own group represented "civic virtue" while the other group was subverting the Republic in the interest of foreign powers (England vs. France) or personal power. One of Madison's main arguments for national government was that factional disputes within individual states would be ironed out at the national level. The rise of national politics cutting across the entire country doomed that dream.

For better or worse, the convention finished its work in the middle of September 1787. In sending the Constitution out to the states, the delegates unanimously endorsed what amounted to a cover letter signed by George Washington on behalf of the entire convention. Unlike the records of what was said during the convention, which were secret, the letter was public and reflected the views of the delegates as a whole. Although it is quite short, it contains some clues as to how they saw the product of their work. They explained the goal that "the power of making war, peace, and treaties, that of levying money and regulating commerce, and the correspondent executive and judicial authorities should be fully and effectually vested in the general government of the Union." Thus, they wanted a strong, effective central government. "But," the letter continued, "the impropriety of delegating such extensive trust to one body of men is evident—Hence results the necessity of a different organization."

In other words, the delegates said they wanted a stronger national government, one in which the corresponding executive and judicial authority were "fully and effectually vested." But they thought it was dangerous to put powers such as the authority to make war, peace, and treaties into the hands of one body (or, presumably, any single person). Consequently, they divided power and created checks and balances. Most of the rest of the book is devoted to arguments about how the Constitution manages this task.

All this would have remained purely academic unless the Constitution was actually adopted, something the convention itself had no power to do. For the new government to go into effect, it would have to be ratified by conventions in nine states, with the delegates elected by the people of the state. It was not at all obvious that the ratification effort would succeed. The Constitution seems like an inevitability now, but it did not seem so then. Things could well have come out differently.

Ratifying the Presidency

Ratification by the State of New York was crucial if the new government was to be launched successfully. Its geographic location, its population, and its economic significance even then made it indispensable to a successful new government. A series of newspaper essays signed by "Publius" undertook a systematic defense of the new Constitution. They became known as the Federalist Papers because advocates of the new, stronger federal government were called Federalists. It was common at the time for essays of this kind to be written under a pseudonym. Besides "Publius," the debate over ratification features important works by "Cato," the "Federal Farmer," and others.

The authors of the Federalist Papers, as it turned out, were Alexander Hamilton and James Madison, with a small initial assist from John Jay. This was as distinguished a group of authors as one can imagine. Madison would become a leader in Congress and then president; Jay would become the first Chief Justice; and Hamilton as the first treasury secretary would essentially found the US financial system. These three men were also key in founding what became our first organized political parties, the Federalists and the Democratic-Republicans. After much morphing, these parties provided the seeds for today's Republican and Democratic Parties. The Federalist Papers have become canonical texts in American constitutional law, partly because of their role in ratification but mostly because of their scope and clarity—and also because of the stature of their authors. I refer to them repeatedly in the chapters ahead. They might be called the most important op eds in American history, although they are longer and more analytic than their modern-day counterparts. It is important to keep in mind that they had no official standing; at the time, no one even knew the authors. They were advocacy pieces intended to persuade New Yorkers to vote for ratification.

Federalist Nos. 67 to 77 dealt with the chief executive. They were written by Hamilton, who had been enthusiastic enough about executive power to have proposed having a president for life at the convention. The Federalist Papers reflect that enthusiasm. In Federalist No. 70, he extolled the importance of energetic execution of policy: "A government ill executed, whatever it may be in theory, must be, in practice, a bad government." To be effective and energetic, the executive needed "unity, duration; an adequate provision for its support; competent powers"—all of which, he said, the Constitution provided to the president.

In particular, energy in the executive (something Hamilton himself had in abundance) was crucial to successful government. Hamilton called it "a leading character in the definition of good government." He went on to say that an energetic executive "is essential to the protection of the community against foreign attacks; it is not less essential to the steady administration of the laws; to the protection of property against those irregular and highhanded combinations which sometimes interrupt the ordinary course of justice; to the security of liberty against the enterprises and assaults of ambition, of faction, and of anarchy."

Hamilton then defended the presidency against possible criticisms. He explained the need for a single chief executive rather than a committee on the basis of the need for energetic government: "Decision, activity, secrecy, and dispatch will generally characterize the proceedings of one man in a much more eminent degree than the proceedings of any greater number; and in proportion as the number is increased, these qualities will be diminished." Nor, he insisted, should the idea of a single chief executive be rejected because of its association with King George III. Federalist No. 69 argued that it was unfair to compare the proposed presidency with the English monarchy for a host of reasons: many of the traditional royal prerogatives were subject to Senate approval (like making treaties), were transferred to Congress (like coining money), or were forbidden out-right (like granting titles of nobility). Instead, he argued, the governorship of New York was a more accurate comparison, no doubt a comparison designed to appeal to his New York audience.

While extolling the potential for energetic executive action, Hamilton was also at pains to explain the existence of checks on executive power. For instance, in Federalist No. 72, Hamilton described something he thought at the time was a beneficial feature of the Constitution: the president's limited power to fire officials. He argued that the ability of top officials to stay in place across presidential administrations would provide government stability. In Federalist No. 77, he added the claim that Senate consent would be required to remove top officials as well as to appoint them. That is not the way the law has developed, nor is it the position he took later. But given that the Constitution says not a word on the subject, there is nothing absurd about Federalist No. 77's view of the limits on presidential power to remove other officers. In Federalist No. 73, he also downplayed the president's veto power. He portrayed the president's veto power as merely a way of getting Congress to give further consideration to legislation. In practice, of course, it much more often operates as a death sentence for proposed legislation. By making the veto power look weaker than it really was, Hamilton was bolstering his argument against comparing the president to the English monarch.

In some of the Federalist Papers, Hamilton stressed the ways that the Constitution blended executive and legislative powers instead of strictly separating them. In Federalist No. 72, Hamilton discussed the role of the Senate in the international sphere. In doing so, he also shed light on the closely connected scope of the president's role. Critics claimed that giving the Senate a role in treaty making improperly involved the legislature in the exercise of executive power, a violation of the separation of powers. Hamilton argued, however, that it was arbitrary to classify treaty making as either purely executive or legislative.

If anything, treaties were more legislative than executive because they created general rules governing future behavior. Yet they were not entirely legislative either, because they created contracts between sovereigns, not ordinary laws binding on citizens. Thus, the power to make treaties seemingly "formed a separate department, and to belong, properly, neither to the legislature nor to the executive." As a practical matter, negotiating treaties fit best with the executive branch, but "the vast importance of the trust, and the operation of the treaties as laws, plead strongly for the participation of the whole or a portion of the legislative body in the office of making them."

One of the earlier Federalist Papers also addressed the concern that the proposed Constitution failed to respect the need for separation of powers. Federalist No. 47 attempted to rebut the claim that the Constitution "intermixed" the powers of creating, executing, and interpreting the laws. Critics argued that doing so violated the maxim that allowing one branch to exercise these multiple powers was the essence of tyranny. Madison replied that this maxim was only true where all the powers of one branch were under the control of another, which was not true of the Constitution. It did not apply where there was more limited mixture of powers. His remark about the "essence of tyranny" is often quoted by critics of modern administrative agencies, but they often leave out that Madison limited that concern to extreme situations. His whole point was that combining the powers of the branches was not ordinarily a worry.

There was one other significant mention of the presidency. Madison, like many of the Framers, was worried about legislative dominance of government, based on the recent experience of the newly formed American states. In Federalist No. 48, Madison spoke about the risk that the legislature would sweep all the power of government into its own orbit, making it necessary to ensure the president's independence through separate election, salary protections, and so forth. Clearly, this part of the constitutional design worked so well in fact that the president has seemed to dominate the government more often than Congress.

Despite our focus on the president today, the presidency was not the primary focus of debate then. Given that the Constitution proposed to revolutionize the relationship between Congress and the states, its defenders were more concerned with issues of federalism and with showing that Congress would behave responsibly. The presidency was also a bit of a sideshow for the Constitution's opponents. They were much more exercised by what they saw as a frightening increase in federal power by institutions they feared would be dominated by elites. Perhaps the lack of attention to the presidency represented a failure of imagination. Surely they would have had more to say on the subject if they had envisioned how much power would be concentrated someday in the White House.

Nevertheless, while the critics' emphasis was elsewhere, they did take some shots at the proposed chief executive. The Anti-Federalists, who were opposed to ratification of the Constitution, could not agree among themselves whether the president would be too strong or too weak. Some worried that a weak president would be susceptible to foreign "intrigues." George Mason, an eminent Virginia lawyer who had been at the convention but refused to sign the final document, worried about the president's advisers. If the president's advisers were the members of the cabinet (as turned out to be true of most early presidents), Mason thought, that would be the worst outcome. Cabinet secretaries would make for "the worst and most dangerous of all ingredients for such a Council in a free country." Mason bemoaned the absence of an official council to advise presidents and rally political support in confronting Congress. He fretted that the president would be surrounded only by what we now call yes-men or would become a tool of the Senate.

Like Mason, other Anti-Federalists worried that the Senate would dominate the president. Because treaties would be the "supreme law of the land," they thought, the Senate and the president could engage in lawmaking on their own. This would leave the House of Representatives, which represented the people, with no voice. This concern was tied to the Anti-Federalists' general fear that the government would be controlled by elites at the expense of the people.

Other Anti-Federalists were worried that the president would be too strong rather than too weak. Writing under the pseudonym Cato, a prominent Anti-Federalist asked, "Wherein does this president, invested with his powers and prerogatives, essentially differ from the king of great-Britain (save as to name, the creation of nobility and some unmaterial incidents)?" Indeed, rather than leave office quietly, there was fear that a president might use the military to overturn the Constitution and become a monarch. It was this fear of a monarchical presidency that Hamilton was pushing back against.

One opponent of the Constitution combined both anxieties. He worried that a strong, ambitious president would reduce members of Congress to "his sycophants and flatterers." On the other hand, a weak president would be a "minion of the aristocrats, doing according to their will and pleasure, and confirming every law they think proper to make." Either way, the government would be dangerously out of balance.

What is most interesting about these Anti-Federalists is their failure to coalesce around a clear idea of how the presidency would operate. They had a variety of concerns about Congress but focused on the fear that it would run roughshod over the states and the people at large. But the presidency seemed to be something of an enigma to them.

Despite opposition, the Constitution won ratification. As expected, George Washington was elected the first president. Washington was not a man of letters like Jefferson, a constitutional theorist like Madison, or a brilliant advocate and organizer like Hamilton. But he was an effective leader, listening carefully to the views of others but then decisive in making choices. He was also perhaps the one person in the country who would have been trusted so universally as the first holder of the office. Although he was not a brilliant intellect, he was deeply respected by others, including Hamilton.

He and the newly elected Congress were faced with the task of translating the Constitution's generalities into concrete actions. The views of the First Congress are often given special weight today. The reason is partly that its membership was so distinguished, including twenty members who were at the Constitutional Convention, with Madison in particular playing a leading role in the House. The actions of the First Congress also get special respect because it did so much to establish the framework of the government, from the internal operations of Congress and the executive branch to the federal judicial system. Washington and his key cabinet members (Hamilton and Jefferson) also did much to fill in the outlines of the executive branch. Congress and the president had their work cut out for them.

Launching the Presidency

Despite all the worries about its new powers, the early federal government was a mere shadow of today's federal government. It was hardly the kind of Leviathan that libertarians today worry about. Even by the mid-1790s the government had only $6 million in tax revenue. The headquarters of the War Department—the equivalent of today's Pentagon—had a staff consisting of an accountant, fourteen clerks, and two messengers. The State Department staff was even smaller: seven clerks (one of whom ran the patent office) and a messenger. But, of course, the polymath Thomas Jefferson was secretary of state, which perhaps counted as more than one full-time employee. The Continental Army and Navy had been essentially disbanded at the end of the American Revolution, though state militias still remained. The military was slowly and fitfully restored, but at the start of the War of 1812, the army and navy combined still had fewer than thirteen thousand men.

Despite this smaller scale, establishing a new government was no easy matter. When Washington took office, it was unclear just how the power of the presidency would be implemented. The discussions prior to ratification did not provide obvious answers. Fortunately, Washington began with a tremendous reservoir of respect and goodwill to draw on, having achieved independence as the leader of the Continental Army.

After the new government was launched, it became clear that there were quite a number of constitutional questions on which the Framers themselves were unclear or in disagreement. Perhaps this reflects the fickleness of the political mind; perhaps it reflects the fact that the Framers had never had a clear shared understanding in the first place. We look today to the Federalist Papers for guidance, but even its authors did not always agree later about the interpretation of the Constitution. Within a few years, a major dispute broke out about the scope of presidential power. Like many disputes to follow, this one found Hamilton on one side and Jefferson and Madison on the other. Indeed, they increasingly found themselves divided on many questions, presaging the rise of the first recognized political parties, the Federalists on Hamilton's side and the Democratic-Republicans on Jefferson and Madison's. One area where they disagreed was presidential power.

Their dispute about presidential power was sparked by a tense international situation. After the French Revolution, England and France came to blows. They were the Great Powers of the era, like the United States and the Soviet Union in the mid-twentieth century. Everyone agreed that the United States, then a very weak power, needed to stay out of the conflict. The question was how to do so. Should America's neutral status be declared by the president or by Congress? Some thought that only Congress could do so. Just as only

Congress had the power to declare a state of war, they argued, it alone must have the power to formally declare that the United States was neutral in the conflict.

Washington did not agree. He issued the 1793 Neutrality Proclamation, which declared the nation a neutral party and prohibited certain conduct by Americans, such as trade in contraband with either side. The proclamation warned that Americans would be subject to "punishment or forfeiture," including criminal prosecution, if they violated the rules governing neutrals under international law. The proclamation was controversial and seen by some as a power grab by Washington. The French Revolution had been a polarizing event. Jefferson and his supporters were favorable toward the French revolutionaries in what they saw as a struggle against despotism. They saw Hamilton and his supporters as partial to the British and closet monarchists. They felt that Washington had allowed himself to become a tool of the Hamilton faction.

Hamilton once again stepped forward as the defender of executive power. He wrote a series of anonymous publications under the name "Pacificus" defending Washington's action. One aspect of his argument has received the most attention over time. In that part of the argument, Hamilton maintained that the president has broad powers beyond the explicit grants in Sections 2 and 3 of Article II. According to Hamilton, the president's power over foreign affairs is limited only by express constitutional language, like the clause giving the Senate a role in making treaties. Specifically, he relied on the vesting clause of Article II, which says that the executive power is vested in the president. The question was, what did the Constitution mean by "executive power"? In Hamilton's view, the clause gave the president powers beyond simply implementing the laws. In fact, the specific presidential powers listed in the Constitution were merely illustrations of the president's broad powers. Since the nation's executive power was vested in the president, Hamilton reasoned, Washington's authority to issue the Neutrality Proclamation was beyond question. Hamilton's argument was the first clear formulation of what has become known as the unitary executive theory, which I examine later.

This was only part of Hamilton's argument, however. In addition to this more famous argument, Hamilton argued that the president was responsible for executing the laws—not just domestic laws, but also "the Law of Nations" (as international law was then called). He also tried to downplay the significance of the Neutrality Proclamation, viewing it as merely a factual statement that the United States was not an ally of either party.

At Jefferson's urgent behest, Madison responded to Hamilton in another series of anonymous pamphlets under the pseudonym Helvidius. He argued that executive authority must "presuppose the existence of laws to be executed," and these laws can be made only by the legislative branch. He also accused Pacificus of deriving his vision of the president from the powers of the English king, insisting that the Framers of the Constitution had rejected this vision of sweeping executive power.

Madison apparently was not entirely happy with his own response, though scholars have conflicting views about why. He may have wished he had come up with better arguments or that he had refused to engage, or perhaps he had second thoughts about the validity of his position. In any event, whatever agreement Madison and Hamilton may once have had about presidential power was clearly becoming frayed only a few short years after the Constitution went into effect.

This dispute between Madison and Hamilton was not the only issue about presidential power to emerge in the early years of the Republic. Given that the Constitution was brand-new, questions about how to interpret it were constantly arising. After all, there were no precedents from the courts or past experience to use for guidance on constitutional issues. The First Congress devoted considerable time to constitutional issues, including those relating to its own powers and the president's. Much of what it did can be seen as filling in the details of the broad outlines that emerged from the Constitutional Convention.

One symbolic but important issue was what to call the president. Some favored "Excellency" or "Highness," lest foreigners think that the president was merely a presiding officer, like the chair of a committee. They wanted to ensure that the dignity of the office received its due. But Madison, who by then was sitting in the House, insisted that "President of the United States" was a sufficient title, arguing that anything else would smack of royalty. This again reflected the desire of the Framers to distinguish the presidency from the still-despised English king. Though not a man insensitive to his personal dignity, Washington seemed happy with the choice. The nomenclature indicated that the president was merely the citizen who at any given time was holding a specific government office, not someone who had somehow been lifted to a higher personal status.

One early constitutional debate in Congress was over the power to remove executive officers who had been confirmed by the Senate. Views in Congress were divided. Some thought the president would have the power to remove officials regardless of what Congress said. Others thought government officials could only be removed by impeachment; still others, that the consent of the Senate would be required for removal as well as appointment. This episode in Congress has received a lot of attention in connection with modern disputes about the president's control over the cabinet and bureaucracy. I will take a closer look later in the book.

Another relevant issue was how much power Congress could delegate to the administration. The First Congress did so quite broadly with regard to patents (inventions "sufficiently useful or important"), in governance of the territories, and in establishing the new seat of government in the District of Columbia (somewhere between the eastern branch of the Potomac and Connoghochegue Creek). On the other hand, the Second Congress specified postal rates and the locations of postal roads, leaving little leeway to the executive branch regarding these details. This is another issue I return to. In this, as in so much, the disagreements of the 1790s have echoes in today's constitutional debates.

In terms of the Senate's role more broadly, Washington initially took the Senate's constitutional right to provide "advice and consent" to treaties literally, seeking the Senate's "advice" in person about a new treaty. The Federalist Papers actually suggest that the Senate was supposed to play that advisory role, and so obviously does the language of the Constitution. But Washington was so unhappy with the ensuing discussion that he left in a huff and never came back, though he sometimes engaged in other forms of consultation. On other occasions, Washington requested the Senate's advice on the meaning of an existing treaty and on what steps he should take if it proved impossible to settle a dispute with Britain over a boundary issue through negotiation.

It was not the Senate alone that took a hand in foreign affairs. In 1793, both branches of Congress took it upon themselves to cancel a treaty with France through ordinary legislation rather than assume only the president could do so. The boundaries of presidential control over foreign affairs remain disputed to some extent even today. I return to these issues in chapter 4.

As I mentioned earlier, the US military was almost nonexistent when Washington took office. In the summer of 1789, he informed Congress that there were 672 soldiers remaining, and he asked for congressional authorization for the army to protect the frontier. Washington also asked certain individuals to act as informal representatives to foreign governments until such time as ambassadors could be chosen and confirmed by the Senate. Once again, he took the initiative during the transition period rather than leave things to Congress.

Washington clearly established a strong role for the president. Given that he was by far the best known and most trusted individual nationally, he naturally became a focal point for government decisions. It is also clear that the drafters and ratifiers of the Constitution wanted a chief executive who would be more powerful than most of the state governors had been. The question of just how much stronger is one that will occupy us for much of this book.

To a surprising extent, the constitutional puzzles of the early Republic remain with us today: Does the president have the power to renounce treaties on his own? Can the president order military actions without congressional consent? In running the government, are there any limits on the president's power to fire officials for whatever reason? Does the president have emergency powers outside of any statute? These are not merely academic questions, as is known to anyone who even dips into the news from time to time. Much of this book is devoted to trying to sort through the arguments that have figured in these sometimes-bitter debates.

2 *Clashing Visions of Presidential Power*

The areas of dispute about presidential power are many, and so are the arguments on each side. But the disputes tend to feature two contesting viewpoints—the same viewpoints that first surfaced in Hamilton's and Madison's dispute about Washington's Neutrality Proclamation. The arguments are nuanced, however, and even people who adopt the same model can disagree about how to apply it. But the two models tug in very different directions and call for different emphases in analyzing the issues. As we turn to specific areas of dispute, such as the president's power to fire government officials or to take military action, we see these same two models clashing again and again.

One model deemphasizes the particular grants of power to Congress or the president in favor of reliance on the first sentence of Article II, the vesting clause. This model is often called the unitary executive theory. Strictly speaking, however, that term applies only to arguments for complete presidential control of the bureaucracy. In that narrow form, it holds that everyone within the executive branch is under total presidential control. The broader theory uses similar arguments to justify an expansive view of presidential power in other areas such as initiating wars and controlling foreign policy, as well as presidential immunity from congressional or judicial oversight.

There's no generally accepted rubric for the broader theory. For convenience, I will call it presidentialism.

Presidentialism has been championed by conservatives like Justices Antonin Scalia and Clarence Thomas in recent years. But it is not an exclusively conservative idea. Presidents and their lawyers, of whatever ideological stripe, are naturally attracted to this theory.

Many presidentialists, though not all, believe that the vesting clause also gives the president a free hand in dealing with foreign countries, including use of the military as needed, and in national security more generally. The basic vision of this presidentialist model is to stake out an area of inherent presidential power and build a high wall around it. The overriding metaphor is the separation of powers. Justices Scalia and Thomas have been among the leading advocates for this view.

The other model tends to speak more of checks and balances among branches than of walls between them. From that point of view, the task is not to give each branch complete autonomy within its domain. Instead, it is to strike a balance between the need for vigorous government and preventing any one branch from getting out of control. Those taking this position often look for workable accommodations between the branches and speak of protecting the core functions of each branch. For instance, although agreeing that the president needs substantial control over the executive branch, checks and balances theorists are also willing to allow Congress to limit the president's removal power when there seem to be persuasive practical reasons for giving an official independence from political control. This approach doesn't come with a label, but I will often refer to it for convenience as the balanced government approach.

Although it is seldom voiced these days, there is also a third possible model, the congressional supremacy model, which is in some ways the mirror image of presidentialism. It basically limits the president to whatever powers Congress chooses to provide, apart from the few specific powers granted in Article II, which are read very narrowly. In particular, this model places heavy emphasis on Congress's power to make laws that are "necessary and proper" for carrying out its own powers and those of the other branches of government. Aspects of this congressional supremacy model crop up from time to time in my discussion. The reason it is not more prominent these days probably has something to do with Congress's relative reticence to assert its prerogatives since World War II. Congress has seemed especially dysfunctional in recent years, which makes it hard to muster enthusiasm for the idea that it should take a dominant role.

Although members of the public may like their own representatives in Congress, they tend to hold the institution itself in low regard. Thus, the congressional supremacy model seems currently dormant, leaving most of the debate to take place between the presidentialist and balanced government approaches. But there are a couple of places where the congressional supremacy model has emerged: it has been championed by liberals in terms of war powers and by conservatives in terms of domestic policy making.

The presidentialist and balanced government models differ not only in their conclusions but also in their methods of analysis. Presidentialists these days think that the original understanding of the Constitution answers most questions about presidential power. They generally consider themselves originalists, giving the original understanding the dominant role in constitutional interpretation. Pragmatists find the text of the Constitution and the historical evidence far less clear, though they do attend to the pragmatic perspectives taken by Framers. They emphasize instead the desire of the Framers for energetic but responsible government. They also tend to think that, in general, the original understanding of the constitutional provisions is only one factor to be considered in interpreting the Constitution. Thus, they tend to favor the idea of a living Constitution whose meaning evolves over time. Because of the importance of this disagreement over the role of history, it is worth a short detour to talk about the debate over originalism.

That debate matters because it frames all the specific issues discussed later in this book. Consider the war power. We live in a world much different from that of the Framers. The United States is a super power, not a second- or third-tier country as it was then. The United States has an enormous permanent military establishment, based on professional soldiers rather than militia members. We and our potential opponents have access to technologies undreamed of in the 1700s, such as drones, nuclear weapons, long-range missiles, and cyberwarfare. For an originalist, none of that is relevant to the scope of presidential power over military hostilities. In fact, for an originalist, nothing that has happened since 1800 or so has much relevance to interpreting the Constitution. Non-originalists disagree.

The Debate over Originalism

The debate over originalism has raged for more than forty years, since the theory was fully embraced by conservatives, and it shows no signs of abating. I will give a quick overview of the arguments on both sides of this debate and resist the impulse to dive deeper into the thousands of law review pages devoted to the subject. Much of the debate seems most relevant to judicial rulings on individual rights, but I will focus on the parts that are most pertinent to presidential power.

Although originalism takes many forms, at heart it is the view that the meaning of the Constitution was fixed on the date it was ratified. Opponents believe that the meaning has evolved as society has changed over the past two centuries. Originalists believe this evolutionary approach gives judges too much power to impose their values on society. Justice Scalia was especially insistent about the need to follow originalism in order to curb judicial activism. Originalists also argue that the Constitution gains its legitimacy from its ratification by the people two centuries ago. For an interpretation of the Constitution to be legitimate, it, too, must be based on their understanding of its meaning at the time. And originalists argue that intent is the usual basis for interpreting legal documents and, in any event, that originalism has always been the main instrument of constitutional interpretation outside of mid-twentieth-century liberal activism.

Critics of originalism are quick to argue that the original intent isn't a sound basis for interpreting the Constitution. It isn't easy to establish what the delegates at the Constitutional Convention thought about many issues. There are big gaps in the historical record, and different historians interpret the record differently. In addition, supporters of the Constitution may not have shared the same understanding of its meaning or expectations about how it would be applied. Madison and Hamilton famously disagreed with each other and sometimes with their earlier selves about the meaning of the Constitution. It is hard to know how to attribute an "intent" to a diverse group of individuals who may not always have agreed. In response to these concerns about reconstructing the original intent, many originalists have switched their focus from "original intent" to "original public understanding." Rather than ask what the authors of the Constitution had in mind, they ask how a reasonable reader in the late eighteenth century would have understood its words.

Despite their differences, originalists are in agreement that the original intent or meaning trumps other approaches to constitutional interpretation (except, perhaps, firmly settled precedent) whenever the original history can be discerned with sufficient specificity to resolve the question at issue. As Justice Scalia once wrote, the "Great Divide with regard to constitutional interpretation is not that between framers' intent and objective meaning, but rather that between original meaning (whether derived from framers' intent or not) and current meaning."

Critics have also challenged the claim that originalism reduces judicial leeway and thereby takes the politics out of constitutional law. Given an unclear historical record, they argue, originalists are likely to find the answers in history that fit their own ideological bent. This is especially true because of originalists' penchant for switching between a focus on original intent and one on original understanding, as well as their ability to frame historical questions in either very specific or very general ways. Critics also question whether lawyers and judges possess the training and historical knowledge needed for expert judgment on questions of constitutional interpretation.

Finally, critics argue that originalism fails to accurately describe the American constitutional tradition. Modern non-originalist opinions by the Supreme Court have banned racial segregation, provided legal protection to advocacy by dissidents, limited discrimination against women and sexual orientation minorities, and allowed federal regulation of matters such as employment discrimination, environmental pollution, and organized crime. Critics portray originalism as an attempt to reimpose an archaic legal order to the detriment of equality values, civil liberties, and a modern, integrated economy and society.

A tension between constitutional meaning and the perspective of contemporary society is inherent in originalism, and it limits the ability of originalist scholars to bridge the distance between the two. Without some distinction between current understanding and original meaning, originalism would be indistinguishable from the "living Constitution" approach that it rejects. However we fill in the blank in the phrase "original ____," whether with "intent," "understanding," or something else, the word *original* highlights that it is not the *present* but the *past* that is of importance.

One problem originalists face is what to do about Supreme Court decisions they consider wrong on originalist grounds. A few originalists, such as Justice Thomas, simply think those decisions should be overruled as soon as possible. But most think it is important to give weight to judicial precedents, as has been the practice in the Anglo-American legal tradition. Just how much weight precedents should have is something originalists disagree about it. For someone like Justice Thomas, the Supreme Court decisions discussed throughout this book don't count for much, but other originalists would give them weight. For those other originalists, the question of when to overrule decisions in the name of original understanding can be a vexing one.

It is only fair to explain my own view about originalism. I have to confess that I have never been able to accept the idea that the meaning of the Constitution was fixed for all time on the day that the ninth state of the thirteen states ratified it, which was all that was required for it to go into effect. This is partly because I believe that the historical record is more complex and ambiguous than many originalists seem to think. But it is also partly because deciding tough issues on the basis of events a century or two ago, without considering the lessons of later history and present realities, seems like a strange way to run a government. In a law review article, I wouldn't put my conclusions this bluntly or simplistically, but all the nuances aren't necessary for my purposes here. Still, like nearly all non-originalists, I think that the history of the framing period is always relevant to constitutional disputes and sometimes deserves heavy weight. That's why I coauthored a book about constitutional history featuring long excerpts from the convention debates and the ratification arguments.

The text and the framing era deserve consideration for several reasons. Both provided the seeds from which the present organization of government came to be. The Framers also articulated values that we share today—recognizing the need for an energetic government with strong leadership, yet concerned about the risks of unrestrained executive power to democracy and individual rights. Canadians call their view of constitutional interpretation the "living tree." That captures the gist of my approach, which is to view constitutional interpretation as firmly rooted but also subject to further growth. In particular, unlike originalists, I think we need to take account of how the branches of the tree have grown, not just the location of the roots and trunk. We need to consider not simply the document created by the Framers, but the structure of government that has evolved over generations of American history. We also need to leave space for renewal in the face of new challenges. Knowing what Americans thought George Washington could do with the militia is not much help for understanding how to govern cyberwarfare or domestic wiretapping.

I realize that many smart people disagree with me about the originalism issue, and the issues are far more complex than the previous paragraph suggests. It is possible that my views are simply a product of the era in which I learned constitutional law, when the dominant view embraced the idea of a living Constitution.

In any event, you don't have to agree with me about originalism for the purposes of this book. The meaning of history is rarely indisputable, so even originalists can reach very different conclusions. In what follows, I try to be even-handed in giving an account of the relevant history. Like almost everyone else who writes about constitutional law, I consider the views of the Framers very important, though I don't consider them as decisive as originalists do. If you think I'm wrong about that, you're welcome to give the historical discussions in later chapters as much weight as you find appropriate. Correspondingly, you're welcome to give less weight to Supreme Court decisions, although if you're like most non-originalists, you won't brush them aside completely. In short, the dispute between originalists and non-originalists is frequently a matter of emphasis, even though legal scholars, including me, have tended to emphasize the theoretical differences over the practical overlap. With this discussion of originalism in mind, it is time to take a closer look at the different models of the presidency.

The Presidentialist Model

What I am calling presidentialism is shorthand for a cluster of views about presidential power. In its narrowest form, it's a theory about the chain of command within the government. In the narrow form of the unitary executive theory, the president is essentially commander in chief of the entire executive branch, not just the military. It would probably be best if the term "unitary executive" had been limited to that single issue of command over executive officers rather than sometimes being applied more broadly to all of what I'm calling presidentialism.

Even that narrow version of presidentialism would have dramatic consequences. If fully adopted, the unitary executive theory would mean some fairly sweeping changes in the way modern government functions. Since the 1880s, when Grover Cleveland was president, we have had independent agencies like the Federal Trade Commission (FTC), the Federal Communications Commission (FCC), and the Federal Reserve Bank. The heads of these commissions have been appointed by the president, but the president needs to show "good cause" to remove them before their terms are up. Modern practice includes not only a variety of independent federal agencies like those mentioned above but also a range of other mechanisms to limit political influence over the operation of the bureaucracy, such as civil service protections, inspectors general, and voluntary state enforcement of federal law. As we will see later, the Supreme Court today seems increasingly sympathetic to the unitary executive vision of presidential control over the executive branch, though it remains to be seen just how far the Court will go.

The term "unitary executive" is also commonly used in a much broader sense. Beyond the issue of the president's control over the bureaucracy, the term is often used to refer to all arguments for inherent presidential power, not just inherent authority to direct executive branch officials. For instance, some scholars argue that the president alone can make certain decisions, such as when and how to take military action. These decisions are "unitary" in the sense that the power is exercised by a single person, the president, rather than the president and members of Congress and judges. Another reason is that many of the arguments for these broader claims overlap with the narrower argument for unbridled presidential control of the executive branch. In particular, like the arguments for a presidential power to remove other officials, the arguments for the president's war powers rely heavily on the vesting clause.

All of the variants of presidentialism can be seen as relying on three major arguments: the constitutional text, the original understanding, and subsequent practice by the executive branch. Here is a brief orientation to these three arguments and some common counterarguments.

Constitutional Text

In terms of the constitutional text, the theory relies first and foremost on the vesting clause. Unitary executive theorists argue that this clause places the executive power in the president, not in some more diffuse body. This understanding of the vesting clause is reinforced by the take care clause, which makes the president personally responsible for ensuring "faithful execution" of the laws. By "vesting" the "executive power" in the president, so the argument goes, the Constitution makes it clear that only the president and subordinates can execute the laws. For advocates of the broader theory, the same language gives the president broad powers over foreign relations and use of the military, which are said to be inherently executive. This theory traces back to Alexander Hamilton's defense of Washington's Neutrality Proclamation.

Critics of the unitary executive theory do not view the vesting clause as a substantive grant of power but rather as descriptive of the general nature of the office, the equivalent of adding the phrase "Executive Power" to the heading "Article II." These critics view the president as an overseer of the executive branch, not as "the decider." They note that other parts of Article II speak of duties or powers of other officers, implying that the president does not hold all executive power in their own hands. In the critics' view, the take care clause requires presidents to do their best to ensure that the laws are faithfully executed but does not imply that the president controls decisions made throughout the executive branch. And, in their view, the take care clause may actually impose limitations on the president's control of subordinates in some circumstances, that is, in cases where presidential control might actually undermine the proper execution of the laws. Critics also emphasize that the necessary and proper clause gives Congress the power to pass laws necessary and proper not only to the exercise of its own powers but also to the powers vested in the other branches of the federal government.

The upshot is that these critics of presidentialism agree that the president must have considerable control over the executive branch but not necessarily the absolute control advocated by the unitary executive theory. In terms of the broader argument about the vesting clause, the critics believe that the president's power over foreign relations and military matters must be linked to the more specific grants of power in Article II, such as the power to act as commander in chief.

Original Understanding

Advocates of presidentialism also point to a body of evidence before and during the drafting and ratification of the Constitution. Well-known political theorists such as John Locke and Montesquieu wrote of the importance of separating the legislative and executive powers in order to avoid tyranny. They also gave broad definitions of executive power. Some opponents of the Constitution advocated an executive council to restrain and counsel the president; the Constitution's supporters pointed to the need for a single head of the executive branch in order to obtain vigorous action as well as accountability. In addition, certain essays in the Federalist Papers, in particular, Federalist No. 70 (discussed earlier), stress the need for an energetic executive, both in enforcing the laws and in foreign affairs. The ratification debates also contained expressions of the importance of the take care clause to ensure the vigorous enforcement of federal law.

Critics of presidentialism point to other historical evidence bearing on the role of the president. Essentially, they accuse unitary executive theorists of cherry-picking statements that give a false picture of clarity and consensus among the Framers rather than portraying the more complex and conflicted process of decision making. Critics instead see considerable dispute and uncertainty at the Constitutional Convention about the meaning of the separation of powers. For instance, to provide another layer of deliberation, Madison had proposed a standing council of revision that would have combined executive and judicial functions. Rather than reflect a strict philosophy of separation of powers, debates turned on more pragmatic considerations. During ratification, according to the critics, the supporters of the Constitution pointed to the need for unity at the top of the executive branch but did not further argue that all officials must be at the beck and call of the chief executive in order to ensure effective government. Indeed, at the time of the founding, a variety of public and private actors enforced the law.

Later Practice

Advocates of presidentialism also rely on post-ratification history to confirm their position. Much of this history concerns actions and statements by early presidents, who asserted the power to direct a variety of other executive branch officials and took the initiative in foreign affairs and military matters. Congress was divided on the issue, but many members believed that the president had the constitutional power to remove executive branch officials, though quite a few others disagreed. Once again, critics contest the evidence. They point to the laws establishing the Treasury Department and the Comptroller General as instances in which Congress took pains to establish the duties of officials independent of the president and in which Congress viewed the offices as enjoying a special relationship with Congress's own activities. Madison seemed to think that officials performing more judicial functions should be shielded from removal. Although the statute establishing the Post Office originally provided that it would operate under the direction of the president, this language was removed almost immediately when the law was amended. On the broader question of foreign affairs and war powers, the critics again point to evidence suggesting a major role for Congress.

I will dive into many of these issues later. I do not expect the debate among legal scholars and historians to be settled any time soon. In terms of the broader claims for presidential power, presidents have definitely dominated the national security sphere for the past century or more, frequently giving minimal heed to whatever prerogatives Congress might claim. But these presidential assertions of power have not gone unchallenged, and from time to time Congress has successfully pushed back.

The mirror image of presidentialism is what has been called the Whig theory of the presidency, after the name of a nineteenth-century precursor of today's Republican Party. This theory was espoused by the Whig Party from the time of Andrew Jackson until it later fragmented, with many northern members forming the core of the new Republican Party. The Whig theory is based on congressional supremacy: Congress sets policy and structures the government, and the president is merely

Congress's agent in carrying out its decisions. This theory was born in reaction to Jackson—whom the Whigs called "King Andrew" because of his penchant for unilateral executive action. The Whig theory came close to describing the operations of the government during the time between Lincoln's death and Theodore Roosevelt's presidency, although presidents were probably never actually as weak as the theory suggested. Even a president subordinate to Congress is a very powerful individual.

The Supreme Court has taken a middle ground between the unitary executive theory and the Whig theory. It has often been broadly supportive of presidential power, but it has been more concerned about checks and balances than unitary executive theorists generally have been. The resulting legal doctrines have not been as crisp and clear as they would be if the Court had fully bought into either of the two more purist approaches. So far, however, the Court has preferred to play the role of referee between Congress and the president rather than give either branch complete dominance.

The phrase "wall of separation" is usually used in the context of the establishment clause, as a barrier between church and state. But it would also be an apt metaphor for presidentialism. Presidentialists view the government as divided into three walled kingdoms—executive, legislative, and judicial—each with complete power within its own kingdom. There are only a small number of doorways between the kingdoms that allow one to intrude on the affairs of another. The president's power to veto legislation is one example. The Senate's power to approve or reject treaties is another.

A different metaphor—"checks and balances"—characterizes an alternative vision of the relationship between the branches. It emphasizes the ability of the branches to prevent abuses of power by each other, though it also leaves room for considerable cooperation between the branches. Indeed, if the three branches were constantly at war, little would ever be accomplished. This more interactive vision has heavily influenced the modern Supreme Court. The one area where presidentialism has made major inroads involves presidential control within the executive branch.

The Constitutional Law of Checks and Balances

We can get a better sense of how the idea of checks and balances works from the leading case on presidential power, *Youngstown Steel & Tube Co. v. Sawyer*, better known as the *Steel Seizure* case. The case arose during the Korean War. After a labor dispute threatened to close American steel mills, President Harry Truman concluded that such a closure would cripple the US war effort. Consequently, he ordered the steel mills to be seized by the government. You may be picturing tanks and armed troops descending on the steel mills, but the seizure basically meant that notices of the takeover were posted in the mills and that the government could set wages and prices. The steel companies continued to operate the mills under protest and challenged the seizure as unconstitutional.

Truman was a Democrat, and every member of the Court had been appointed by him or Franklin Roosevelt, his Democratic predecessor. Several had been political allies or had served under one president or the other. The majority opinion was written by Justice Hugo Black, who had attained his position by being a ferociously loyal Democratic senator. You might expect that the Court would rule in Truman's favor. But in a bluntly worded opinion, Justice Black rebuffed Truman's action.

Before deciding constitutional issues, the Supreme Court typically considers whether there is a nonconstitutional basis, such as a federal statute, that would decide a case. Justice Black began by asking whether Congress had authorized Truman's action. He observed that while two statutes did allow the president to seize property under certain circumstances, neither statute was applicable, and

Congress had provided other mechanisms for dealing with labor disputes. Thus, any justification for Truman's action would have to come directly from the Constitution rather than any authority delegated by Congress.

Black then examined possible sources of constitutional authority for the president's action. He dismissed the argument that the seizure was an exercise of the president's power as commander in chief: "We cannot with faithfulness to our constitutional system hold that the Commander in Chief of the Armed Forces has the ultimate power as such to take possession of private property in order to keep labor disputes from stopping production." That, he said, was "a job for the Nation's lawmakers, not for its military authorities." Similarly, he was unwilling to rely on the president's executive power as a source of authority. "In the framework of the Constitution," he said, "the President's power to see that the laws are faithfully executed refutes the idea that he is to be a lawmaker." Rather, Congress has the lawmaking power, and the Constitution "did not subject this lawmaking power of Congress to presidential or military supervision or control." Finally, Justice Black found it irrelevant that previous presidents had sometimes seized property without statutory authority in wartime or emergencies, for "even if this be true, Congress has not thereby lost its exclusive constitutional authority to make laws necessary and proper to carry out the powers vested by the Constitution 'in the Government of the United States, or in any Department or Officer thereof.'" Because in his view Truman's seizure of the steel mills lacked either congressional or constitutional authorization, Justice Black concluded that it was unconstitutional.

Justice Black's opinion was joined by four other justices, making it the official majority opinion. But those four apparently did not fully agree with Black. They all filed concurring opinions to explain their views, three of which deviated from his reasoning and considered the seizure invalid because it was at odds with congressional policy.

Instead of Justice Black's opinion, the more nuanced concurring opinion of Justice Robert Jackson has come to be seen as the authoritative statement of the law.

Justice Jackson's opinion is especially interesting because, as attorney general under President Roosevelt, he had endorsed strong executive action, including one industry seizure that the Truman administration cited in defense of the steel seizure. He had also gone out on a limb to support some of FDR's actions in the run-up to World War II. But he was also acutely aware of the importance of interactions between the president and Congress. Given his history as attorney general, he might have seemed likely to support Truman's action. He did not take that route, but he did not adopt Black's rigid view of presidential power either.

Justice Jackson pooh-poohed the possibility of defining presidential power based on the original understanding. In a striking turn of phrase, he said that "just what our forefathers did envision, or would have envisioned had they foreseen modern conditions, must be divined from materials almost as enigmatic as the dreams Joseph was called upon to interpret for Pharaoh." The inability to find clear historical answers was not for lack of trying, he contended, for "a century and a half of partisan debate and scholarly speculation yields no net result but only supplies more or less apt quotations from respected sources on each side of any question." Thus, Jackson was no fan of what we now call originalism, at least in the context of presidential power.

Rather than focus on original intent, Jackson thought, it was more important to view the issue of presidential power in the context of practical realities. He emphasized the working relationships between the branches of government, as they had struggled with the problems of governance over the years. Or as put more eloquently by Justice Jackson, "While the Constitution diffuses power the better to secure liberty, it also contemplates that practice will integrate the dispersed powers into a workable government. It enjoins upon its branches separateness but interdependence, autonomy but reciprocity."

With this idea in mind, Justice Jackson divided issues of presidential power into three categories, each with its own rules. The first category strongly favors the president. Congress has authorized the president's action, and the president's powers are at their maximum because the president exercises the combined powers of both branches.

In the second category, Congress is silent, but the president claims independent authority. Here, past practice can be important. In this category, outcomes are more doubtful. According to Justice Jackson, "When the President acts in the absence of either a congressional grant or denial of authority," there is a "zone of twilight" in which the division of powers is unclear. Consequently, "congressional inertia, indifference or quiescence" can enable and perhaps invite the president to act. Justice Jackson found it difficult to prescribe rules for this category, believing that "any actual test of power is likely to depend on the imperatives of events and contemporary imponderables rather than on abstract theories of law."

In the third and final category, the president acts in the face of a congressional prohibition, and here "his power is at its lowest ebb." The president's "claim to a power at once so conclusive and preclusive must be scrutinized with caution, for what is at stake is the equilibrium established by our constitutional system." In fact, in the nearly seventy years since Jackson wrote, there is only one case in which the Court has ruled for the president in a category 3 case.

Justice Jackson placed President Truman's steel seizure in the third category because Congress had provided other mechanisms for dealing with labor disputes, including those with national impact, and had refrained from authorizing government seizures. Jackson then scrutinized all the specific constitutional sources of presidential power and decided that none of them applied.

He first rejected the argument that the vesting clause gave the president unlimited powers: "The example of such unlimited executive power that must have most impressed the forefathers was the prerogative exercised by George III, and the description of its evils in the Declaration of Independence leads me to doubt that they were creating their new Executive in his image." Similarly, he did not think the commander in chief clause power applied. He felt sure that "the Constitution did not contemplate that the title Commander in Chief of the Army and Navy will constitute him also Commander in Chief of the country, its industries and its inhabitants." Finally, Justice Jackson rejected the government's reliance on the take care clause, which he viewed as extending presidential power as far as there is law to enforce, while the due process clause means that government power extends no *further* than law exists to authorize it. Finding no explicit grant of power to the president that might override congressional disapproval, Jackson held the seizure unconstitutional.

The *Steel Seizure* case shows that exercises of presidential power are on strongest ground when they can be traced to some specific grant of authority, either in a specific clause in the Constitution or in a statute enacted by Congress. Relatedly, the case establishes that with certain exceptions, the lawmaker (Congress) gets to control the law enforcer (the president).

The status of Justice Jackson's opinion was cemented three decades later in an opinion written by Justice (later Chief Justice) William Rehnquist. Rehnquist, perhaps not coincidentally, had been a law clerk for Justice Jackson the year the *Steel Seizure* case was decided. This case arose from dramatic events in Iran. Students, who were generally thought to be acting on behalf of the anti-American government, seized the American embassy in Tehran and took the embassy staff hostage. President Ronald Reagan negotiated an agreement with the Iranian government for the release of the hostages. In return for their release, the United States agreed to release

Iranian funds held in America, suspend all legal actions in US courts against the government of Iran, and refer all claims against Iran to an international tribunal. The major constitutional dispute involved the suspension of litigation in the US courts. Although no statute directly authorized the suspension, the Court upheld it because it concluded that Congress had implicitly endorsed the practice of entering into such agreements. The Court relied on a long practice of presidential settlement of private claims against foreign governments and congressional legislation implementing these settlements. The Court also made it clear that *Steel Seizure* provided the appropriate framework for analysis, though not a rigid set of rules.

The *Steel Seizure* framework sees congressional and presidential powers as overlapping and sometimes unclear. When Congress and the president work together, their powers reinforce each other. But when they conflict, Congress wins, unless a power expressly granted to the president is impaired. This is quite a different way of thinking about power than the wall of separation. Both views claim to embody the rule of law and democratic accountability but in different ways.

This conflict will appear again and again in this book, first with regard to disputes over the president's control of foreign affairs in the next chapter. Congress has generally been content to give the president leeway in dealing with foreign nations. But it has tried to intervene on various occasions. When it has done so, disputes about the president's constitutional power over foreign affairs are seen in stark relief.

3 The President and Foreign Affairs

Domestic policy is ultimately in the hands of Congress. It is Congress that creates major domestic programs, from civil rights laws to environmental laws to the multi-trillion-dollar response to the coronavirus pandemic. But outside our borders, it is the president who takes the initiative. Foreign affairs are near the core of presidential power.

We see examples of this all the time. For decades, the United States treated the government of Taiwan as the legitimate government of China while refusing to have contact or engage in trade with the People's Republic of China. President Richard Nixon first began to reverse that stance, a process that continued under a series of his successors. When relations with China became chillier, it was President Trump who made the key policy decisions.

Another recent example involves climate change. The Clinton administration negotiated the Kyoto Protocol, a major international effort to cut carbon emissions from developed countries. When George W. Bush was elected, he decided that the agreement placed too many economic burdens on the United States, and he decided not to send the proposed treaty to the Senate for ratification. With Obama's election, US policy shifted again, and he signed the Paris Agreement, in which countries around the world agreed to address their carbon emissions. Trump denounced the Paris Agreement and began the process of withdrawal soon after taking office. Congress and the courts sat on the sidelines throughout this process.

The dominant presidential role in foreign policy goes back much further than Trump. As early as George Washington, presidents have taken the initiative in this area and have done their best to relegate Congress and the courts to the sidelines. Their ability to do so has ebbed and flowed, but during the past century they have succeeded far more than they have failed. These actions directly affect the lives of Americans: troops who are sent on dangerous missions abroad, Americans whose phone calls and emails are swept up into investigations of foreigners, and diplomatic spats leading to trade sanctions that affect the economy or immigration limits that affect families.

Presidents not only stake a claim to power over foreign affairs, but they are also eager to exclude Congress, the courts, and state government from this arena. Those institutions in turn claim that their own prerogatives are being violated. So these disputes over presidential powers are turf wars but turf wars with very high stakes.

War and foreign affairs, the subjects of the next two chapters, overlap along many dimensions. Both involve national security. At the extreme, foreign policy blurs into outright warfare. There is a gray area between them involving covert actions. And with the exception of the Civil War, military hostilities have always involved foreign actors. Thus, warfare, diplomacy, and treaties are all connected. So are the presidential and congressional powers relating to those issues. It is not surprising that the Framers of the Constitution often lumped both subjects together as "the powers of war and peace." But trying to cover war and foreign affairs in two chapters is hard enough: there is more than enough for a separate book on each subject. Trying to cover everything in a single chapter would be completely unmanageable.

I will begin with foreign affairs—meaning everything about our relationship with foreign countries except for the use of armed force.

This includes diplomacy but also other activities such as intelligence gathering, foreign aid, and recognition of foreign powers. The issues here are not just about diplomats in fancy clothes sitting around talking. I will also discuss whether the president has the power to engage in wiretapping in the United States without congressional authority, whether the president (and only the president) has the power to tear up treaties, and whether the president can direct the actions of state governments to advance US foreign policy.

As always, we start with the text of the Constitution. Article II gives the president three powers specifically relating to foreign affairs: the power to receive foreign ambassadors, the power to appoint US ambassadors, and the power to make treaties. The latter two powers require the advice and consent of the Senate. Presidents have built their control of foreign affairs on a generous interpretation of these powers, buttressed by a suite of other arguments.

While the clauses granting these powers could be read narrowly to make the president the mouthpiece of Congress, it is reasonable to interpret them as giving the president complete control of diplomacy, meaning all formal communications with foreign governments, including treaty negotiations. In the arena of foreign affairs, presidents also have relied on the general "executive power" they claim under the vesting clause. And from the beginning, they have pointed to a practical justification: dealing with foreign countries involves the kind of decisiveness, secrecy, and information available only to the executive branch. Today, they can also point to a history of presidential dominance of foreign affairs as an accepted feature of American government.

The constitutional text clearly does not give presidents the only role in dealing with other countries. While presidents have exercised broad discretion in foreign affairs, the Constitution also gives Congress important foreign affairs powers. Even in terms of diplomacy, Congress is not completely without influence. The Senate must approve treaties and the appointment of ambassadors. Historically, the power to approve treaties has included the power to add "reservations," in effect, exceptions and conditions on ratification. Thus, unlike the president's power to approve or veto legislation, which is limited to a simple yes or no, the Senate plays a more active role in shaping international commitments.

Congress has other powers as well. The commerce clause gives Congress the power to regulate international trade, not just interstate commerce. Congress also has the power to punish "Offences against the Law of Nations," meaning conduct that violates international law. Congress can influence foreign affairs using other powers, such as conducting oversight hearings and refusing to appropriate funds for some activity abroad that the president wants to pursue. A further limit on presidential exclusivity is that even state governments can play some role. They can enter into "compacts and agreements" (but not "treaties") with foreign powers, so long as Congress consents.

Congress's powers can be used to initiate policy or counter presidential initiatives. Of course, they can also be used—and frequently are used—to delegate additional authority to the president beyond that which the Constitution conveys directly. To take recent history as an example, President Trump aggressively used tariff increases as a policy instrument, relying on a federal statute that authorizes tariffs to protect US security. He also relied on statutory authority to restrict travel from China and Europe in response to the coronavirus, and earlier to make controversial arms sales to foreign countries.

There are many questions in the area of foreign policy that have never been addressed by the courts, leaving Congress and presidents to fight things out. Courts are wary of intervening in these battles. They often say that these cases present "political questions" over which they have no jurisdiction, meaning that the issues are relegated to the "political" branches of government to work out. Later in the book, I will take a closer look at this political question doctrine.

For now, it's enough to say that it has left many constitutional conflicts to the other branches of government. In the absence of a neutral judicial arbitrator, disputes between Congress and the president have no necessary end point.

Advocates on both sides have developed their own stock arguments based on the constitutional text and structure, evidence of the original understanding, whatever precedents exist, and historical practice, sometimes augmented by arguments about practicalities. The executive branch has been especially assiduous in marshaling legal arguments. Legal opinions by the US attorney general, or in more recent years the Office of Legal Counsel in the Justice Department, now constitute a formidable body of "precedents" that presidents can cite. Congress has been less systematic about making its arguments, but it does not lack for advocates. With the courts often refusing to act as referees, some of the arguments seem to go on forever.

One of the dividing lines in this debate is whether the vesting clause gives the president unbridled control of foreign affairs. Although all supporters of the unitary executive theory agree that the vesting clause gives the president inherent "executive" powers, they don't all agree on whether this includes inherent control of foreign affairs. Some leading conservative scholars argue for presidential hegemony over war and foreign affairs, but other conservatives view the original understanding as completely contrary to that view.

Pragmatists are also divided. They agree that the president has broad foreign affairs powers, but they do not necessarily agree about what kinds of checks Congress can apply. There is a pragmatic argument for presidential dominance in this area, based on the need for decisive, unified government action and the president's unique access to intelligence. But there is also a pragmatic argument that these decisions are too important to be left to a single person in the Oval Office and that unlimited presidential power creates too much risk of abuse.

In terms of legal arguments, pragmatists generally don't rely on the vesting clause. In support of presidential power, they may give broad interpretations of specific grants of power, such as the president's power to receive foreign ambassadors and appoint American ones. Or else they simply fall back on pragmatic arguments and historical practice, as opposed to the constitutional text. Other pragmatists, those who wish to check presidential authority, give broader interpretations to Congress's powers, as well as wanting the courts to play a more active role.

In looking at the allocation of powers over foreign affairs, it makes sense to begin with the vesting clause and then turn to the pragmatist approach, to which the Supreme Court seems inclined in the form of the *Steel Seizure* case.

For the present, I want to focus primarily on diplomacy and nonmilitary options available to the president. The line is admittedly a blurry one, since presidents can use nonmilitary options such as covert operations and cyberattacks, which blend into the outright use of force. There is one important issue that is common to both the military and foreign affairs authority: the claim that the vesting clause gives the president sweeping powers in both these domains.

At its most dramatic, the question is whether the president can take the country to war without congressional approval. Although government lawyers and respected scholars have made the vesting clause argument, it has had only modest support from the Supreme Court. Instead, the Court has taken a more measured view of presidential power, which looks much like the *Steel Seizure* approach of Justice Jackson.

Foreign Affairs Powers, Express and Otherwise

The Constitution gives the president some powers relating to foreign affairs, such as the power to appoint US ambassadors and receive foreign ambassadors. But these powers, on their face, do not encompass matters like presidential control of intelligence operations, use of trade sanctions, or overriding state laws. Thus, presidents have often looked elsewhere in their search for power.

If there is one case that presidents most frequently cite in arguments about foreign affairs powers, it is *Curtiss-Wright*. This 1930s case grew out of an increasingly brutal war in South America. Congress passed a law giving the president the power to ban exports of weapons to either side if doing so would help bring the war to a close. The president issued such a ban. An arms manufacturer was indicted for selling fifteen machine guns to Bolivia in violation of the ban. The manufacturer challenged the constitutionality of the president's action. Although the *Steel Seizure* case was still some years in the future, the Court rejected this argument on grounds that we can now see as referring to the first category of Justice Jackson's classification scheme. The Court emphasized the breadth of presidential power where Congress has authorized an action in the foreign sphere and where the president also has independent authority.

The Court's opinion was written by Justice George Sutherland, one of the leading conservatives on the New Deal Court. The language of the opinion went well beyond the facts of the case. The Court first stated that the foreign affairs power, unlike domestic legislative power, was already vested in the Union as an aspect of national sovereignty prior to the adoption of the Constitution. The Court then argued that this inherent national power was then conferred on the president. "Not only . . . is the federal power over external affairs in origin and essential character different from that over internal affairs," the Court found, "but participation in the exercise of the power is significantly limited." Consequently, "in this vast external realm, with its important, complicated, delicate and manifold problems, the President alone has the power to speak or listen as a representative of the nation." Conceptually, this argument is different from the vesting clause claim just considered; it relies on the general nature of the federal government rather than on any specific clause. But the practical implications seem very much the same.

In addition to this theoretical argument, the Court relied on practical considerations, such as the need for secrecy in the conduct of diplomacy and the president's access to confidential information. "In short," the Court wrote, "we are here dealing not alone with an authority vested in the President by an exertion of legislative power, but with such an authority plus the very delicate, plenary and exclusive power of the President as the sole organ of the federal government in the field of international relations."

The *Curtiss-Wright* theory of inherent foreign affairs powers, derived outside the power grants in the Constitution, has not been repeated in later opinions. This is perhaps because the theory is in serious tension with the foundational idea of a national government of limited, enumerated powers. Historians have not been particularly kind to Justice Sutherland's version of history. But lawyers for the executive branch never tire of quoting the language about presidential supremacy in foreign affairs. In modern times, however, the vesting clause has provided the go-to argument for the president's lawyers.

The executive branch's focus on the vesting clause contrasts with the Supreme Court's method of analyzing foreign affairs cases. Cases since *Curtiss-Wright* have focused on specific constitutional grants of power to the president and on evolving practices under the Constitution. Thus, the more recent cases have more in common with the *Steel Seizure* model of the presidency than with the freewheeling presidential powers portrayed by Justice Sutherland. But this does not mean that the president must always give way before Congress.

A 2015 case, involving whether Congress or the president controls passport language, exemplifies the approach taken in recent decisions. The parents of a child who had been born in Jerusalem wanted his passport to identify that city as part of Israel. At the time, long-standing US foreign policy was to avoid classifying the city as part of any country, given that both the Israelis and the Palestinians claim Jerusalem as their capital. (President Trump later reversed that policy, but he didn't take office until after this case). Despite the long-standing, contrary presidential policy, Congress passed a statute allowing individuals born in Jerusalem to have Israel listed as the location of their birth on their passports. President Obama's State Department refused to implement this law. The Supreme Court used the *Steel Seizure* case to back Obama's position. This was one of those cases in which Congress and the president are in conflict. The Court reasoned that Article II powers, such as the power to receive ambassadors, carry with them exclusive presidential control of the recognition of foreign governments—that is, deciding which government's ambassadors should be received at all. Moreover, in the Court's view, recognition of a foreign government involves not only accepting the government as legitimate but also determining its boundaries. The Court further reasoned that passports are communications between the United States and foreign governments and thus are also under presidential control.

The Court also looked to history. The Court said, "The President since the founding has exercised this unilateral power to recognize new [nation] states—and the Court has endorsed the practice." The Court considered recognition of governments and determination of their boundaries to be parts of the power to receive ambassadors. Thus, the president's use of that power could not be countermanded by Congress.

Interestingly, although he generally championed presidential power, Justice Scalia argued for a narrower view of executive authority in the passport case, siding with the parents over Obama. "Recognition," he said, "is a type of legal act, not a type of statement." In his view, it was "a leap worthy of the Mad Hatter to go from exclusive authority over making legal commitments about sovereignty to exclusive authority over making statements or issuing documents about national borders." In a different mode from his earlier expansive view of presidential power, he emphasized that the Framers "considered a sound structure of balanced powers essential to the preservation of just government, and international relations formed no exception to that principle." As this opinion illustrates, it is a mistake to oversimplify the views of any one judge or scholar.

Overall, the Jerusalem passport case was a narrow win for the president. The Court did not speak in sweeping terms about the president's power over our relations with foreign countries. Instead, it relied on the long-standing tradition that the power to receive ambassadors includes the power to determine whether they represent legitimate governments and on the president's control of official communications with other countries. Passports can be regarded as communications from the US government, though they are equally important these days as a way to reenter the United States. Presidents engage in many other activities involving foreign nations such as managing and sometimes ending foreign aid, control of the CIA and other intelligence agencies, and protecting the nation's borders. *Curtiss-Wright* could be read to give the president free rein over all these activities. But the Court in the passport case, by ruling narrowly, conspicuously steered clear of any broad endorsement of presidential autonomy in foreign affairs.

The Court's reluctance to give presidents a blank check also figured in a 1985 case involving treaty enforcement. The case arose from a dispute over the right of foreigners to consult their countries' consuls (local diplomatic representatives) when arrested. Under the Vienna Convention on Consular Relations, the United States and other countries have agreed to give each other's citizens the right to contact their countries' consuls. Some US states did not comply with this requirement, including Texas in the case of Mexican citizens arrested there and later facing the death penalty. Skipping over some complications, the upshot was that the US Supreme Court said that it would not force states to comply with the Vienna Convention.

President George W. Bush issued a directive telling the states to comply with international law in their criminal cases. The federal government argued that this directive was binding on state courts because of the president's inherent power over foreign affairs. In an opinion by Chief Justice John Roberts, the Court rejected this assertion of presidential authority. Because the treaty was intended to have no domestic legal effect until implemented through legislation, the president's action was questionable under the *Steel Seizure* case's analysis. Unlike the president's power to settle foreign claims (at issue in the Iranian case), Roberts wrote, "the Government has not identified a single instance in which the President has attempted (or Congress has allowed) a presidential directive issued to state courts." He added that the president was even less able to cite a previous example that "reaches deep into the heart of the State's police powers and compels state courts to reopen final criminal judgments and set aside neutrally applicable state laws."

This opinion by Chief Justice Roberts reaffirms that Justice Jackson's concurrence in the *Steel Seizure* case is firmly established law. It also reflects the Court's attentiveness to historical practice in this area, although the Court is always careful to note that past practice would not validate clearly unconstitutional conduct. Both of these aspects reflect a judicial recognition that disputes over the boundaries between Congress and the president are primarily resolved between these two branches through the political process.

Presidents have wanted a more sweeping definition of their powers than these recent cases seem to provide. They have turned to the vesting clause as a way to justify everything from wiretapping in the United States to covert operations against foreign countries, even in the face of congressional restrictions. Since these disputes often involve issues that are unlikely to be heard in the courts, and since the

Supreme Court has not squarely rejected the vesting clause theory, presidents have felt free to act on the basis of this theory. When the Constitution vested the "executive power" in their office, they contend, it gave them control of foreign affairs and the military.

The question of whether the vesting clause gives the president broad power is hotly contested. And no wonder, because this interpretation could give the president inherent power to engage in a suite of actions regardless of statutory restrictions, for example, invading or bombing other countries, undertaking intelligence and covert activities, preventing foreigners from entering the country or deporting them for security reasons, and so forth. Naturally, this interpretation is congenial to presidents. The debate over this interpretation has been mostly waged in terms of the original understanding.

If this seems like a purely academic debate, it has also had real-world consequences. The George W. Bush administration used this argument as the basis for a secret surveillance program, involving interception of data from electronic communications on a vast scale. The administration claimed that the president had authority under the vesting clause to create this program as part of his inherent power over national security. A federal statute called the Foreign Intelligence Surveillance Act (FISA) seems to prohibit this type of surveillance without a warrant. But in the administration's view, the vesting clause trumped the statute: Congress simply had no power to interfere with any program instituted by the president to protect national security. This broad claim turned out to be more sweeping than the Bush administration later proved willing to defend. But the vesting clause remains an important part of constitutional argument about foreign affairs law.

There is ammunition for both sides of the debate in the historical record. Interpreting the evidence is complex because even when a Framer said the president has power to do X, we cannot always know the Framer's specific reason. There is more than one path to concluding that the president has broad power over some particular issue. During the drafting and ratification of the Constitution, speakers did not often lay out their analyses in great, lawyerly detail. Even when they did, advocates of presidential power felt free to mix and match whatever arguments supported a particular possible presidential action.

The arguments get very complex. Although I generally have tried to avoid getting too deeply into the weeds of constitutional argument here, this issue is so important that I feel the need to make an exception. Because there is a lot of back and forth between contesting arguments, a dialogue form seems like a natural way to convey the arguments. In a bow to history, let's call one of our speakers Alexa Hamilton and the other Jamie Madison.

MODERATOR: Thanks for joining us for this discussion about the vesting clause thesis. To get started, Alexa, maybe you can explain the thesis to us.

ALEXA: Glad to. It's really very simple and very obvious. Article II of the Constitution, which is about the president, begins by saying, "The executive power shall be vested in a President of the United States." That's the vesting clause. Except for some powers that the Constitution shifted to Congress, we think that this "executive power" includes all the powers traditionally held by the chief executive in England. That includes complete control of foreign affairs and the military. It also includes complete control of all aspects of the executive branch.

JAMIE: I can't refrain from pointing out that what Alexa calls the "chief executive in England" was actually King George III.

MODERATOR: Okay. Let's talk about the text of the Constitution. Jamie?

JAMIE: Alexa is taking one sentence out of Article II but ignoring the rest of it. If Alexa is right, that first sentence gives the president all the authority that could ever be needed. So how does she explain the fact that Article II goes on to provide some additional powers, like receiving ambassadors. And if the vesting clause already gave the president complete control of the executive branch, why does Article II go on to grant the power to get written opinions from cabinet members? This seems completely unnecessary and even trivial if the president already had such broad authority from the vesting clause.

ALEXA: Admittedly, some of those additional grants of powers do seem unnecessary, but it's not unusual for legal documents to contain excess language that was added just in the interest of clarity. Anyway, Jamie, if the president's powers over foreign affairs and the military don't come from the vesting clause, where do they come from? And what is the vesting clause *for*, if not to grant power to the president?

JAMIE: The Constitution does give the president specific power to appoint ambassadors and consuls with Senate consent. It also makes the president commander in chief. That's enough to give the president the sole role to act as official spokesman for the United States internationally and to oversee the military. But that's a lot less than the complete power over foreign affairs and warfare that you think the vesting clause gives the president.

MODERATOR: Well, it sounds to me like both of your theories have a few problems with the constitutional language to contend with. Let's turn to the original intent of the vesting clause. Alexa, what did the Framers mean when they said "executive power" was vested in the president? What was the original intent?

ALEXA: That's a great question, though I would rather call it the original public understanding. The great political and legal thinkers of the era—Locke, Montaigne, and Blackstone—all viewed the executive power as including the foreign affairs power and the war power. The Framers had that in mind when they used the term "executive power" in the Constitution. You can find statements everywhere that foreign policy and warfare involve exactly the things that the executive does best: decisive, unified action; secrecy; and access to secret information. Those aren't exactly what Congress is good at.

JAMIE: All well and good, but we don't really know that the Framers were informed about the fine points of those writers' works. And yes, you can point to people saying this and that about what the president could possibly do. But I noticed that you used the phrase "original public understanding." What we're talking about now is *not* what the public in 1787 generally thought about presidential power. It's what the public under-stood by the phrase "executive power." If they thought that phrase gave the president such tremendous power, it's just amazing that absolutely nobody ever said so explicitly. The first time the argument was made was by your ancestor, Alexander Hamilton, well *after* the Constitution was already adopted.

ALEXA: If you're right, however, there's a big mismatch between what they said about presidential power and what they actually wrote in the Constitution. That's hard to believe too.

JAMIE: Maybe so, but your theory that they meant to give the president the powers of the British monarch goes way too far. The supporters of the Constitution insisted over and over again that the President was not going to be like the king. Even your ancestor, who loved the idea of executive power as much as anyone, wrote about that at length in the Federalist Papers.

MODERATOR: I would like to change the topic a bit. I know that the Supreme Court often looks at how the early Congress and presidents implemented the Constitution. What does that history have to say about presidential power?

ALEXA: I'll stick to a few bullet points. Congress conceded early on that the president could send special envoys to communicate with foreign governments without asking for anyone's approval. George Washington also gave up on including the Senate in treaty negotiations after one abortive effort. And, of course, Washington also issued the Neutrality Proclamation, keeping the United States out of the war between Britain and France. That's the action my ancestor Alexander so brilliantly defended in his discussion of the vesting clause. Jefferson went to war against the Barbary pirates without asking Congress.

JAMIE: I'll try to be brief too. Each of those events is a lot more complex and nuanced than Alexa would like to admit. And there were also some striking examples of Congress taking the initiative. Congress made President Adams turn over copies of diplomatic communications with France (the famous "XYZ" letters), so it could consider whether there was a basis for going to war. Congress also declared that an existing treaty with France was no longer in effect rather than leave that to the president. Furthermore . . .

MODERATOR: I'm sorry to interrupt, but I think we're going to have to end right there. Sadly, I think we're out of time. Thanks to both of you for those spirited explanations of your viewpoints.

Let me say a little bit about how I view this debate. In my opinion, the fact that the historical debate has continued this long is an indication that it is possible to interpret the evidence in more than one way. It is not impossible to support the vesting clause theory based on the historical record. But I come out clearly on Jamie's side of this question, not Alexa's. For me, the strongest piece of evidence is the silence about the vesting clause in the debates over the Constitution. In terms of the drafting and ratification of the Constitution, it is hard to find anyone who explicitly argued that the president has inherent powers of this kind.

In fact, it's not clear that anybody at all said that the vesting clause gives the president complete control of maintaining peaceful relations or starting wars, or the like. It is easy, on the other hand, to find statements vehemently denying that the president would be anything like the still-hated English monarch. There were also many statements that the powers of war and peace were not the president's (or at least not the president's alone). If the clear meaning of the vesting clause had given the president such unchecked powers, for example, the power to start wars without congressional approval, it seems likely that someone would have said so explicitly. The Framers certainly spent enough time talking about far less weighty issues.

If advocates of the vesting clause thesis were right, the president would have nearly unchecked power to break treaties, impose sanctions, and even use military force, with only narrow exceptions. Yet the Framers feared the abuse of power and were well aware of the grave consequences of such actions for the nation. Assuming they meant to write the president a blank check thus seems at odds with the general tone of founding-era thought.

Since I'm not an originalist, I can't just rely on my reading of the historical record. I agree that there are strong practical reasons for the president to take the lead in foreign affairs and control of the military. The president is the person in charge of managing the government. It's reasonable to assume that the manager is in charge of handling crises in the absence of instructions to the contrary. We expect even a clerk to grab a fire extinguisher when the place is in flames. But while the president has the initiative, I don't see any reason for eliminating a role for Congress. These issues are too important to be left to any single individual.

Despite advocacy by presidential lawyers and some notable legal scholars, I do not expect the Supreme Court to embrace the vesting clause thesis for matters of national security. The reason is partly precedent. But it is not irrelevant that most Americans believe some recent president has grossly abused these powers. For some, it was Barack Obama's bombing campaign in Libya, against the advice of administration lawyers, or wiretapping a suspect with foreign ties who was connected with Trump's 2016 presidential campaign. For others, it was Donald Trump's use of emergency powers to fund a wall on the Mexican border or his unilateral immigration restrictions. The one thing both sides agree on is the danger of unrestrained executive power. It is strong medicine to say that these powers are unlimited and that Congress and the courts are powerless.

Executive Agreements and the Role of the Senate

A special problem arises with respect to presidential agreements with foreign powers. Article II empowers the president to make treaties but only with the consent of the Senate. Presidents make agreements with foreign countries all the time, however, without ever submitting them to the Senate for approval. A recent example is the Paris Agreement on climate change entered into by President Obama, from which President Trump then withdrew. But this example is only one of hundreds, perhaps thousands, of executive agreements.

The two leading cases on the subject of executive agreements arose from President Franklin D. Roosevelt's decision to give diplomatic recognition to the Soviet Union in the 1930s. The Soviet government had seized Russian corporations after the Russian Revolution. In connection with the decision to give diplomatic recognition to the Soviet regime, Roosevelt had entered into a complex executive agreement dealing with claims between Americans and the Soviet government. The state courts refused to enforce legal rights in the hands of the Soviet government that had been seized from Russian corporations. They said recognizing the Soviet seizure of the corporations violated the state's public policy. The question was whether Roosevelt's executive agreement could overturn a state's policies.

In an opinion by Justice Sutherland, the Court upheld Roosevelt's executive agreement and held that it overrode state law. Sutherland, a leading conservative, also wrote the paean to presidential power in *Curtiss-Wright*. In the executive agreement case, Sutherland again emphasized the president's role as the sole international representative of the United States. He also emphasized the established presidential practice of entering into executive agreements. As he wrote, "An international compact, as this was, is not always a treaty which requires the participation of the Senate. There are many such compacts." Consequently, the Court held that the executive agreement was valid. In a related case, the Court warned that US foreign policy might be thwarted if "state laws and policies did not yield before the exercise of the external powers of the United States"; indeed, the "nation as a whole would be held to answer if a State created difficulties with a foreign power."

The Court upheld another executive agreement in the context of the Iranian hostage crisis arising out of the seizure of the US embassy in Tehran in 1979. When President Reagan took office, he negotiated an agreement to free the hostages. In return, the United States agreed to a process for dealing with legal claims by Americans against Iran. Basically, the United States agreed to stop all lawsuits against the Iranians in our own courts, leaving Iran free use of all its bank accounts and other assets in this country. Rather than being decided in the courts, private claims against Iran would be decided by a special tribunal established by the two governments.

The Supreme Court upheld the executive agreement. It relied heavily on a long history of the executive branch settling claims between the United States and foreign nations. Congress had never rejected this practice and had sometimes passed laws implementing those agreements. It seemed unlikely at the time that the Court would disown the hostage agreement, since doing so would hamper the government's efforts to make deals in similar future emergencies.

If executive agreements have the same legal force as treaties in preempting state law, you may wonder where the distinction lies and why presidents ever bother submitting treaties to the Senate. As to the first question, there is no real guidance from the Supreme Court. The cases involving the Soviet Union and Iran could be interpreted narrowly. Those cases involved agreements made in connection with giving formal recognition to a foreign government or in areas like settling legal claims involving foreign countries, where there is a long-standing practice of presidential agreements. But these cases could also be read much more broadly. There are many executive agreements in a wide range of areas—far more than the number of formal treaties. The State Department has developed a set of criteria that it weighs in deciding whether Senate approval is required, including past practice for similar agreements, the proposed duration of the agreement, and whether congressional implementation will be required. In practice this is likely to mean that the decision to submit an agreement to the Senate will often be based either on a desire to give greater reassurance to other countries through the formality of Senate ratification or on congressional pushback against the use of an executive agreement. Given that many agreements require at least some congressional implementation, if only in the form of funding, presidents may be reluctant to use executive agreements if the Senate insists that a pact really amounts to a treaty.

The Paris Agreement limiting carbon emissions is an interesting example of how these decisions are made. Other nations wanted this agreement to be a formal treaty. The Obama administration said that this would be unacceptable. If the agreement were legally binding, it could no longer be considered an executive agreement because of the significance of its provisions. Thus, it would have to be submitted to the Senate, which was unlikely to ratify it. Other participants in the negotiations gave way in order to have the United States join. For that reason, the only legally binding portions of the Paris Agreement relate to less substantive matters such as procedures for monitoring and verifying carbon emissions. If the emission limitations were themselves legally binding, then the agreement would have been so important that it would have required Senate approval, which would clearly not happen. The Obama administration's view was that provisions that were legally binding were minor enough to be adopted through an executive agreement. Notably, when President Trump announced his decision to withdraw from the agreement, he undertook to comply with the withdrawal procedure provided by the agreement itself. Thus, he chose to treat the Paris Agreement as legally valid without Senate confirmation.

There is a third form of international agreement that has become particularly common recently. These are called executive-congressional agreements. Such agreements are negotiated by the president but then enacted as statutes by Congress using one of its legislative powers, such as the power to regulate interstate or international commerce. Since many agreements do involve matters within Congress's legislative powers, this mechanism can potentially replace many Senate-confirmed treaties. This has been the preferred route for creating trade agreements. It was used for the North American Free Trade Agreement (NAFTA), the first trade agreement between the United States, Canada, and Mexico. It was also used for President Trump's replacement agreement, the United States-Mexico-Canada Agreement (USMCA).

There are unsettled constitutional issues relating to executive-congressional agreements. It is unclear whether there are any matters reserved to the treaty power (excluding the House and requiring a Senate supermajority). For example, could a peace treaty after a war take the form of an executive-congressional agreement? It is also undecided whether executive-congressional agreements can be revoked unilaterally by the president. It's hard to see how a president could have the power to terminate an executive-congressional agreement, which takes the form of a statute. The Constitution gives Congress, not the president, the power to pass and repeal statutes. Of course, a particular executive-congressional agreement may itself authorize the president to terminate the agreement, which is a different matter.

Historical practice has been ambiguous about the power to terminate formal treaties. Congress has cancelled some treaties by statute. Presidents also take the position that they are free to revoke treaties. But the issue still has to be considered unsettled. This issue came before the Supreme Court in a 1979 case. President Jimmy Carter had recognized mainland China and withdrawn from an existing treaty with the government in Taiwan (which at that time claimed to be the legitimate government for all of China). In the end, only one justice actually took a position on the president's power to terminate treaties. That justice argued that the president has the power to unilaterally withdraw from treaties. The other justices dodged the issue on various procedural grounds. So it remains unsettled.

As I discuss in a later chapter, the Supreme Court has often done in other cases what it did in the Taiwan treaty case: refuse on jurisdictional grounds to decide important disputes about the limits of presidential power. This is particularly true in the area of foreign affairs, where the Court is especially cautious about intervening. That is one reason there are so many unsettled issues in this area. So the battle for control of foreign affairs continues, with each side repeating its stock arguments.

As we have seen, presidential power in foreign affairs is controversial. But that is nothing compared to the controversy over the president's war-making powers. That topic is the subject of the next chapter.

4 Taking the Country to War

One of the most fraught issues in constitutional law is the president's ability to use military force without Congress's approval. Lives are literally on the line in this situation, and the debates are inevitably heated. The language of the Constitution has not changed, but that is not true of the ways that presidents and Congresses have made decisions on the use of military force. The institutional realities may or may not correspond to what the Framers had in mind.

In this area, there is a ragged trail from practices at the founding to practices today. Congress is sometimes passive in the face of presidential unilateralism but sometimes pushes back. Whether because of changes in constitutional understandings or in the political balance of power, presidents over the past century have taken a more expansive view of their power to use military force independent of Congress. Some recent examples include President Obama's bombing campaign in Libya and air strikes in Syria by both Presidents Trump and Biden. This chapter follows the history of presidential unilateralism from the framing of the Constitution to today.

It is always wise to begin by looking at the Constitution itself. National defense was certainly on the Framers' minds. After all, the country had just emerged from a long, bitter struggle against Britain. The text of the Constitution reflects their concerns about national security. According to the Preamble, one of the Constitution's main purposes was to "provide for the common defense." More specifically, the Constitution makes the president the commander in chief of the military. But the Constitution also vests a bevy of powers in Congress. Most notably, Congress has the power to "declare war." In addition, the Constitution gives Congress five other military powers:

1. Taxing and spending to "provide for the common Defense." This provides authority to finance the government's national security activities.
2. Granting "letters of marque and reprisal," which were used in earlier times to authorize private ships to attack and seize enemy ships, and making rules about captured enemy property or blockade runners.
3. Raising and supporting the army and providing and maintaining the navy.
4. Making rules for the "governance and regulation" of the military.
5. Providing for calling out the militia (today's National Guard) to suppress insurrections and repel invasions.

Congress has some additional powers that are granted only obliquely by the Constitution. When required by rebellion or invasion, the writ of habeas corpus may be suspended—meaning that dangerous individuals can be jailed without a judicial hearing. The Constitution does not say who exercises this power, but it has always been understood that Congress (and maybe *only* Congress) can suspend habeas.

The Constitution also says that the federal government shall protect each state "against invasion." The Constitution does not specify which branch of government is responsible for providing this protection.

To round out the picture, it is worth noting that the states are left with some military authority of their own. Each state controls its state militia, or National Guard, when it has not been called into federal service. Moreover, with the consent of Congress, states can maintain their own army or warships in peacetime. In theory, Congress could override a presidential veto to authorize this and thus give states their own militaries. Moreover, if states are invaded or in imminent danger of invasion, states can "engage in war" on their own.

In terms of the constitutional text, there is also the vesting clause to be considered. Especially during the George W. Bush administration, defenders of presidential power relied on the vesting clause as authority for allowing the president to initiate the use of military force at will. I will not repeat the extensive discussion of the vesting clause in the previous chapter. My own view is that the vesting clause at most gives the president power over the execution of the laws, not remnants of King George's royal powers, such as attacking other countries. But even if I am right about that, it only eliminates one of the arguments for a dominant presidential role; it does not settle the issue.

Since the Constitution gives Congress powers relating to the military, including the power to declare war, we cannot define presidential power without simultaneously defining congressional power. In particular, the scope of Congress's power to declare war is hotly debated. To some scholars, it is crystal-clear that only Congress can authorize the use of military force. But others argue that formal declarations of war had fallen into misuse by the late 1700s, accompanied by a wide understanding that wars could be started without them. We need to take a deeper look into the history to try to sort out this debate.

As is usual with history, what you learn depends partly on what questions you ask. If you ask what the Framers understood to be the powers of a commander in chief, you get one answer. Presidents have leaned heavily on that power. But there is only modest evidence that the Framers understood that language to give the president unlimited control of military force. Originalists who care about "original meaning" or "original understanding" would put special weight on this question. If you ask whether the Framers thought that the president had a special role in national defense, the answer may be different. And if you ask about the lessons of the past century, you may get different answers yet again. Theories of constitutional interpretation matter here, because they dictate which of these questions is most relevant. At least some Framers thought the president should have broad power, but they did not say specifically where that power came from. Key Framers agreed broadly about the general need for a strong, energetic executive, especially in dealing with other countries. Thus, the pro-president case might be stronger for originalists who believe in looking at the "original intent" than for those who focus on the "original meaning" of the text. Still, there is also a lot of evidence that suggests a robust role for Congress. The recent history shows both bold claims of unilateral authority by presidents and some equally bold actions. Yet it also shows efforts at accommodation between Congress and the president.

The War Power and the Framers

We begin where our history as a nation begins, with the War of Independence. George Washington was commander in chief of the Continental Army, but he was far from all-powerful. His actions were closely directed by Congress, sometimes in painful detail. On occasion a committee of the Continental Congress would go to the front to gather information or give Washington directives. Their instructions covered matters such as how to deploy troops and how to treat enemy prisoners. Washington frequently wrote Congress to get permission to move ahead with his proposals, but Congress did not always agree or even respond. For instance, after the British Redcoats won the Battle of Long Island, Washington wanted to burn New York

City so that the British couldn't use it as a base. Congress refused to allow him to do this or to give him permission to abandon a vulnerable fort at the north end of Manhattan. When a high-level British prisoner complained to Washington about his treatment, Washington responded, "[I am] not invested with the Powers you suppose; and it is as incompatible with my authority as my inclination to contravene any determinations Congress may make." As time went on, this close oversight by Congress became unworkable. Congress ultimately realized it was impractical to micromanage a commander in the field and granted Washington broader discretion to act on his own.

Under the Articles of Confederation, which went into effect in 1781, the Continental Congress had the "sole and exclusive right and power to determine on war and peace." There were exceptions, which were later carried over into the Constitution, if a state was attacked or about to be attacked immediately. Since there was no separate executive branch under the Articles of Confederation, Congress also controlled the conduct of war. It took the votes of nine states out of thirteen to appoint a commander in chief.

After independence, state constitutions varied in their provisions for power over the military. Some state constitutions required the governor to consult an executive council before calling out the militia. South Carolina required the consent of the legislature. The Massachusetts constitution gave the governor extensive powers as commander in chief of the military. The New Hampshire constitution gave the governor full power to use the militia within the state against any foe "as shall, in a hostile manner, invade, or attempt the invading, conquering, or annoying this commonwealth." Those powers, however, had to be "exercised agreeably . . . to the laws of the land," leaving them subject to legislative control, as was also true in Massachusetts. And the consent of the New Hampshire legislature was required to use the militia outside the state, as was the case with the

Massachusetts constitution. All of this formed the background for the drafting and ratification of the Constitution.

War Powers at the Founding

The Philadelphia convention met less than eight years after General Cornwallis's surrender at Yorktown ended the War of Independence. Although the Constitution contains important language relating to the military, there was relatively little discussion of the power to go to war. An early draft of the Constitution gave Congress the power to "make war." One key moment at the convention involved an amendment to this language, changing "make war" to "declare war." Unfortunately, it is not terribly clear just why this change was made or what it meant.

James Madison's cryptic notes of the discussion regarding the change have been pored over by generations of lawyers and scholars, searching for hints about the implications of the change. The notes are brief enough to quote in their entirety.

"To make war."

Mr. Pinkney [*sic*] opposed the [vest]ing [of] this power in the Legislature. Its proceedings were too slow. It wd. meet but once a year. The Hs. of Reps. would be too numerous for such deliberations. The Senate would be the best depository, being more acquainted with foreign affairs, and most capable of proper resolutions. * * *

Mr. Butler. The Objections agst the Legislature lie in great degree agst the Senate. He was for vesting the power in the President, who will have all the requisite qualities, and will not make war but when the Nation will support it.

Mr. M[adison] and Mr. Gerry moved to insert "*declare*," striking out "*make*" war; leaving to the Executive the power to repel sudden attacks.

Mr. Sharman [*sic*] thought it stood very well. The Executive shd. be able to repel and not to commence war. "Make" better than "declare" the latter narrowing the power too much.

Mr. Gerry never expected to hear in a republic a motion to empower the Executive alone to declare war.

Mr. Mason was agst. giving the power of war to the Executive, because not (safely) to be trusted with it; or to the Senate, because not so constructed as to be entitled to it. He was for clogging rather than facilitating war; but for facilitating peace. He preferred "*declare*" to "*make.*"

There was clearly some diversity of views. James Madison and Elbridge Gerry, who proposed the change of language from "declare" to "make," explained it as authorizing the president to repel sudden attacks. Pierce Butler wanted to give the president full control, which George Mason, Roger Sherman, and Madison opposed. We do not know what others said, or even the precise language used by these speakers, which makes this brief discussion hard to interpret with confidence. Clearly, the change was intended to shift some of the power to use force from Congress to the president, at least in response to impending or actual attack.

One unanswered question is whether the term "declare war" was used in its colloquial sense of authorizing hostilities or in its technical sense. The practice of the time seemed to indicate that technically a formal declaration of war was not necessary in order to start a war. But a declaration of war *was* legally necessary before a country could take action against residents or property from the other country, or against the other country's shipping. So it is possible that the Framers meant to adopt the technical meaning of a declaration of war, meaning that it was not necessary before going to war but only to authorize certain measures like seizing enemy property. On the other hand, this technical interpretation does not fit very well with Madison's explanation about defensive responses to sudden attacks, which seems to suggest that only Congress could authorize offensive military actions. Madison's notes leave a lot of room for interpretation, and plenty of people have been willing to leap into that space.

As to why the subject did not get more discussion at the convention, I suspect the reason was that the United States was in no position to start wars with other countries. We were a relatively weak nation with a huge war debt that had yet to be paid off. The possibility that we would someday have the world's most powerful military must have been far from the delegates' minds.

There was also discussion of war powers during the ratification process. The Federalist Papers do address warfare, though only in passing. In Federalist No. 41, Madison responded to arguments that federal powers were too extensive. As federal powers "over foreign dangers," he listed the powers to declare war, grant letters of marque, raise armies and fleets, regulate and call out the militia, and levy and borrow money. Madison argued that all of these powers were necessary to defending the country. He then devoted most of the rest of Federalist No. 41 to rebutting claims that the Constitution would result in a large standing army that would threaten democracy. His focus seems to have been on congressional powers. He said nothing specifically about the president. Perhaps the most relevant comment, for our purposes, was about the significance of declaring war. Madison said no one would argue against the necessity of giving the government the power to declare war. That suggests that he thought this power was important, not merely a technicality or an outmoded relic.

Federalist No. 69, by Hamilton, is a review of presidential powers, more or less clause by clause. When he got to the commander in chief clause, he explained it as "nothing more than the supreme command and direction of the military and naval forces, as first General and admiral of the Confederacy; while that of the British king extends to the *declaring* of war and to the *raising* and *regulation* of fleets and armies." The emphasis is in the original.

Hamilton then added that "direction of war implies the direction of the common strength, and the power of directing and employing the common strength forms a usual and essential part in the definition of the executive power." That language might be read, at least in isolation, as an argument for inherent executive power over warfare, but here Hamilton is speaking of a specific clause, the commander in chief clause. In passing in Federalist No. 72, Hamilton also refers to the "direction of the operations of war" as part of "the administration of government" and hence properly given to the president. Note, however, that he does not say "starting wars," which definitely is not merely a matter of "administration."

In Federalist No. 74, Hamilton wrote again about the president's control of the military. He explained that the commander in chief power was similar in many state constitutions. He added that it was obvious that "direction of war most peculiarly demands those qualities which distinguish the exercise of power by a single hand." "Peculiar" meant something like "to a special extent" rather than "odd" or "weird" as it does today.

That's about it, in terms of discussion of the war power. The version of the Federalist Papers that I am using is over 550 pages. These discussions take up about 1 or 2 percent of that space. Perhaps the reason that the authors, like the delegates at the Constitutional Convention, gave so little attention to the question of who could go to war was that it seemed like an academic question. Of course, it is also possible that they all agreed and did not think the matter needed mentioning. If so, it would be nice if we knew the nature of this silent consensus.

Issues about the military also came up in the ratification debates. In the Virginia debates, the opposition was led by Patrick Henry (of "give me liberty or give me death" fame) and George Mason, who had been a delegate at the Philadelphia convention but refused to sign the final product. Madison was the most important advocate for ratification in Virginia. All three were involved in discussions of the president's power as commander in chief. It is worth noting, though, that this was a somewhat haphazard discussion, with individuals speaking to the topic on separate occasions and sometimes in the midst of a speech that was mostly about something else.

Mason and Henry were eloquent in describing the possibility that a president, after successfully leading the military against an internal revolt, might turn around and march the military back to the capital to conduct a coup. "Can he not," Henry asked, "beat down every opposition" as the head of the army? "Away with your president!," he continued. "We shall have a king: the army will salute him monarch: your militia will leave you, and assist in making him king, and fight against you: and what have you to oppose this force?" According to the notes of the debate, "Here Mr. Henry strongly and pathetically expatiated on the probability of the President's enslaving America, and the horrid consequences that must result."

Mason, too, raised the specter of the president as the proverbial man on horseback, leading an army that might seize control of the government. He thought the consent of Congress should be required before the president could command the army in person. Because the president remains in office during an impeachment trial, Mason also worried that "when he is arraigned for treason he has the command of the army and navy, and may surround the Senate with 30,000 troops."

In one response to these arguments, Governor Edmund Randolph contrasted the powers of a monarch with those of the president: "In England, the king declares war. In America, Congress must be consulted." Indeed, he went on to say, "I cannot conceive how his powers can be called formidable. Both houses are a check upon him. He can do no important act without the concurrence of the Senate."

In another response, Madison argued that Congress held the purse strings and thus ultimate control of the military. He spoke of the Constitution as putting the power of the purse in one set of hands and the power of the sword elsewhere. He did not mention Congress's control of declaring war as a check on the president's use of the military. Advocates of presidential power argue that this meant that only the president had power to decide when and how to use the military, with Congress having only financial control as leverage. But as usual, there are also other interpretations. An alternative explanation is that Henry and Mason had been focused on domestic use of the military, making the power to declare war largely irrelevant. And giving the president "power of the sword" might merely mean control of operations rather than control of the decision to go to war. Madison spoke of more than the power of the purse. He also said members of Congress "have the direction and regulation of land and naval forces. They are to provide for calling forth the militia—and the president is to have the command; and, in conjunction with the senate, to appoint the officers."

Advocates for presidential power to initiate wars find themselves in the odd position of relying more on the accusations of the opponents of the Constitution than on its supporters. They do have a fair point, however, in that the pro-Constitution Federalists put little emphasis on Congress's possession of the power to declare war as a check on the president.

The War Power in the Early Republic

As guidance about how the Framers thought powers over war were divided, we can also look at the views expressed soon after the Constitution went into effect. Two episodes during the Washington administration seem particularly relevant. The first involved the debate over Washington's Neutrality Proclamation, which was intended to keep the country out of the war between France and Britain. This incident was mentioned earlier, but it deserves deeper examination. In his anonymous defense of the proclamation, Hamilton seemed to concede that only Congress could start a war: "If the Legislature have a right to make war on the one hand—it is on the other the duty of the Executive to preserve Peace till war is declared." Since this was the same piece in which Hamilton came up with his vesting clause argument, it seems plain that he did not consider the vesting clause as giving the president authority to start wars.

Madison responded by emphasizing that the Constitution had carefully given the power to conduct a war to the president and the power to initiate wars to Congress: "Those who are to *conduct a war* cannot in the nature of things, be proper or safe judges, whether *a war ought* to be *commenced, continued,* or *concluded.* They are barred from the latter functions by a great principle in free government, analogous to that which separates the sword from the purse, or the power of executing from the power of enacting laws" (emphasis in original). Declaring war was inherently legislative, not executive: Rather than executing an existing law, it "has the effect of repealing all the laws operating in a state of peace, so far as they are inconsistent with a state of war: and of enacting as a rule for the executive, a new code adapted to the relation between the society and its foreign enemy."

The second episode involved military conflict with an Indian tribe. Congress had authorized the use of the militia to support the regular army in defending the frontier. It seemed to assume that the president needed no special authority to use the regular army itself for defense purposes. In an episode involving the Wabash Indians, Washington apparently read his authority as extending to attacks in reprisal for Indian marauders. This was criticized by at least one senator as beginning a war without a congressional declaration.

Washington may have thought that reprisals were encompassed within the authority to defend the frontier, but he apparently did not think he was authorized to conduct purely offensive operations. There was pressure on Washington to take the offensive. He responded that he had been preparing for offensive measures against that tribe whenever Congress gave the word: "The Constitution vests the power of declaring war with Congress; therefore no offensive expedition of importance can be undertaken until after they have deliberated on the subject, and authorized such a measure." Apparently, he did not have in mind a formal declaration of war, which was never issued, but Congress did vote to support the offensive measures Washington advocated. Thus, Washington seemed very clear about who had the power to start an offensive war. And it wasn't him.

Washington was succeeded by John Adams. Under Adams, the United States entered what has been called a quasi-war with the French. Although there was no open state of warfare, the United States restricted trade with the French. Congress authorized naval measures against them. This led to some important Court rulings. In one case, the Court observed that since Congress had the power to declare war, it also had the power to limit the means used in a war. In another case, a statute authorized the navy to seize merchant ships *traveling to* French territory. President Adams ordered the navy to seize ships traveling to or *leaving* French territory. The ship's owners sued a captain who had seized their ship leaving French territory. The Court admitted that it was very reasonable for the government to interpret the law to cover ships sailing from French territory. Nevertheless, Congress had only authorized attacks on ships going the other direction. Consequently, the Supreme Court held the captain personally liable for damages to the ship owners. The Court took for granted that the executive branch could not go beyond the specific war-fighting authority that Congress gave.

Jefferson had pressed Madison to advocate limitations on presidential power in the dispute over Washington's Neutrality Proclamation. As president, however, Jefferson apparently changed his mind.

American ships in the Mediterranean were being seized and their crews held for ransom by the Barbary pirates. Without authority from Congress, he secretly ordered the navy to attack the pirates and the North African rulers supporting them. The strength of this precedent is diminished, however, by the fact that he misrepresented his orders to Congress, apparently unwilling to publicly admit he had acted beyond his authority.

As we have seen, the debate over the original understanding of presidential war powers is complex. Advocates of presidential power can point to several bases of support: a strong tradition of executive control of the use of force, the decreasing importance of formal declarations of war internationally, and the lack of emphasis on the congressional power to declare war in the ratification debates. But there is also evidence on the other side, suggesting that "any offensive expedition of importance," to use Washington's phrase, would require authorization by Congress.

The actual division of power between the president and Congress has evolved since the Framers' era of muskets and wooden sailing ships. To understand the current state of affairs, we need to take a closer look at that later history.

The Ebb and Flow of Presidential War Powers

Whatever may have been the intentions of the Framers, later history has much to say about the president's power to go to war. Unfortunately, the lessons of that history are controversial. There has been considerable variation in how the president and Congress have interacted regarding the decision to use military force. To make the discussion easier to follow, I'll divide the history into three large time periods: pre–World War I, World War I to Vietnam, and post-Vietnam. Although each era had its own complexities, the three eras mark important evolutionary stages.

From the War of 1812 to World War I

Prior to the Civil War, the United States engaged in two wars with other countries, the War of 1812 with England and the Mexican-American War (1846–48). The 1812 war was sparked by British seizure of former British sailors on US ships or territory, as well as resentment against the English ban on other countries trading with its enemy, France. James Madison, who by then had become president, told Congress that the English had committed acts of war against the United States. He thought it was up to Congress to decide how to respond. "Whether the United States shall continue passive under these progressive usurpations," he said, "is a solemn question, which the Constitution wisely confides to the Legislative Department of the Government." Congress did declare war. That turned out to be a big mistake. The United States suffered a humiliating loss, including the sacking of Washington, DC, and the burning of the White House. Many Americans think of the war as a victory because of General Andrew Jackson's success in the Battle of New Orleans. But due to poor communications, that battle was actually fought after the war was already over.

The Mexican-American War was fought over Texas. While he purported to leave the decision to Congress, President James Polk seems to have deliberately provoked an attack by sending US troops into disputed territory, thereby forcing Congress's hand. Polk had already promised Texas that he would protect it against an invasion from Mexico as long as negotiations were ongoing over Texas entering the Union. The outcome of the war was a mixed blessing. It added the Southwest and California to the United States. By reigniting the debate over slavery, however, the US victory over Mexico helped pave the way to civil war.

In terms of casualties, the Civil War was by far the largest war in US history. It also prompted expansive uses of power by President

Lincoln. After the South seceded and opened fire on Fort Sumter, Lincoln took a number of emergency actions while Congress was not in session, including a blockade of southern ports. Under international law, a blockade was an act of war. The legality of the blockade was challenged after several ships and their cargoes were seized by the navy. It was not until several months later that Congress was back in session and authorized the use of force against the Confederacy. The issue, then, was whether Lincoln had the authority to go to war in the meantime, before receiving authority from Congress. A related issue, of less relevance today, was whether the conflict could qualify as a war even though, in the government's view, secession was illegal and the southern states therefore remained part of the United States.

The legal issues reached the Supreme Court in the *Prize* cases. The Court ruled in favor of Lincoln. First, the Court said, civil wars do not call for declarations of war. Rather, "when the party in rebellion occupy and hold in a hostile manner a certain portion of territory; have declared their independence; have cast off their allegiance; have organized armies; have commenced hostilities against their former sovereign, the world acknowledges them as belligerents, and the contest a war." Second, the Court concluded, when faced with invasion or rebellion, the president must respond rather than wait for congressional authorization: "The President is not only authorized but bound to resist force by force," and "he is bound to accept the challenge without waiting for any special legislative authority." Finally, as to whether southerners could be treated as enemies under the laws of war, rather than simply as criminals under domestic law, the Court wrote that they "have cast off their allegiance and made war on their Government, and are none the less enemies because they are traitors."

The *Prize* cases make it clear that the president can respond to attacks on the United States without awaiting congressional authorization, but the Court has provided little guidance about presidential power to use armed force under other circumstances. Since the Civil War period, the Court has basically stayed mum about the legality of decisions to go to war, dodging any effort to have it decide the issue. One reason for the change is that warfare changed. Early Court rulings generally related to the seizure of vessels as part of blockades or similar actions. But that situation became increasingly rare, though there were a few cases as late as World War I.

During the fifty years after the Civil War, the United States managed to stay out of major conflicts, with the exception of the Spanish American War. That war was declared by Congress in retaliation after a US ship blew up in Havana Harbor, in what historians now think was probably an accident rather than the result of an attack. The ensuing war with Spain gained the United States control of Spanish colonies in the form of Cuba, Puerto Rico, and the Philippines.

Throughout much of the nineteenth century, the United States engaged in small-scale military actions against weaker countries. For instance, there were repeated forays before the Civil War into the Fiji Islands and Africa. Some of these actions are poorly documented. Some were taken by military commanders acting on their own initiatives. Others were responses to attacks on US citizens or property, often in areas that were outside effective control by their own governments. By today's standards, the United States and European nations were remarkably overbearing and belligerent. After someone threw a bottle at the US minister in a Nicaraguan town, the navy secretary sent a ship to demand an apology. When the apology wasn't forthcoming, the ship shelled and destroyed the town. This apparently went a little too far. It sparked a major controversy, and President James Buchanan later backed away from attempts to justify the action. In 1900, President William McKinley sent five thousand soldiers to help European countries put down the Boxer Rebellion in China, on the asserted justification that he was protecting American property. McKinley seems to have felt no need for congressional authorization. It seems plain that during this period, the executive branch felt free to engage in these smaller-scale military actions without specific authority from Congress. That has continued to be true in later periods as well.

World War I to the Vietnam War

World War I was the first time that the United States played a major role on the world stage. As ferocious trench warfare continued in Europe, US ships were attacked at sea by an increasingly aggressive German submarine campaign. While contending that he had the power to act alone, President Woodrow Wilson asked Congress to authorize him to arm US merchant ships for self-defense purposes. Senate rules at the time placed no limit on debate, and the bill was killed in a filibuster by antiwar senators. Wilson accused this "little group of willful men" of making the United States "helpless and contemptible." (In response to this incident, the Senate later adopted the "cloture" procedure, allowing a supermajority of senators to cut off debate.) Wilson went ahead and armed the ships on his own authority. The Germans began sinking US vessels, a clear act of war. Wilson said it was "neither right nor constitutionally permissible" to go to war without Congress, and Congress duly declared war.

When World War II broke out in Europe, President Franklin D. Roosevelt was sympathetic to the beleaguered British, who desperately needed military equipment to continue the war effort. He was hamstrung, however, by congressional neutrality legislation that was designed to keep the United States out of the war. The administration developed workarounds in an effort to evade the statutory restrictions. It is debatable whether these workarounds were actually valid, but clearly Roosevelt felt the need to avoid open violations of congressional mandates. All of this became moot after the Japanese attack on Pearl Harbor. The attack led to formal declarations of war against both Japan and Germany, which had declared war on the United States in the meantime. Thus, the two world wars were declared by Congress, although the president took unilateral action in the windup to war in both cases.

The Vietnam War Era and Beyond

World War II was followed almost immediately by the Cold War between the United States and the Soviet Union. During this era, US troops were often moved into risky situations without congressional approval. This trend paved the way for the only major war fought outside the United States without express congressional authority, the Korean War. President Harry Truman's legal theory was that Korea was not a "war" in terms of international law, because the United Nations had requested armed assistance to enforce international law. Given that the conflict was not technically a war, no declaration of war was needed or even appropriate. In Truman's view, use of the US military to enforce the dictates of the Security Council did not require any additional congressional approval beyond the US agreement to join the UN. It seems clear that Truman could have obtained congressional approval if he had wanted to, but his advisers feared that a formal declaration of war would make it more likely that the Chinese and perhaps the Soviets would intervene. After the Korean War, the United States engaged in covert activities abroad but not in open warfare—until Vietnam.

It is hard to say the exact moment the Vietnam War began. President John F. Kennedy placed US troops in South Vietnam as "advisers" well before the United States officially entered the conflict. The United States also began a series of covert actions against North Vietnam. Under President Lyndon B. Johnson, the United States escalated its presence dramatically. Congress came into the picture after a minor naval scrimmage in the Bay of Tonkin. A small-scale exchange of fire took place between North Vietnamese gunboats and a US destroyer. (Radar seemed to show signs of another threatened attack a few days later, though in retrospect this seems to have been wrong.) Johnson believed he had the power to respond unilaterally, but he preferred to get support from Congress. Congress then passed the Bay of Tonkin Resolution, approving the use of the military in the region. Citing a US treaty with Southeast Asian countries, the resolution authorized the president "to take all necessary steps, including the use of armed force," to assist any of those countries "requesting assistance in defense of its freedom." The president's authority would terminate "when the President shall determine that the peace and security of the area is reasonably assured."

Johnson's effort to get the Bay of Tonkin Resolution from Congress was motivated more by politics than by the belief that the authorization was required. Johnson's lawyers believed congressional authorization was unnecessary. In the modern world, they contended, a threat to US security could occur anywhere in the world. Thus, they argued, Vietnam was essentially a defensive war by the United States. Many members of the Nixon administration also believed that the president did not need congressional authorization to fight in Vietnam. Indeed, Nixon expanded the war to include Cambodia and Laos. In 1971, increasing public opposition to the war led to the repeal of the Bay of Tonkin Resolution.

Over Nixon's veto, Congress passed the War Powers Resolution of 1973 in an effort to assert control of the use of military force in general. (Despite the name, the "resolution" is a federal statute, not just an expression of Congress's views.) The resolution is intended to avoid situations in which the president introduces US troops into a conflict and leaves Congress the choice between funding the military intervention or being accused of failing to support the military. Section 1543 requires the president to report to Congress when the Armed Forces are introduced into hostilities, "into situations where imminent involvement in hostilities is clearly indicated by the circumstances," or "into the territory, airspace, or waters of a foreign nation." Section 1544(b) requires the president to withdraw the Armed Forces sixty days after giving notice unless Congress authorizes the use of force. The statute also states Congress's view that the "constitutional powers of the President as Commander-in-Chief to introduce United States Armed Forces into hostilities, or into situations where imminent involvement in hostilities is clearly indicated by the circumstances, are exercised only pursuant to (1) a declaration of war, (2) specific statutory authorization, or (3) a national emergency created by attack upon the United States, its territories or possessions, or its armed forces." There is no definitive resolution of the constitutionality of these requirements, and their effectiveness is disputed, as is the extent to which presidents have complied with them.

In the summer of 1974, Congress passed legislation cutting off funding for combat operations in the Vietnam War. After Nixon resigned under threat of impeachment, President Gerald Ford was left to wind up the war. In managing the US withdrawal, he stretched some of the language of the funding restrictions to the extent he could but felt compelled to comply.

Although there were smaller-scale military actions in the intervening years, the next major war effort came in response to Iraq's attack on Kuwait in 1990. The UN Security Council almost immediately condemned the invasion and authorized economic sanctions and a blockade. When this proved unsuccessful, the Security Council gave Iraq a deadline to withdraw and authorized the use of military force thereafter. After assembling an international coalition and launching a PR campaign in the United States, the George H.W. Bush administration obtained congressional authorization for the use of force against Iraq. The measure authorized the use of military force to defend against the "continuing threat posed by Iraq" and to enforce the UN resolution. The war was a rapid success, and things remained relatively quiet for another decade, until terrorists attacked the Twin Towers and the Pentagon on September 11, 2001.

In response to the 9/11 terrorist attack, President George W. Bush opened negotiations with Congress to obtain its authority to use force. His first proposal would have authorized the use of force not only in response to 9/11, but to "deter and prevent any future acts of terrorism and aggression" against the United States. The final text of what became the Authorization to Use Military Force was much narrower. It authorized "necessary and appropriate" military force against the people and groups responsible for 9/11 or against others harboring them.

Behind the scenes, however, the administration claimed much more sweeping authority derived from the Constitution. A classified memo held that the president had unlimited ability to use military force, even to start a full-scale war. When the administration decided that an invasion of Iraq was warranted, many of Bush's advisers did not believe that congressional authority was required. Nevertheless, Bush decided that it would be better to get authorization. Congress overwhelmingly approved the measure.

Although the United States has remained mired in Iraq and Afghanistan, to date there have been no new large-scale military initiatives. Both President Obama and President Trump, however, have engaged in drone attacks and small-scale raids, notably, a raid under Obama to kill Osama bin Ladin, who planned the 9/11 attacks, and a drone attack under Trump that killed a high-ranking Iranian defense minister who was in Iraq at the time. The attack on bin Ladin was done under the auspices of the post-9/11 authorization to use military force. The legal rationale for the attack on the defense minister was hotly disputed.

Concluding Thoughts on the War Power

This history seems to offer several lessons. The first is that the president has the power to respond to attacks on the United States without prior congressional approval. The second is that presidents have generally sought congressional approval before engaging in major hostilities, with the Korean War as the one exception. And the third is that presidents have taken smaller military initiatives without congressional approval, though Congress has sometimes pushed back.

Neither the text of the Constitution nor what we know of its origins and early implementation gives the President a blank check for use of the military. The broad suite of military powers given to Congress makes it clear that it has a major role to play. This is consistent with the historical practice of obtaining congressional authority for major military actions. The difficult problem is posed by small-scale military actions. It seems unrealistic to think that we need a vote in Congress before the president can launch the rescue of Americans who are held hostage or threatened by imminent violence. But unrestricted power to engage in "small hostilities" can lend itself to abuse, including escalation to major warfare.

My own view is that the War Powers Resolution seems consistent with the general historical pattern, requiring congressional approval for major actions but not for short-term, minor interventions. (Recall George Washington's view that he could not begin any "major offensive action" without congressional authorization.) It also seems to provide a reasonable balance of the competing interests. It gives the president some power to take urgent action while requiring consultation with Congress and congressional authority for prolonged hostilities. Finally, there are good arguments for the constitutionality of the resolution's restrictions on presidential authority. If we apply the *Steel Seizure* framework, presidential violations of the resolution fall into the category where presidential powers are at their weakest, that is, when Congress has taken the opposing position. The president then needs to rely on a grant of authority by the Constitution, presumably from either the vesting clause or the commander in chief clause. Opinions would differ whether this is the right legal analysis, but I lean toward the view that the War Powers Resolution is constitutional.

When running the military, engaging in foreign policy, or implementing domestic legislation, the president is not alone. The executive branch is full of other decision makers, including cabinet secretaries and their supporting teams on down, who advise them and carry out their decisions.

Ultimately, the effectiveness of any given presidential initiative nearly always depends on the cooperation of thousands of others. What tools does the president have to ensure that cooperation is forthcoming? We now turn to the constitutional issues surrounding that question.

5   The Bureaucrat in Chief

The president is one of the most powerful individuals in the world, perhaps *the* most powerful. But that does not mean that the president can govern alone. The federal government has two million civilian workers. Their duties are manifold. They operate Social Security. They handle the activities required to staff, equip, and deploy the military. They collect taxes, bring criminal cases, issue regulations, conduct inspections, investigate crimes, and operate facilities. They staff embassies around the world. The president can issue executive orders, but in most cases someone else must carry them out. Presidents do make key decisions, but their practical power to implement those decisions requires the obedience of many others. Being the head of an enormous bureaucracy is not a glamorous aspect of the president's job, but it is a crucial one.

The president's legal authority over the bureaucracy primarily stems from two sources. The first is the power to hire. The president chooses cabinet secretaries and other higher-level officials, subject to Senate approval. By statute, the president also has the power to appoint many officials without Senate approval. Moreover, many of the officials that the president appoints also have the power to appoint their own subordinates, expanding the number of political appointees. Presidents used to allow cabinet officers to select their own nominees for the deputy and assistant secretaries in their departments, but today the White House is heavily involved in those selections. Thus, the most influential positions in government are staffed by the president's people.

The second source is the power to fire, which is as important as the power to hire. Although the presidential appointments power is governed by Article II of the Constitution, the text says nothing explicit about the president's power to remove officials. As we will see, however, the Supreme Court has implied a broad, but not unlimited, removal power. The powers to hire and fire are the key levers of presidential control of the bureaucracy, buttressed by the president's ability to influence how much money agencies receive from Congress.

Appointments and firings can be used for many purposes. They can be used to select talented, energetic experts and to get rid of the incompetent or lazy. They can also be used to ensure that the people running government programs agree with the president's policy views. Or they can be used for less appealing purposes, such as rewarding cronies or political supporters or punishing independent thinkers, regardless of competence. As currently designed, the system attempts to shield non–policy makers from political influence. With some narrow—and constitutionally controversial exceptions— policy makers are at the president's beck and call. The ultimate question is how politicized our government will be.

Given the size of the bureaucracy, no one person could possibly exercise effective oversight. The presidency today is not just one individual, but an institution. In the early days, presidents had little or no staff. But the Executive Office of the President is now a bureaucracy in its own right, with four thousand employees, sitting above the larger bureaucracy that is formally charged with implementing the laws. The Executive Office includes not only the White House staff— the president's immediate circle of advisers—but also powerful organizations such as the National Security Council (about fifty employees) and the Office of Management and Budget (over five hundred employees). This bureaucracy amplifies the president's ability to set policies and policy priorities.

Take the Environmental Protection Agency (EPA) as an example. Many recent presidents have taken office with the desire to make major changes in environmental policy. There's an old saying, "People are policy." By nominating people for the top positions in the agency who share the president's agenda, the president can go a long way toward controlling results. These days, however, the president can do much more. Under a series of executive orders going back to President Ronald Reagan, agencies like EPA cannot issue any significant regulations without having them approved by the White House. If the head of EPA fails to comply with that process, that person is almost immediately out of a job. Moreover, that person's congressional testimony and public speeches also have to be cleared by the White House, as does EPA's budget request. Again, noncompliance is punishable by firing.

Some see this increased centralization as a good thing, making government more accountable and better organized. Others see it as a threat to objective decision making. They fear that politicized agencies will drift away from the missions assigned them by Congress. Regardless of which side is right, the trend toward great centralization over the past forty years is unmistakable, regardless of who occupies the White House.

The president's powers to hire and fire are the key to control over the executive branch. The legal issues in this area may seem very technical and dry, but the stakes are important. The ultimate issue is whether Congress can insulate some federal officials from political oversight in the interests of objective decision making. The benefit may be to lessen the risks of presidential abuse of power and politically biased decisions. But there is also a cost. Limiting presidential powers means that government policy will be less coherent and less responsive to electoral mandates.

Constitutional rules about presidential hiring and firing have their own special jargon. Here is a brief glossary and some basic rules.

Principal officers. These are officials, like cabinet secretaries, who have substantial legal power. They must be nominated by the president and require confirmation by a majority of the Senate. Most can be fired at any time the president chooses. Under current law, however, Congress can require the president to show good cause for firing officials from some positions.

Inferior officers. These are people who exercise significant authority but at a lower level. Congress can give either the president or the department head the power to hire the person. Under Supreme Court doctrine, the power to hire and the power to fire are linked. If Congress gives the president the power to appoint, the Constitution automatically gives the president the power to fire. But if Congress instead gives a department head the power to hire, Congress also can constitutionally give the department head (not the president) exclusive power to fire.

Employees. These are people in the executive branch who do not exercise enough legal authority to be considered officers. It is up to Congress to prescribe how they are hired or fired, except that the personnel decisions cannot be made by Congress itself. Congress has put many of these positions in the Civil Service system, which requires appointment on the basis of merit and prohibits firing except for good cause.

Because these categories have different rules, many disputes involve where to pigeonhole a particular position. All large organizations have similar issues regarding how to classify employees, and the decisions have a big impact on hiring and firing.

There are important disputes about how much power Congress has to limit presidential control. In particular, believers in the unitary executive theory argue that the president should be able to fire any official in the executive branch of government at any time.

The Appointment Power

The Framers of the Constitution took a keen interest in the appointment of officials, having observed developments in England. The king used appointments to lucrative offices as a way of cementing control, which the Framers considered an insidious form of corruption. At the same time, they recognized that if Congress controlled all appointments, it would dominate the executive branch. Their effort to balance these factors takes up much of Article II, Section 2.

The resulting rules and their interpretations by courts are arcane and technical, but they determine the extent to which the president can install supporters in the bureaucracy. Restrictions on presidential appointment powers really matter. One feature of the Trump era was pushback by high-level career professionals against the administration—viewed by some as the "deep state in action" and by others as "speaking truth to power." The presence of these high-level professionals is a reflection of the limits of the president's ability to install supporters in the bureaucracy. Where Senate confirmation is required, the Republican Senate generally approved Trump's nominees but sometimes pushed back in cases where nominees were considered unqualified or had serious conflicts of interest. So it matters whether Senate confirmation is required or not. The technical rules I discuss below determine which positions the president has free rein to fill and which are subject to restrictions. Basically, these are the sorts of rules that outside the federal government are the domain of Human Resources managers. The HR people generally use

Frequently Asked Questions to explain these rules, and I think it makes sense to use the same approach here.

Q: What does the Constitution say about Senate approval for appointments?
A: The Constitution specifically requires Senate approval for ambassadors, consuls, and judges. Congress can require Senate approval for other positions if it so wishes.

Q: What positions are appointed by the president?
A: Presidential appointment is required for ambassadors, consuls, and judges. Presidential appointment is also the default for all other "officers."

Q: Can Congress provide a different procedure for appointing officers?
A: Only for "inferior officers." (Non-inferior officers are often called "principal officers.") Congress can give the power of appointing inferior officers to the president (with or without Senate approval), to the "heads of departments," or to the courts.

Q: What happens if an appointment requires Senate approval but the Senate is not in session?
A: If the Senate is not in session, the president can make a "recess appointment." There has been a history of gamesmanship between the Senate and the president in which a president claims that a recess exists and the Senate then changes its procedures to prevent a gap in its activities.

Q: The Senate sometimes leaves town for extended periods but continues to have pro forma sessions. What does that mean, and are those sessions enough to keep the president from making recess appointments?

A: Typically, in a pro forma session, a senator is chosen to call daily sessions to order, which are almost always immediately adjourned without any business taking place. The Supreme Court has ruled that the Senate is not in "recess" during these sessions. So the president cannot make recess appointments.

Q: *If a president wants to avoid the process of Senate confirmation, are there other options besides recess appointments?*
A: Yes. Under the Vacancies Reform Act, the president can making Acting appointments. There is a limit on how long these "Actings" can serve, but it's a pretty generous limit. This has created a lot of room for the executive branch to avoid Senate confirmation.

Q: *Congress can take the power of appointment away from the president for inferior officers. What is the difference between inferior officers and principal officers?*
A: The Supreme Court has struggled with this. After Watergate, Congress provided for the appointment of independent counsels (ICs), who were appointed by the courts. That is one of Congress's options for inferior officers but not for principal officers. The Court decided that the ICs were inferior officers in *Morrison v. Olson*. The Court considered the IC an inferior officer because the investigations had to comply with Justice Department regulations, the appointments were temporary and limited to a particular event or official, and the IC could be removed for good cause by the US attorney general.

Q: *Does Morrison continue to provide the test for determining whether someone is an inferior officer?*
A: This is unclear. The Court seemed to waffle about the appropriate test in a later case involving an accounting board that was under the

Securities and Exchange Commission (SEC). The Court considered not only the SEC's power to review the board's decisions but also its ability to remove members of the board. Another case focused on a single factor to determine whether a military appeals judge was an inferior officer: the degree of supervision by other officials.

Q: Is every government employee an "officer"?
A: No. The Constitution does not explicitly distinguish between "officers" and other government employees. But it would make no sense to require that every file clerk and janitor employed by the federal government be appointed by the president or a cabinet officer. Of the two million civilian workers, around 4,000 are political appointees, of whom about 1,200 require Senate confirmation. The rest are simply employees.

Q: How are employees appointed?
A: There is some history here. Beginning with Andrew Jackson, presidents followed the adage, "to the victors belong the spoils," packing the entire government with the party faithful. After President James Garfield was assassinated by a disappointed office seeker, his successor, Chester Arthur, led the creation of the Civil Service system with appointments based on merit. But only "employees," not "officers," can be included in this merit-based system.

Q: What is the difference between an officer and an employee?
A: This issue came to the Supreme Court in a case involving investment fraud. The head of an investment company marketed a retirement savings strategy called "Buckets of Money." In the SEC's view, he used misleading presentations to deceive clients. He claimed that the sanctions against him were invalid because the person conducting the hearing was an "officer" who had been invalidly appointed rather than an employee. Even though the hearing officer's decision

could not become final without review by the SEC, the Court concluded that control of the conduct of the hearing process was enough to constitute significant legal authority. Consequently, he was an officer and could not be included in the merit-based appointment system. This was a potentially major decision. There are scores of hearing officers across the government, handling many important administrative cases. Until now, most have been subject to merit selection processes, not political appointment.

Q: Do the distinctions between various categories of bureaucrats depend on their job descriptions or their actual power?
A: The distinctions are based on their job descriptions. Under many presidents, the second most powerful person in the executive branch is the White House chief of staff. But the chief of staff has no legal authority—"only" the ability to speak credibly on behalf of the president. For that reason, the chief of staff is classified as an employee, just like the person who empties the wastebaskets at the White House.

These rules determine the extent to which the president can ensure that the higher-ups in the bureaucracy support his program. Correspondingly, they also determine whether Congress can insulate a position from politics or oversee appointments by requiring Senate confirmation.

The Implied Removal Power

The president's decision to fire an official is typically more visible than the decision to hire. The Watergate scandal came to a head when President Nixon fired—or rather, had his acting attorney general fire—Special Prosecutor Archibald Cox, the Harvard law professor who had been assigned to investigate criminal activity involving Nixon himself and his subordinates. But the importance of the removal power goes well beyond such high-profile cases. Officials who serve at the pleasure of the president or cabinet officers have limited ability to engage in independent judgment. Their lack of independence may be a bad thing if you want to depoliticize decision making or a good thing if you want presidents to be able to steer the government. Really, it's both, in proportions that can vary with different presidents.

The removal power has been far more legally contentious than the appointments power. In part, as we will see, this is because the Constitution does not speak to the issue directly. The constitutional issues are politicized. Since the New Deal, conservatives have attacked independent agencies like the Federal Trade Commission (FTC), whose commissioners can only be removed by the president for good cause. Other examples are the Federal Reserve Board and the Federal Communications Commission. Conservative critics contend that these agencies' independence from presidential control makes them politically unaccountable and allows them to work at cross- purposes to the rest of the government. Their primary arguments are based on the unitary executive theory. Liberals, on the other hand, worry that politicizing these key agencies will give too much influence to the powerful industries they regulate while at the same time allowing presidents to engage in political favoritism.

Given that the Constitution does not address the subject, at least directly, several different inferences might be drawn. The necessary and proper clause gives Congress authority to pass laws to implement its own powers and the powers of the other branches. You could argue that the terms and conditions of government officers were left to Congress under this clause. Alternatively, you might infer that the same procedures apply for removal as for appointment, meaning that removal of a principal officer requires the consent of the Senate. Alexander Hamilton took that position during ratification, though he changed his mind later. The Supreme Court has not taken either of these approaches. Instead, the Court has held that the president has the implied constitutional power to remove all executive branch officers, subject to some exceptions.

Myers v. United States, which was decided in the early twentieth century, is the favorite case of advocates for unlimited presidential removal power. Although the case is cited in high-flown constitutional arguments, it was really about who would have control of patronage appointees. At the time, postmasters were plum patronage appointees. *Myers* involved the removal of a local postmaster by the postmaster general, despite a statute requiring Senate approval for removals. The question was whether that requirement was constitutional.

Why had Congress resurrected Hamilton's pre-ratification idea about Senate approval for removals? The reason can be traced to the aftermath of the Civil War. The Senate had come within one vote of removing President Andrew Johnson from office in a dispute over Reconstruction. The specific ground of impeachment was that Johnson had violated a federal statute prohibiting him from firing the secretary of war or other officials without the Senate's consent. The law relating to postmasters was passed later, based on the same model of Senate-approved removals. Because postmasters were patronage appointments, the effect was to limit the president's ability to enforce discipline within his own political party by firing postmasters who decided to back rival factions.

Mr. Myers was one of the 12,000 loyal Democrats rewarded with appointments to run a post office after Woodrow Wilson's election. Myers was appointed for a four-year term when Wilson fired all the Republicans and replaced them with loyal Democrats. Myers was apparently a poor manager who had bad relations with his staff. Wilson did not seek the consent of the Senate before firing him. As a political science professor at Princeton, Wilson's pet theory had been that Congress had become too dominant in the years since the Civil War.

Professor Wilson had argued that the country needed a stronger presidency, and President Wilson emphatically agreed. Myers waited until his four-year term as postmaster would otherwise have expired. Then he sued for back pay for the time between the firing and the normal end of his term.

The opinion of the Court was written by Chief Justice William Howard Taft. Not surprisingly, Taft, a former president, was a vigorous supporter of presidential power. He reasoned that presidential removal power was necessary to preserve the unity and coordination of the executive branch. In matters subject to presidential discretion, executive branch officials operate as the president's agents. Thus, he endorsed the unitary executive theory that everyone in the executive branch is the president's assistant.

Interestingly, the two best-known justices of that period, Oliver Wendell Holmes and Louis Brandeis, dissented. Brandeis provided an alternate view of the relevant history, while Holmes was more dismissive. Holmes called Taft's argument based on the vesting clause and other clauses in the Constitution "spider's webs inadequate to control the dominant facts." He stressed that the office of postmaster owed its existence to Congress, which could abolish it tomorrow.

But the majority was unpersuaded by Holmes's rhetoric or by the other dissenters' account of history. Instead, it emphasized the Framers' desire for energetic presidential leadership of the executive branch and the views taken by early presidents. The majority also relied on the vesting clause as a source of support. For these reasons, *Myers* is as close as the Court has ever come to endorsing the unitary executive theory.

The majority opinion gave great weight to what it called the Decision of 1789, in which Congress extensively debated the removal power. This was not a court decision but a series of votes when Congress was first setting up the federal government. There is definitely support for Taft's position in this episode but not as much support as he claimed.

The episode began when Rep. James Madison filed a motion in the House to establish the first cabinet department, making its secretary removable by the president. In the preliminary consideration of this motion, Madison successfully fought off an effort to make removal conditional on Senate approval. Another House member argued that Congress needed to provide for removal one way or another. He thought it made good sense for Congress to give this power to the president. Another representative thought that it was not necessary for Congress to say anything about removal, because removal was an executive power that the president would have anyway. The House then passed a motion "in favor of declaring the power of removal to be in the President." The motion did not clarify whether this was a constitutional requirement or a policy decision made by the House. When the matter returned to the House from the Senate for a vote on the legislation, the debate continued regarding whether removal was inherently within the executive power. To resolve the dispute, the bill was amended to drop any direct statement giving the power of removal to the president. Instead, the amendment stated only that the duties of the office would go to the secretary's clerk whenever he was removed by the president. This implied that the president could remove the secretary but did not specify the source of the president's authority. This amendment passed the House.

What should we make of this train of events? It is clear that there was considerable House support for the idea of an inherent presidential removal power. That is consistent with Taft's later interpretation of the episode. But the meaning of the final House vote is unclear, because the amendment was supported by two groups with opposing views on the constitutional issue: those who believed the president had inherent power and those who thought he had to get that power from Congress. The Senate was evenly divided, leaving the vice president to break the tie in favor of the "whenever" formulation. Congress then used the same "whenever" language in the statutes setting up the other two departments, Treasury and War.

The episode seems more ambiguous than Taft was willing to admit. On the one hand, many members of Congress believed the Constitution gave the president removal power. On the other hand, if the vesting clause was a grant of this power, many members of Congress seemed quite oblivious to this supposedly clear meaning. The one thing that seems clear is that most members of Congress thought the president should be able to remove cabinet officers, whether for constitutional or policy reasons.

Opponents of the unitary executive theory also have some history to cite. They point to the laws establishing the Treasury Department and the Comptroller General to show that government officers were not just presidential appendages. In both cases, Congress took pains to establish the official's duties independent of the president, and Congress clearly viewed these officials as enjoying a special relationship with its own activities. Thus, Congress did not view these officials as merely the president's alter egos. As the first secretary of the treasury, Hamilton was tasked by Congress with reporting to it on the economy and recommending legislation, a task that he zestfully undertook. Even Madison seemed to think that officers performing more judicial functions should be shielded from removal. Although the statute establishing the Post Office originally provided that it would operate under the direction of the president, this language was removed almost immediately when the law was amended. Thus, the vision of presidential hegemony that underlies *Meyers* has some historical support, but the history is not unambiguous.

Myers used sweeping language regarding the removal power and the president's power to supervise the executive branch, but the opinion also contained some equivocations. Taft conceded that if

Congress gave the power of appointing an inferior officer to the head of a department, Congress could also protect that officer from arbitrary removal.

Moreover, Taft seemed open to considering whether Congress might have valid reasons for protecting some officers from removal, regardless of who appointed them. Congress might delegate discretion specifically to an officer with special knowledge, raising a question whether the president would have control over the decision. And there might be officers whose duties were "quasi-judicial," whom Congress might be able to protect from removal by the president. That left some ambiguity about what power the president might have to remove officers with judicial or quasi-judicial duties, such as judges in US territories or in the District of Columbia's local courts. Such an exception might also cover administrative hearing officers. Finally, *Myers* involved the requirement of Senate approval for removal rather than some more modest limitation on presidential removal, such as requiring the president to have good cause.

In the end, it is hard to care one way or another about who can fire the manager of a local post office. But during the New Deal, the Supreme Court was faced with a much bigger issue. Starting in the post–Civil War period, Congress created a series of independent regulatory commissions. The Interstate Commerce Commission was the first one, with the task of ensuring fair rates for railroad shipping, which was then the nation's lifeblood. This commission was abolished when freight markets changed drastically after trucks took over much of the country's shipping. But similar commissions remain active today, such as the Federal Communications Commission (the FCC), the Occupational Safety and Health Commission (OSHA), and the Federal Energy Regulatory Commission (FERC).

These agencies fit a common template. Their commissioners are appointed by the president with Senate approval. Rather than serve at-will, they have fixed terms, and the president can only remove them for incompetence or misconduct. Although it is not organized as a commission, the Board of Governors of the Federal Reserve Bank has similar rules regarding appointment and removal. Congress seemed to want to ensure that the president would not be able to bring political influence to bear on the decisions of these commissioners. And by having staggered terms, Congress could ensure that no one president could pack these commissions with political supporters.

Conservatives have always hated these independent agencies, in part because of the lack of political control but also because the whole mission of the agencies is to regulate the economy. At the core of the unitary executive theory is the argument that all the commissions are unconstitutional because of their independence from immediate presidential control.

This is an important dispute, but it has to be kept in perspective. Nearly all of what the federal government does happens outside of these commissions. These days, many of the most important regulatory agencies, like EPA, are completely subject to presidential control. But the independent agencies are still significant. Because they are somewhat insulated from politics, they tend to move more incrementally and to be a bit less prone to ideological disputes. But this insulation from politics and from shifts in presidential administrations raises constitutional issues, given Taft's general endorsement of the presidential removal power.

That constitutional issue reached the Supreme Court after President Franklin Roosevelt removed a Republican member of the Federal Trade Commission. The Supreme Court apparently considered the issue extremely simple, since it took only a month to decide the case. Conservative justice George Sutherland wrote the opinion for a unanimous Court upholding the statute protecting FTC commissioners. Justice Sutherland's opinion limited *Myers* (the postmaster case) to purely executive officers, who do not exercise what Sutherland called quasi-legislative or quasi-judicial powers. Thus, he seems to have picked up on Taft's intimation that different rules might apply to officers whose duties were not purely executive. Members of the FTC were not purely executive in that they were charged with interpreting the broad language of the statute prohibiting unfair trade practices. That made them quasi-legislative. And they also decided cases dealing with the conduct of individual companies, making them quasi-judicial.

Even the liberals on the Court, who might have been expected to support Roosevelt, took sides against him. Justice Louis Brandeis, who had dissented in *Myers,* privately expressed concern about the implications of an unlimited presidential removal power. He feared that preventing the members of such powerful agencies from exercising independent judgment would leave the United States little better than a dictatorship. Imagine the risks, he said, if someone like the Louisiana demagogue Huey Long became president. Roosevelt, however, was outraged by the result, which he considered an attack on the presidency and on himself personally.

The leading—and by far the most controversial—modern removal power case is *Morrison v. Olson.* The portion of the case dealing with the independent counsel's appointment was discussed earlier, but the more important portion dealt with removal of the IC. To prevent the president from short-circuiting investigations into wrongdoing in the White House or the cabinet, Congress provided that the IC could be removed "only by the personal action of the Attorney General and only for good cause."

Ted Olson was a Justice Department official in the Reagan administration who allegedly gave false testimony to Congress regarding an investigation of EPA. Others were accused of wrongfully withholding documents. Alexis Morrison, a Washington lawyer with government experience, was appointed IC to investigate these charges. When Olson was subpoenaed to provide evidence to a grand jury convened by Morrison, his defense to the subpoena was that the IC law was unconstitutional. The Supreme Court rejected that defense and upheld the IC law.

Chief Justice Rehnquist's majority opinion abandoned the distinction between purely executive and quasi-legislative or quasi-judicial officials. Instead, his opinion upheld the "good cause" removal provision on broader grounds. As discussed earlier, in deciding the appointments clause issue, the Court held in the same case that the independent counsel was an inferior officer with limited jurisdiction, a temporary term of office, and a degree of oversight by the attorney general. Limitations on the removal of such an officer might be invalid if they undermined presidential control of the core functions of the executive branch. But the Court did not believe that this was true of the independent counsel.

Justice Scalia alone dissented. It would be an understatement to say the dissent was emphatic. In his view, "If to describe this case is not to decide it, the concept of a government of separate and coordinate powers no longer has meaning." The vesting clause, he said, "does not mean some of the executive power, but *all* of the executive power" is solely in the hands of the president. Consequently, he said, the statute would be unconstitutional under "fundamental separation-of-powers principles" if two questions were answered affirmatively: whether the conduct of criminal prosecution and investigation is "the exercise of purely executive power" and whether the statute deprived the president of "exclusive control over the exercise of that power." For Scalia, the answers were obvious: "To ask these questions was indeed to answer them, since prosecution is commonly considered a core executive function and the whole purpose of the statute was to limit presidential control over investigations of high officials." Of course, the majority did not agree that these were the right questions to ask.

Justice Scalia lambasted the broad ruling of the Court. "As far as I can discern from the Court's opinion," he said, "it is now open season upon the President's removal power for all executive officers." The president functioned at the mercy of the Court: "The Court essentially says to the President: 'Trust us. We will make sure that you are able to accomplish your constitutional role.' I think the Constitution gives the President—and the people—more protection than that." It remains a puzzle to me why Scalia thought unbridled political control over law enforcement was a safeguard rather than a threat to liberty.

Morrison established the constitutional standard for assessing whether restrictions on the president's removal power are constitutional. Both the outcome in that specific case and the constitutional standard remain controversial to this day and are obviously unacceptable to adherents of the unitary executive theory. Arguably, the Court underestimated the extent to which the IC law undermined the functioning of the presidency before that law expired. The constitutional standard established in *Morrison* is still the law today, at least as applied to inferior officers. But unitary executive theorists continue to press their arguments, and there are clearly receptive ears among the current justices.

The Supreme Court's latest ruling on the removal power marks a further step toward adoption of the unitary executive theory. This 2020 ruling involved the Consumer Finance Protection Bureau (CFPB). Congress established the CFPB to protect consumers against abusive or fraudulent financial practices. Rather than a multimember commission, the CFPB's chief decision maker is its director, who is appointed by the president for a five-year term. Congress took special care to insulate the director from political pressure because of fear of the enormous political influence of the finance industry. The director may be fired only for "inefficiency, neglect of duty, or malfeasance in office"—the same language the Supreme Court had previously approved for independent commissions. But this time the result was different.

Chief Justice Roberts wrote for the five-justice majority, holding that the head of the CFPB is removable by the president. He found the case distinguishable from precedents involving independent commissions because the CFPB's director was even more insulated from presidential control than the heads of other independent agencies. Unlike the typical commission, there was only one member, so there was no guarantee that an appointment would come up during any given president's term. Unlike in multimember commissions, the president lacked the power to determine which member would serve as chair. For those reasons, Roberts found prior cases distinguishable. And because of the CFPB's unusual financing arrangement, the president could not even hope to use budgetary influence on the agency. The majority believed that the need for removal power was especially important because of these other features of the CFPB structure. It was in vain that Justice Elena Kagan argued for the four dissenters that the majority had overlooked considerable contrary evidence about the original understanding, the actual functioning of the executive branch, and the justifications for those unique features of the CFPB.

The unique features of the CFBP perhaps make it distinguishable from other independent agencies. What augurs poorly for those other agencies, however, was Roberts's general language about the removal power. Based on selective quotations from the framing era, primarily featuring Madison, the Court found an unmistakable conscious decision by the Framers to give the president full control of all executive functions. In Roberts's view, the Framers' "constitutional strategy" was clear: "Divide power everywhere except for the Presidency, and render the President directly accountable to the people through regular elections." The Framers viewed the legislature as the greatest threat to liberty, he said, while they wanted energy and decisiveness from the executive branch. So the Framers settled on a simple arrangement. "In that scheme," Roberts said, "individual executive officials will still wield significant authority, but that authority remains subject to the ongoing supervision and control of the elected President." The result, according to Roberts, is to uphold the electorate's control of the administration of the laws, via the president. Through the president's oversight, "the chain of dependence [is] preserved," so that "the lowest officers, the middle grade, and the highest" all "depend, as they ought, on the President, and the President on the community."

This might be called mythic originalism. As we have seen, while there is definitely some evidence to support Roberts's view of the original understanding regarding the presidential removal power, attributing a unified vision to the Framers as a whole is dubious. For one thing, Alexander Hamilton was apparently quite unaware of this "simple arrangement" when he wrote about the issue in the Federalist Papers and thought Senate approval was required to remove cabinet officers. Apparently, he did not discern the clear link between his robust vision of executive power and the presidential removal power that the majority of the Court now finds so obvious. And the Framers definitely did not consider the president's "dependence on the community" as a sufficient protection against abuses of power. If they had, they could have dispensed with checks and balances entirely. The clarity that Roberts purports to see in history is the clarity of his own conception of executive power, not the clarity of the historical record.

Be that as it may, the effect of this recent series of opinions is at best a severe limit on Congress's ability to restrict presidential removal power. *Morrison* now applies (at most) only to inferior officers executing the law but lacking policy authority and multimember commissions subject to other forms of presidential control. In the short run at least, the future of presidential removal power depends on whether

Roberts is prepared to maintain those narrow exceptions from the otherwise unlimited power of the president to fire subordinates.

It is important not to lose sight of the core issue in these disputes over the president's control of hiring and firing. Everyone agrees on the importance of the president's ability to have subordinates who can be trusted to follow administration policy. The question is whether there are limits to how far that principle extends. And that in turn involves the question of whether the entire executive branch should be a creature of the president's will or whether there is sometimes a need for independent judgment.

From a president's point of view, appointment and removal have political value, but they are mostly means to an end: to ensure that the government carries out the president's policies. That brings us squarely to the question, How much power does the president have to set policy? We turn to that question next.

6   *The Domestic Policy Czar*

No one doubts the importance of the president's power over foreign policy and use of the military abroad. But concerns closer to home predominate for most Americans. The public wants to know what the president is doing about economic issues, the environment, health care, and law enforcement. As I write, the novel coronavirus and its economic repercussions top the agenda. Whether they think there is too much regulation or too little, voters want the president to do something about national problems. When there is a crisis, whether a financial panic, a bombing, a hurricane, or a pandemic, people look to the president. They assume that the president must have the power to address these problems. And presidents do have vast powers, some implied but many conferred by Congress. Yet there are limits, as the Supreme Court has made clear throughout US history.

Within the domestic sphere, some powers are directly in the hands of the president. The president can declare national emergencies, raise certain tariffs, and block entry to the United States simply by issuing an order. Other powers are granted by Congress to administrative agencies like the Treasury Department or EPA, so the president can't simply sign orders in the name of those agencies. That has to be done by the agency heads. But the president can generally hire and fire the agency heads. (Basically, an administrative agency is any civilian part of the executive branch outside the White House.) The president has limited power over the independent agencies discussed in the previous chapter, such as the Federal Trade Commission. But much more of the federal government is subject to direct presidential supervision. Some examples are the IRS, EPA, the State Department, the FBI, the Defense Department, and the CIA.

The president has always controlled these nonindependent agencies as a matter of legal theory. But the president's effective control of the sprawling federal bureaucracy is much greater than it used to be. The appointees to these agencies are carefully vetted for loyalty to the president's agenda. Much of what they do is directly overseen by the White House, including all significant regulations they issue, their communications with Congress, and their budgets. No leader's control of an organization is absolute, even in a dictatorship, but the upshot is that the vast bulk of the government is subject to presidential oversight and direction.

Consider the ways open to the president to make policy. Nearly all of what the executive branch does involves implementing laws passed by Congress. Congress has empowered the executive branch to implement laws by issuing regulations, bringing criminal cases, issuing or rescinding permits, or making various kinds of spending decisions. One of a new president's primary goals is to change the direction of the executive branch toward implementing that president's policies. The transitions from Barack Obama to Donald Trump and then to Joseph Biden illustrate this process, with overnight changes in the direction the government was moving in areas such as immigration, civil rights enforcement, and the environment.

Most of the changes in policy involved actions by administrative agencies within the executive branch. President Trump opposed the climate change regulations that EPA issued under President Obama. He appointed a new agency leadership team and directed them to reconsider the regulations. To no one's surprise, EPA then began the process of repealing the regulations. Trump also opposed the Obama administration's priorities in enforcing the immigration laws. There are far more people who are legally subject to deportation than the government has the resources to pursue. The Obama administration focused on deporting immigrants who had violated criminal laws. Trump changed the policy in favor of a more sweeping use of deportation powers. He also clamped down on refugees seeking asylum in the United States. Biden again reversed course.

This kind of presidential influence on domestic policy is central to the modern presidency. This chapter asks three questions about the president's constitutional power to make policy within the domestic sphere. First, what can the president do without congressional authorization? It is clear that in the international sphere the president has some degree of constitutional autonomy, but there seems to be less room for unilateral action in the domestic sphere. Second, how much policy-making authority can Congress give the president? The answer to this question may be in flux, with a possible majority on the Court preparing to limit Congress's ability to give the president control of major policy issues. In the short run, this would mean that some important regulatory statutes would be declared unconstitutional, leaving gaps in regulation until Congress is able to give more detailed directives to the executive branch. Third and finally, what obligation does the president have to affirmatively carry out Congress's directives? In many situations, simply doing nothing— deciding not to engage in prosecution or deportations—may be a powerful way of making policy. But again, there may be limits. I will begin with the first of these questions.

Presidential Action without Congress

In the domestic sphere, nearly everything the president does, either directly or through others in the executive branch, is based on authority granted by Congress. Nearly everything, but not quite everything. At least since Lincoln, presidents have claimed an inherent power to deal with crises. The Supreme Court has taken up the issue several times, trying to accommodate the need for presidential flexibility with the need to limit the potential for arbitrary abuse. Line drawing is difficult given the need to accommodate the realities of modern government while preserving checks and balances. For that reason, this is an area where the tug-of-war between Congress and the president is especially important in setting boundaries. History has been an important factor: presidents are given more judicial leeway where Congress has been willing to give the president maneuvering room, less where actions are unprecedented or have been the subject of congressional pushback.

Although constitutional issues arise when the president acts independently of Congress, this is rarely necessary today because Congress has given the president so many powers. As early as 1792, Congress gave the president the power to call up the militia "whenever the laws of the United States shall be opposed or the execution thereof obstructed ... by combinations too powerful to be suppressed by the ordinary course of judicial proceedings." It was this power that President Lincoln used immediately after the Confederate attack on Fort Sumter, when he called out 75,000 militiamen and made it clear that the North was serious about resisting secession. Today, there are over a hundred statutes that give the president special powers after declaring a national emergency. President Trump invoked some of those statutory powers after he declared the coronavirus pandemic a national emergency.

Given the existence of these statutory emergency powers, presidents have less need to fall back on claims of inherent power. Nevertheless, there may be gaps in these statutes, where the president may need to rely on inherent powers. The *Steel Seizure* case indicates that these inherent powers are by no means unlimited. There are a handful of Supreme Court decisions dealing with inherent powers. They indicate that the president has at least some implicit authority directly from the Constitution to deal with emergencies, particularly when those emergencies have an impact on government operations. Each of these decisions has some broad language, but it is not clear how much weight to give that language.

The issue of inherent presidential power has been around a long time. An 1833 Supreme Court opinion still provides presidents with some apt language to quote. The case itself, however, could not have been more mundane. Under a long-standing practice, a navy clerk had been paid a small commission based on the amount of claims he processed. The claims in question mostly involved pension payments and other amounts owed by the navy. During a financial dispute between the clerk and the navy, the navy claimed that the clerk's commissions had been illegal because they were not authorized by a specific statute. The Court ruled in favor of the clerk, rejecting the claim that the navy needed to show specific authority for everything it did.

The Court's opinion contained some language about presidential power that goes beyond the specific facts. It said that expecting Congress to regulate "the minute movements of every part of the complicated machinery of government" would "evince a most unpardonable ignorance on the subject." The law could not provide for every detail: "There are numberless things which must be done, that can neither be anticipated nor defined, and which are essential to the proper action of the government." If you are thinking that this case is less than a dramatic vindication of executive powers, you would be right. But it does suggest that the president and other executive branch officials have some power to fill gaps in statutory authority.

The 1833 case involved only the internal operation of the government. In several other cases, however, presidents have taken actions that had a direct impact on the public without statutory authority. An 1890 case involved a lurid backstory. A US marshal had been assigned to protect a Supreme Court justice who was thought to be at risk of physical attack. The threat arose from a salacious divorce case, an offshoot of which had been heard by the justice. The lawyer representing the woman later married her, and the couple had threatened the justice. While the justice was on a train between two court hearings, the lawyer approached and hit him. The marshal saw, or said he saw, the lawyer reaching for a knife and shot him dead. The state government arrested the marshal for murder.

The marshal claimed he could not be tried by the state because he was acting within the scope of his duties as a federal officer. There was no statute explicitly authorizing this kind of protective duty by marshals. The Supreme Court stressed the obvious need for the government to be able to protect its own personnel and operations from violence. The national government, the Court thought, should not have to rely on state governments to protect it, any more than it should have to rely on the states to guard federal property. Thus, no statute was really required. In the end, however, the Court concluded that there actually was a statute that authorized use of the marshal to protect the judge, though not in so many words.

Five years later, the Court upheld a more dramatic presidential action. When a nationwide strike threatened to close down the railroads in 1895, the government went to court for an injunction against union leaders. This was at a time when the courts regarded strikes as illegal conspiracies. The government alleged that the strike had resulted in violence, endangered interstate commerce, and prevented the delivery of the mail. The Court upheld the national government's power to protect interstate commerce and the mail from unlawful interference by private parties. Even without any specific grant of power from Congress, the government could exercise that power by suing in the courts to vindicate its rights rather than use troops to guard the railroads.

To the extent that the opinion suggests an inherent executive power to protect interstate commerce, the case goes beyond other cases dealing specifically with threats to government operations. The opinion is preoccupied with showing that the federal authority extends to such strikes (a federalism issue) and that the government was a proper party to bring suit. The union leaders do not seem to have argued specifically that the president was exceeding his powers under Article II; in fact, the word *president* does not appear in the 1895 opinion, although the president was the one behind the lawsuit.

In the early twentieth century, the Court followed up with another decision upholding executive power. Oil companies had raced to extract all the oil from government land in California, based on a statute allowing this use of public lands by anyone who found oil or minerals there. The companies were essentially competing to see who could remove the most oil the fastest, raising the prospect that the oil fields would soon be pumped dry. In order to get fuel, the navy had to buy back the oil at market price after giving it away to the oil companies in the first place. President Taft issued an order "withdrawing" the lands, so the public (including the oil companies) would no longer have free access. One of the oil companies sued in an effort to invalidate this order.

Taft's rationale was that he needed to halt the oil operations so that Congress could decide what to do in this situation. The problem was that the statutes governing public lands said nothing about reclassifying them as no longer being open to exploitation. Nevertheless, presidents had engaged in such reclassifications for a long time, without objection from Congress.

Despite the president's lack of express statutory authority, the Court stressed the practical reasons for respecting this long-standing practice: "Both officers, lawmakers, and citizens naturally adjust themselves to any long-continued action of the Executive Department, on the presumption that unauthorized acts would not have been allowed to be so often repeated as to crystallize into a regular practice." More generally the Court said, "Emergencies may occur, or conditions may so change as to require that the agent in charge should, in the public interest, withhold the land from sale." General legislation by Congress could not anticipate all the specific issues that could arise across millions of acres of government land.

These cases establish that the executive branch does not need specific congressional authority for every action and that it has some ability to improvise to deal with unexpected or urgent situations. Although there is language in the opinions that has proved useful to presidents, the cases are quite limited in other ways. All of them involve assertions of power relating at least in part to the operation or property of the government itself. Most involve long-standing government practices. And none of them involves violations of any statutory limitation on executive power.

The *Steel Seizure* case probably comes as close as possible to providing a framework for understanding these earlier cases. As *Steel Seizure* shows, the Court has not been willing to give the president a blank check for nonstatutory actions. But neither has it closed the door entirely.

Delegated Authority and the President

The cases discussed above are unusual. In practice, within the domestic sphere at least, presidential power nearly always stems solely from a grant of authority by Congress. Sometimes Congress delegates power directly to the president. For instance, President Trump approved a controversial pipeline from Canada to the Gulf Coast under authority of a law giving the president the right to issue permits for cross-border projects. (Obama had previously refused to issue the permit, and Biden later withdrew the permit granted by Trump.) Much more often, however, Congress delegates authority to administrative agencies, which are part of the executive branch.

Congress has established all government agencies, beginning under George Washington, when it created the State Department and the Treasury Department. Agencies get their powers from Congress. Sometimes Congress gives very precise marching orders to an agency, such as instructing it to issue contracts to the lowest qualified bidder. At other times, Congress gives more discretion to the agency in exercising those powers. For example, the Wage and Hour Division in the Department of Labor enforces minimum wage laws. In doing so, the department has to decide things like whether a short lunch break counts as part of the workday. Congress sets the level of the minimum wage, and the president cannot change it or repeal the requirement that employers pay the minimum wage. But what the president *can* do is influence—and often control—how the agency exercises its discretion. A president who believes in the importance of the minimum wage can ensure that the agency exercises its discretion in favor of employees by doing things such as classifying lunch breaks as part of the workday. A president who thinks minimum wage laws distort the free market can give the opposite marching orders. The agency thus has two obligations: one is the obligation to carry out the laws passed by Congress, and the other is to carry out the president's policies within the confines of those laws. The task of the agency is to implement the administration's policies to the extent that it can do so without violating the mission assigned by Congress.

The highest-profile decisions by agencies often involve issuing regulations. Since this is an unfamiliar process for most people, a brief description may be helpful. The following is a fairly mundane example. When I was just out of law school, I was a law clerk for Philip Tone, a federal court of appeals judge in Chicago. He wrote an opinion in a case involving water pollution standards for slaughterhouses and packinghouses. The Clean Water Act requires EPA to issue regulations setting pollution standards that industries must meet by a certain deadline. The pollution standards were supposed to be based on the "best practicable control technology" for that industry's pollution. The regulatory process began with a detailed study of the industry that was commissioned by EPA. EPA concluded that a particular system of pollution treatment called the three-lagoon system was the best practicable technology. It used that technology as the basis for setting limits on water pollution by the industry. EPA then published its proposed regulations and received comments from the industry and others. It issued a final regulation along with responses to the comments. (Today, if a regulation is considered controversial or economically significant, EPA would have to clear it through the White House. But that was not true then.)

The industry's trade association asked the federal appeals court to overturn the regulation, which is where my judge came into the process. The industry did not contest EPA's selection of the three-lagoon system as the best practical way to control pollution. Instead, it argued that even if EPA's three-lagoon system were used, industry still would not be able to achieve the pollution reduction that EPA was requiring. For that reason, the industry wanted the regulation to be sent back to the agency to allow higher levels of pollution. The court concluded that by and large EPA had given reasonable explanations tying its conclusions to the evidence. The court also rejected an argument that EPA could only issue guidelines, not binding regulations setting pollution levels. Thus, the industry had to comply with the pollution reductions that EPA was requiring.

This case wasn't front-page news at the time, and I may be the only person who remembers it today. But it illustrates a process that is used in much higher profile decisions. For instance, the Trump administration wanted to repeal an Obama-era regulation that limited carbon emissions from power plants. President Trump told EPA to reconsider that regulation, and EPA issued a proposal to replace the Obama regulation with a much weaker requirement. The proposal contained a detailed discussion of the evidence and arguments that the Trump EPA relied on. EPA provided about four months for public comments. It received 1.5 million of them. The most important were from state governments like California and from environmental groups like the Sierra Club. EPA then issued a final rule and a detailed explanation of why it rejected criticisms of its proposal. It was immediately sued by critics of the rule, who contested both EPA's interpretation of the statute and its use of evidence.

Presidents like to claim early credit for agency actions, which is one reason people are confused about the process. For example, President Trump issued several executive orders that criticized Obama-era regulations and directed agencies to consider repealing them. Often Trump's executive orders were issued with much fanfare at carefully staged signing ceremonies where the president would take credit for eliminating overreaching, "job-killing" regulations. Many people thought that the Obama regulations were wiped out by a slash of Trump's pen. Actually, he had done nothing of the sort. Trump did not *order* EPA to repeal the regulations. He only told the agency to think about it. Nothing happened to the existing regulations until the agency went through the whole process described above. Trump could have achieved the same result with a private phone call to the head of EPA, but that would have put less pressure on the agency and limited the public credit he was seeking for the repeals. Still, nothing changed legally until EPA itself took action. Until EPA actually issued new rules that repealed or replaced the Obama rules, the Obama rules remained on the books.

It would be a mistake to single out Trump, however. The practice of using these theatrical executive orders goes back at least to President Bill Clinton.

Whether delegation of powers is directly to the president or to an agency, these powers are the basis of much of modern government. Using delegated power, government agencies regulate drug safety, pollution, food safety, securities fraud, and much more. Delegated powers are also used to assess and collect taxes, pay Social Security, reimburse Medicare claims, and build military bases, and that is only the beginning. Some of these statutes are quite broad. The FTC is charged with preventing "unfair trade practices," and the SEC is charged with issuing rules to prevent "manipulative and deceptive practices." Earlier statutes tend to give general directives, while later ones tend to set more detailed rules. For instance, the version I have of the Clean Air Act is around two hundred pages of small print. Even so, the statute rarely gives numerical standards for particular pollutants or industries. Rather, it uses general terms like "best available technology" or "protecting public health with an ample margin of safety."

There is a constitutional issue lurking here: Is there a limit to how much discretion over policy Congress can give presidents and agencies (most of which are under presidential control)? The answer is clearly yes, but the question is how much of a limit. As we will see, the answer seems to be in flux.

Partying Like It's 1935

The Supreme Court has repeatedly said Congress lacks the ability to delegate its legislative power and that there are limits on the amount of discretion Congress can give administrators. To date, the Court has actually found a violation of the nondelegation doctrine in only two cases in its history, both dating from 1935. They involved laws with very sweeping delegations. One gave private bodies the power to make binding regulations, and the other gave the president the right to ban certain products from interstate commerce at will. Since the 1920s, the Court has said that a congressional grant of authority to an agency is valid only if it is governed by some "intelligible principle" setting its boundaries. In practice, this has meant that Congress can give very broad, but not unlimited, discretion to agencies—

and that the president can have a huge impact on domestic policy via control of those agencies.

For the past eighty-five years, it seemed to be completely settled that Congress can give the executive branch broad discretion in implementing regulatory statutes. If I had written this book two years earlier, the issue would probably have deserved only one or two paragraphs of discussion. But now, there is a real move to go back to the 1935 decisions and start declaring regulatory statutes unconstitutional. We cannot be sure where the Supreme Court is going on this. The one thing that we can be sure of is that there is now real doubt about something lawyers, judges, and legislators used to take for granted. If the constitutional standard does shift, the result might be to eliminate only a few extremely wide-open laws, or it might put at risk major portions of the federal regulatory system, such as the Clean Air Act, the food and drug laws, and the securities regulations. Given that the justices backing this constitutional shift are openly skeptical of federal regulation, there is a chance that they may use some new constitutional doctrine to wipe important regulatory laws off the books.

Until this recent development, the Court had been willing since 1935 to give Congress nearly unlimited authority to delegate powers to the executive branch. Almost anything seemed to qualify as an "intelligible principle." A case in 2000 illustrates the application of the intelligible principle test. The case involved a statute giving EPA the power to set air quality standards necessary to protect public health. Implementing these standards is central to the statute. In one sense, this was a narrow delegation, in that EPA was only allowed to consider public health, not other issues like industry cost. Also, the statute covers only certain especially widespread air pollutants. But setting the air quality standards is by no means cut and dried. There are often scientific disputes about the implications of current research. Moreover, the statute says that EPA must allow an "adequate margin of safety." How much of a margin is "adequate" is obviously a judgment call. It would be a mistake to say that EPA has a completely free hand. The statute requires the agency to give public access to the scientific information and the studies it relies on, and EPA must give a detailed explanation of how it evaluates the evidence. A court then decides whether EPA's explanations are reasonable. Nonetheless, EPA has real leeway, and small differences in the standard can have big economic repercussions and a major impact on public health.

A lower court held that the statutory standard was too open-ended and would therefore be unconstitutional unless EPA based its decision on cost-benefit analysis. The Supreme Court held that the statute prohibited cost-benefit analysis, but it went on to unanimously uphold the law anyway. Justice Scalia wrote the opinion. His views were a bit surprising in that he was no fan of government regulation and a strong advocate of cost-benefit analysis. Scalia found that this air pollution provision had language similar to a number of other statutes that had come before the Court. He paraphrased the law as requiring EPA to set air quality standards at the level "that is 'requisite'—that is, not lower or higher than is necessary—to protect the public health with an adequate margin of safety." He found that this discretion was well within constitutional bounds. Scalia observed that in its entire history, the Court had struck down federal statutes only in the two 1935 decisions, where Congress provided essentially no limits on discretion. The entire discussion of the delegation issue takes only a few paragraphs. Scalia devoted much more attention to the statutory issue of whether cost-benefit analysis was required.

Government delegations have been criticized on the ground that Congress is merely passing the buck to avoid the political costs of making tough decisions. Instead of being made by the people's representatives, critics argue, key decisions are being made by unelected bureaucrats. The part about unelected bureaucrats is largely out of date. Today, in the large majority of cases, those bureaucrats are under White House control, so in practical terms this is largely a complaint about giving too much policy authority to the president. This is especially true in terms of major changes in government policy, which almost always come from the top. If the Supreme Court forces Congress to write more specific, detailed laws, presidents will have much less room to influence domestic policy.

There is an ideological dimension to the campaign to strike down existing regulatory laws and send them back to the congressional drawing board for rewriting. Given the difficulty of getting legislation enacted, requiring more regulatory decisions to be made by Congress effectively means that there will be fewer regulations. It is clearly not practical for Congress to decide every detail about what counts as part of the working day, the numerical pollution standards for every pollutant and every industry, or exactly what kinds of financial derivatives are too risky for banks to invest in. Moreover, the Court can strike down legislation faster than Congress could pass new legislation supplying the missing details. Thus, it is not surprising that many of the voices calling for a more robust nondelegation doctrine are actually more concerned about the *existence* of regulations than about who enacts them. For them, reviving the delegation doctrine is a means of deregulation.

Until now, there has not been any doubt about the constitutionality of these federal laws and the regulations issued under them. But that may be about to change, and the change could potentially render much of current federal regulation unconstitutional. The first warning sign involved a 2019 case, *Gundy v. United States*. The case involved a fairly obscure statute regulating sex offenders, but some have seen it as a harbinger of the destruction of the modern administrative state. The statute establishes a national system for registering sex offenders. Congress was apparently unsure about whether to require registration for sex offenders who were convicted before the law was passed. The statute left that decision to the attorney general. The statute does not specify what standard the attorney general should use to make that decision.

The suit was brought by Herman Gundy, who sexually assaulted a minor before the statute was passed. However, he never registered as a sex offender. After he was prosecuted for his failure to register, he challenged the constitutionality of the law allowing the attorney general to require past offenders to register. It seemed to be an easy case, at least if you assumed the Court would follow precedent. Every federal appeals court had rejected similar claims. It turned out that the Supreme Court was badly divided, with no majority opinion. The Court rejected Gundy's argument that the law gave the attorney general too much discretion in deciding whether to require people like him to register. Yet the justices were split 4-1-3. Only eight justices voted because Justice Brett Kavanaugh did not participate in the case.

Four of the justices joined in an opinion by Justice Kagan interpreting the statute to require the attorney general to include sex offenders in the registration system to the maximum extent feasible. They considered feasibility an intelligible principle and rejected the constitutional challenge. But the other four justices who participated in the case expressed an interest in using a stricter constitutional standard. Of those four, one (Justice Samuel Alito) voted to uphold the statute but said he was open to reconsidering the standard in a later case if there was a majority on the Court for changing it. Justice Neil Gorsuch dissented, in an opinion joined by Chief Justice Roberts and Justice Thomas. Gorsuch's dissent called for a dramatic rethinking of the Court's approach to regulatory statutes.

Gorsuch began by noting that different attorneys general had taken very different approaches to the statute. He viewed the statute as leaving the treatment of preenactment offenders completely at the will of the attorney general. He decried the statute for investing the attorney general with the power to make "unbounded policy choices" with "profound consequences for the people they affect." Gorsuch characterized the "intelligible principle" standard as a twentieth-century innovation that opened the door to broad delegations of authority to the executive branch. He called for a return to earlier legal doctrine.

Gorsuch identified several circumstances in which Congress can delegate authority to agencies. First, when Congress has "made the policy decisions," it may leave it to an agency to "fill in the details." Second, once Congress has made the policy decisions, it can delegate fact finding to the executive branch. For instance, it could make a trade embargo contingent on a presidential finding about whether a country had stopped interfering with American shipping. In another part of the opinion, he added that Congress has to set the criteria and facts that the agency can consider. Third, Congress can broadly delegate authority in areas where the president has inherent authority, such as foreign affairs or national security.

After his suggested reformulation of the law, Gorsuch returned to the sex offender law itself, which he found blatantly unconstitutional. Congress, he declared, had failed to make the policy decision. Indeed, he said, Congress had said nothing at all about how the attorney general should make this policy, and he did not consider the question of whether prior sex offenders had to register a mere detail. Thus, the statute failed his test. This is not surprising, since if it were interpreted to give the attorney general completely unlimited discretion, the law would have failed the intelligible principle test as well.

How would Gorsuch's test apply in other cases? Consider the national air quality standards that were upheld by Justice Scalia. On the one hand, the level of the air quality standards is a very consequential decision, not easily described as a "detail." Many other parts of the Clean Air Act regulating industry are keyed to achieving these air quality standards. Much of what EPA does could be considered fact finding regarding public health risks, but there are also judgment calls about when a risk is too uncertain or too minor to matter. The statute also involves a policy decision about how ample the margin of safety should be.

On the other hand, EPA is not left completely unrestrained. The statute does limit the agency to considering a single factor, health risks. As Scalia ruled, it cannot take into account other factors such as cost. And the statute does make what is probably the crucial policy judgment, that risks to public health must be avoided without regard to cost. The federal courts have found it possible to engage in meaningful judicial review, satisfying the concern that courts and the public should be able to decide whether the boundaries of the law were crossed.

Gorsuch's test is vague enough that we cannot be sure how it would be applied. But it is hard for me to believe that the Court would invalidate this provision and in the process knock out three quarters of federal air pollution law. Anything is possible, of course, but that would be a radical move, particularly given that the conservative icon Scalia wrote the key opinion upholding the statute a few years ago. Other portions of the pollution laws seem even less likely to be threatened. Requirements that sources use the best available technology, like the slaughterhouse regulation I discussed earlier, nearly always give a list of factors to be considered and some general indication of their weight. Moreover, if applying such standards isn't filling in the details, it's hard to see what would be. Surely, we could not expect Congress to make such determinations on an ongoing basis for myriad industries.

Assessing the impact of Gorsuch's approach is difficult because of these questions about how it would be implemented. He argued that his approach would not dismantle the modern administrative state, assuming there was a societal consensus on new legislation. Congress, he said, can still give agencies the power to fill in details, even a large number of details, to find facts, and to engage in activities other than issuing regulations like permit decisions. It could also ask agencies to study issues and propose legislation for Congress to consider. But many observers believed Gorsuch was making unrealistic demands on Congress, such as requiring it to set numerical pollution standards for every industry or reevaluating the scientific evidence of pollution risks every few years.

Gorsuch contended that his approach comported with the original understanding of the Constitution. Some scholars argue, however, that the Framers may actually not have seen any constitutional problem with very open-ended delegations. Admittedly, there were statements in that period to the effect that legislative powers cannot be delegated. But these arguably referred only to permanent transfers of legislative powers rather than transfers that Congress kept the power to repeal. In other words, they may have meant that Congress could not make permanent gifts of its powers but that it could loan them out. If we look at what the Framers did rather than what they said, it is not at all clear that the majority was worried about delegating legislative powers. Before and after ratification of the Constitution, there were some very open-ended delegations, such as ones authorizing territorial governors and legislatures to pass whatever laws they thought appropriate or a tax law giving commissions broad discretion. Congress also gave the president a blank check to regulate commerce with Indian tribes.

Advocates on the Gorsuch side of the argument find ammunition in a debate in 1791 over a proposal to establish post roads and post offices. Some prominent figures like Madison argued that Congress could not constitutionally delegate the power to designate post roads. Others argued that this kind of decision should be left to the executive branch. The problem is that it is not clear how many others agreed with Madison's constitutional argument.

There were important local interests involved in the choice of post roads, which may have been at least as important as constitutional qualms. Having a post office or being located on a post road were economic boons to a town. For instance, Madison succeeded in getting a post road within a few miles of his plantation.

If a majority in Congress was really seriously worried about the constitutional issue, it is hard to see why they were not concerned about other broad delegations in the very same law. Congress itself designated the post roads, but it also authorized the executive branch to put post offices wherever it wanted and to designate any additional post roads it wanted. In context, the decision that Congress would designate the post roads itself seems more like what we would today call pork barrel politics than an exercise of high-minded constitutional principles. At the end of the day, it is hard to attach great significance to a few statements cherry-picked from the debate over this bill.

Gorsuch may also have been wrong in thinking that there had been a radical shift in doctrine because of the New Deal. A survey of more than two thousand pre-1940 state and federal decisions involving the delegation doctrine concluded that even before the New Deal, the doctrine never truly constrained delegation of authority to administrative agencies. Thus, the historical foundations of Gorsuch's approach are debatable, though other legal scholars have chimed in to defend his view of the history.

Apart from the historical merits of Gorsuch's position, there is the question of whether it will command a majority on the Supreme Court. Justice Kavanaugh did not participate in the sex offender case. In connection with a later case, he floated his own version of the delegation doctrine. He read Gorsuch's opinion as requiring that Congress specifically authorize major extensions of agency power where a statute is ambiguous. Under his interpretation, Congress would have to "expressly and specifically decide the major policy question itself and delegate to the agency the authority to regulate and enforce." For example, although a federal statute arguably gives the FCC the power to mandate net neutrality, Kavanaugh would consider this a major policy decision that Congress must make. Under Kavanaugh's test, Congress could apparently give an agency unlimited power to reduce existing legal protections but not to expand them.

One problem with Kavanaugh's formulation is that it is not at all clear what constitutes a "major question." The same term is used in an administrative law doctrine that the Court has found difficult to apply. It is also not completely clear whether Kavanaugh was ready to make a drastic change in delegation doctrine anyway. In the end, he equivocated, saying only that Gorsuch's scholarly and thoughtful opinion "raised important points that may warrant further consideration in future cases." Kavanaugh made the statement in the context of the Court's decision not to hear a case. Those decisions are not considered precedents, so justices generally feel no need to speak. The fact that he took the occasion to discuss Gorsuch's opinion at all, when he could just as easily have remained silent, was widely interpreted as siding with Gorsuch's approach, but perhaps that is reading too much into it.

Time will tell whether this will all turn out to be a tempest in a teapot or whether the Court is prepared to turn the regulatory clock back to 1935.

Enforcement Discretion

So far, I have been talking about ways that a president can make policy, either by taking action or by having an administrative agency do it. That way of making policy is proactive: issuing or repealing government regulations. But administrators can also make policy by sitting on their hands. Their decisions about what rules to enforce and against whom can be as important as the rules themselves. For instance, when a president does not view monopolies as a concern, the way that perspective is implemented is by the Justice Department allowing mergers to go forward rather than challenge them in court. Thus, a passive-aggressive strategy of inaction can sometimes make a big difference.

Presidents and their subordinates lack the power to repeal laws passed by Congress. The executive branch is called that because its core function is to execute Congress's legal mandates. The Constitution underlines this point by saying that the president "shall take care that the laws be faithfully executed." But no president or administrative agency has ever had the resources to enforce every law in every case. Congress generally gives administrative agencies far more duties than resources, leaving those agencies with the need to set priorities. Priority setting is not just a financial exercise, however. Consider a US attorney, a lawyer appointed by the president to supervise federal criminal prosecutions in district court in a particular area. A prosecutor must decide how to allocate resources between serious and less serious offenses, which obviously involves some value judgments. With oversight from the attorney general, the US attorney must decide which individual cases have sufficient prospects of winning to make them worthwhile investments of resources. One president's Justice Department may place a high priority on prosecuting gun crimes while another's may deemphasize those cases and concentrate on drug cases.

These priority decisions are obviously important for the individuals in particular cases, but they can have broader societal significance. For instance, the number of prosecutions for violations of environmental regulations goes dramatically up and down, depending on whether a conservative or a liberal is in the White House. On a larger scale, the government may decide that certain laws have such low priority that they are generally not worth the use of prosecutorial resources or that some types of criminal activity are better left to state prosecutors. Regulatory agencies have to make similar decisions. There are more potential subjects for regulation than the agency can pursue. The agency (generally under White House direction) has to set priorities. For instance, under the Trump administration, the top priority was repealing existing regulations rather than expanding regulatory protections.

Setting government priorities involves a great deal of discretion. And that discretion is generally not reviewable by courts. When the Food and Drug Administration (FDA) was first asked to regulate the use of drugs in executions, it declined to do so, saying that even if it had jurisdiction it would exercise its discretion to leave the issues alone. (Later, under the Obama administration, it did end up regulating the drugs using a different law, only to reverse course in 2019 under Trump.) The Supreme Court refused to review the FDA's pre-Obama decision not to regulate. The Court said that "an agency's decision not to prosecute or enforce, whether through civil or criminal process, is a decision generally committed to an agency's absolute discretion." The reason is that enforcement decisions require balancing so many different factors.

There seem to be a couple of possible exceptions where review by the courts may be appropriate. One involves situations in which the agency fails to regulate because of a mistaken belief that it lacks the power to do so. The other involves a wholesale surrender of agency powers, simply giving up on doing its job. The second of these possible exceptions points to a conundrum. The executive has the duty to enforce the laws, highlighted by the Constitution's specific mandate that the president faithfully execute the laws. The president does not have the power to repeal laws; only Congress can do that. At what point does a failure to enforce become an abdication of duty?

The legalization first of medical use of marijuana and then of recreational use in many states poses this issue in a clear form. In several policy guidelines, the Department of Justice announced that it did not believe federal enforcement in those states was a generally good use of resources in terms of federal policy goals like preventing drug dealing by gangs. Effective state regulations could serve those goals without federal intervention, although the department reserved the right to bring individual cases where federal policies such as drug dealing by gangs were at issue.

In 2018, under Attorney General Jeff Sessions, the Justice Department rescinded those previous guidelines in order to "restore the rule of law." Instead of having any special rule for marijuana, prosecutors were told to "weigh all relevant considerations, including federal law enforcement priorities set by the Attorney General, the seriousness of the crime, the deterrent effect of criminal prosecution, and the cumulative impact of particular crimes on the community." So far as I can tell, the new guidance had no real effect. Marijuana or its derivatives remained available at stores across California, including my corner grocery.

A much more complicated situation is presented by the Obama administration programs that provided a path to long-term residence for some noncitizens who lacked immigration papers. The first program applies to people who were brought to the United States as children and who meet other requirements for citizenship. The second applies to parents who are unlawfully in the United States but whose children have green cards or were born here (and are therefore citizens). Members of these two groups could apply for deferred action, meaning their deportation will be indefinitely postponed and they become eligible for authorization to work in the United States.

What makes the issues here so knotty is the complexity of immigration law. Immigration law is a snarl of rules, exceptions, waivers, and exceptions to the waivers. The executive has tremendous discretion to excuse or delay deportation in individual cases. Some experts seem to think that the Obama programs are consistent with established immigration laws and past practices. Others think the contrary.

If immigration officials had decided to grant deferrals in individual cases to people in these categories, probably no one would have batted an eye. But these programs created tremendous controversy for two reasons beyond the strong feelings that surround immigration issues today. First, because these programs apply to whole categories of people, they may seem like efforts to repeal or suspend parts of the immigration laws through administrative fiat. And second, these programs came only after efforts to pass immigration reform in Congress fell apart. They were seen by many as an effort to achieve policy reforms that the administration could not get through Congress.

This is a book about constitutional law, not immigration law. My concern here is whether by directing the adoption of these immigration programs, President Obama violated his constitutional duty to take care that the laws be faithfully executed. If these programs were adopted as reasonable, good faith efforts to implement immigration law, it is hard to see why they should be considered unconstitutional even if it turns out that the administration was wrong on the legal issues. On the other hand, if the idea was just to cook up a pretext for a tacit repeal of immigration requirements, then at the least the programs were skating close to the constitutional line.

With both the nonenforcement of federal marijuana laws and these immigration programs, the answer is that elements of both motivations were probably present. That is, nonenforcement was seen as both a wise use of federal resources and a way to respond to changed circumstances since the laws were passed. The federal drug laws were not passed in a world in which marijuana use is considered harmless and acceptable by much of the population and many state governments. The immigration laws were not passed in a world in which more than ten million people, many of whom came as children, are unlawfully in the United States. It would be unrealistic to expect presidents (or attorneys general or individual prosecutors) to give no thought to their own policy preferences in these situations. But this must viewed against the background of their general duty to enforce the laws made by Congress, not the laws they wish Congress had made. If the take care clause means anything, it means that policy disagreement is not a sufficient stand-alone reason for nonenforcement.

Current efforts on the Supreme Court to revive the nondelegation doctrine may reduce the president's ability to make dramatic changes in regulation. Even so, the president will still have an important role in domestic policy with their powers to shape myriad smaller-scale regulatory changes and control enforcement policy. Those decisions may be less visible to the public, but they would still have potential to change the government's direction in important ways.

This concludes my discussion of the outer limits of presidential authority. Under anyone's reading of the Constitution, the presidency is a tremendously powerful office. It includes wide-ranging powers in foreign affairs and military matters, oversight of the huge federal bureaucracy, control of enforcement discretion, and implementation of broad congressional mandates (even if the Court may be poised to declare some of the very broadest unconstitutional). Having seen the tools available to the president, we will now see how other branches of government can use their powers as checks on the presidency.

7 Presidential Power versus Individual Rights

The presidency was established in the original Constitution, which contained no Bill of Rights. There were only a few scattered constitutional protections for individual rights, such as the requirement of jury trials in criminal cases. Opponents of the Constitution complained bitterly about its lack of a Bill of Rights to prevent federal overreach. In response, supporters of the Constitution promised constitutional amendments entrenching individual rights. The First Congress quickly passed a dozen amendments, ten of which were quickly ratified by the states. Those ten amendments became known as the Bill of Rights. The First Amendment protected freedom of speech and religion, the Fourth Amendment limited government searches and seizures, the Fifth Amendment guaranteed due process of law, and the Sixth Amendment expanded the catalog of protections for criminal defendants. The executive branch has no more power to violate these rights than Congress does. The Supreme Court has now developed a rich body of precedents interpreting and enforcing these rights.

There is an exception, however, to the normal rules for scrutinizing the constitutionality of government actions. When the president takes action in the name of national security, especially in wartime, the attitude of judges changes. They are often leery of intervening in situations where the president has access to secret information, the stakes are extremely high, and the government must act quickly. Yet they have not given presidents a blank check. While courts intervene cautiously, they do intervene from time to time.

These issues were relatively quiescent until the national cataclysm of the Civil War, and it is there that we begin our story.

The Civil War

Presidential power is needed most during a national crisis, when business-as-usual government institutions are overwhelmed. The key is the president's ability to respond flexibly, forcefully, and decisively. This kind of crisis response requires enormous discretion, because every crisis is different. That discretion is subject to abuse, posing a threat to the rule of law. The tensions between presidential power and the rule of law are at their highest in time of war, when presidential authority is at its peak. It is then that individual rights are most in peril.

Never have these tensions appeared in starker form than during the Civil War, when the rule of law was put under severe pressure. Civil wars create unique challenges. Southerners were legally classified as enemies, as in any other war, but they were also classified as US citizens. Further complicating matters, the North contained Confederate sympathizers, especially in border states like Maryland, Kentucky, and Missouri. Even farther north, there were strong pockets of sympathy with the South and opposition to the war effort. For some, this was just a political view, but others gave support to the Confederate cause financially or even militarily.

Lincoln's first problem after the war broke out was protecting Washington. There was only a skeleton military force in the city itself, and with the secession of Virginia, the only access to Washington was through Maryland. Union troops seeking to reach Washington had to march from one train station to another in Baltimore, where they were attacked by mobs. Meanwhile, Maryland legislators were actively considering secession, which would have left Washington completely cut off. To address the crisis, one of Lincoln's first actions was to issue a proclamation suspending habeas corpus. Habeas is an ancient court writ that allows a prisoner to challenge detention in court. It is the ultimate safeguard against illegal detention. The effect of this proclamation was to allow the military to arrest the rioters and their leaders and hold them long enough to restore order.

The Constitution provides that "the privilege of the writ of habeas corpus shall not be suspended, unless when in cases of rebellion or invasion the public safety may require it." Note that this clause does not specify who has power to suspend the writ. (There is a good reason we teach law students to avoid using the passive voice in drafting briefs and other documents.) Suspending the writ has generally been done by the legislature, first the English Parliament and then the US Congress. It makes sense to require a different body to determine whether to unleash the executive's power to detain suspected rebels or invaders (or their supporters). But Congress was not in session and would have taken weeks to assemble, assuming they were able to reach Washington at all. Given the urgency of the situation, Lincoln felt it necessary to act alone.

Lincoln's order led to the arrest of a Maryland man named John Merryman. Merryman had been involved in burning railroad bridges to block troop movements. To obtain Merryman's release, his lawyer filed for a writ of habeas corpus against the commanding officer of the district. The judge hearing the case was Chief Justice Roger Taney. Taney, who had been appointed by Andrew Jackson, came from a family of Maryland slave owners. He wrote the *Dred Scott* opinion, generally considered the single worst decision in Supreme Court history. That opinion held that blacks could never be US citizens and that Southerners had a constitutional right to bring slaves into federal territories. Taney also opposed the use of force to prevent secession.

Not surprisingly, Taney quickly issued a writ to the commander of the fort where Merryman was being held. In response, one of the commander's subordinates appeared and politely refused to produce Merryman in court. He asked for a continuance to consult superiors, citing Lincoln's suspension of habeas. Taney immediately held the commanding officer in contempt. When the US marshal went to the fort to arrest the commanding officer, he was refused admittance. Clearly, the government was not about to bow down to the Chief Justice.

Taney then quickly released an opinion saying that the habeas suspension was illegal but that the courts were powerless to overcome military force. It is unclear whether Lincoln was aware of the case until later, given that Taney raced to judgment in only two days and that telegraph lines to Washington had been cut. The conventional story is that Lincoln directed the military to hold Merryman or other detainees regardless of court orders. That seems plausible, but we cannot be sure about Lincoln's personal involvement. It does seem, however, that General in Chief Henry ("Old Brains") Halleck had directed the commanding officer in Merryman's case to resist Taney's order. (The nickname was bestowed because Halleck actually "wrote the book" on military strategy at the time.) I have little doubt that if asked, Lincoln would have agreed that Merryman should be detained despite Taney's order. Thus, *Merryman* posed two vital issues: whether Merryman had the right to be freed from military detention and whether the government could ignore a court order, even an erroneous one.

Lincoln addressed the issues in his first message to Congress when that body reconvened. He argued that his suspension of habeas was indeed constitutional, so that the military had the right to detain suspected rebels. As an alternative, he argued that his action was compelled by necessity even if it was not strictly constitutional. Pointing to his duty to "take care that the laws be faithfully executed," he argued that it was impossible to enforce federal law in the

South unless he took decisive action to protect the government in the North. As he famously asked, "Are all the laws, but one, to go unexecuted, and the government itself go to pieces, lest that one be violated?" Lincoln's attorney general followed up with a formal opinion defending the constitutionality of suspension. He argued that it would be absurd to say that enemy soldiers captured by the army could be freed by a federal court.

The strongest legal defense of Lincoln's initial suspension is probably the president's power to take emergency action to protect the government rather than any general presidential power to suspend habeas. There is also an argument, supported indirectly by later precedent, that the Militia Act provides implicit power to detain dangerous individuals in circumstances where the civilian courts cannot enforce the law. Although I am inclined to accept those arguments, this may be a minority view among scholars.

Lincoln's necessity argument was a fallback, suggesting some uncertainty about the legality of his action. The necessity argument itself has a bit of the flavor of a "get out of jail free" card—a dangerous card to put into the hands of the holder of such a powerful office. Note that in raising the necessity argument, Lincoln was claiming that if his action actually was illegal, necessity required him to violate the law. There is a factual basis for that claim: if Lincoln had not suspended habeas, he might not have been able to restore order in Maryland, and there is a good chance that Washington would have fallen to the Confederacy.

Still, we should be deeply wary of the argument that upholding the Constitution sometimes requires violating it. Given the importance of habeas as a guarantee of individual liberty, unlawfully suspending habeas presents grave risks to democracy and the rule of law. Nonetheless, Lincoln faced a dire situation: not only a state of war, but an emergency threatening to shatter the country, combined with the unavailability of Congress to approve the suspension. And at the beginning at least, the suspension was limited to the region most at risk. Thus, the situation presented the strongest possible setting for invocation of this dangerous justification. Moreover, Lincoln did not argue that he was entirely above the law. Unless Congress agreed and ratified his actions, he would be subject to civil liability if the courts ruled that the detention was illegal. (As I discuss later, that would not be true today, since the Supreme Court now gives blanket immunity to presidents for their official acts.)

The emergency argument applied only to the first months of the war, before Congress reconvened and had the opportunity to act. But the scope of the habeas suspension expanded over time, until it eventually encompassed the entire country. The eventual number of arrests was in the thousands. Most arrests took place in the South when it fell under Union control, but hundreds occurred in the North. Congress eventually eliminated the constitutional issue about halfway through the war. A March 1863 statute authorized detentions at the order of the president, ratified previous suspensions, and gave executive officials immunity for past detentions.

Despite this support from Congress, there can be no doubt that the power to conduct arbitrary arrests was abused. General Halleck had a Missouri man arrested for saying he would not use the flag even as toilet paper, and a drunk in Baltimore was arrested for saying he would be the first man to hang Lincoln. A newspaper editor in Dubuque, Iowa, was seized for allegedly discouraging enlistments. Lincoln sometimes reversed these decisions, but many did not receive his attention.

During the Civil War, military detention could end in release but could also lead to trials before military tribunals rather than civil courts. The most defensible military trials took place within areas of active military operations, under immediate threat of invasion, or under military occupation. Imposition of martial law in those areas does not seem to have been controversial. Similarly, martial law was often imposed in areas of active guerrilla operations, such as much of Missouri. And in occupied territory, military rule was necessary to ensure that the area remained subdued.

The law was clear about the validity of martial law in areas where it was needed to restore order. Over a decade earlier, the Supreme Court had upheld the use of martial law to deal with an armed insurrection in the *Luther v. Borden* case. The insurrection had taken place in Rhode Island in a dispute over the existing state constitution. Chief Justice Taney wrote the opinion for the Court. Seemingly contrary to his views when the South seceded, Taney found it unquestionable that a government can use military power, including martial law, against an insurrection that could not be controlled by civilian authorities. This rule was reaffirmed in a later opinion by Justice Oliver Wendell Holmes.

The validity of military rule was also clear in occupied territory. The Supreme Court had ruled during the Mexican-American War that the law applicable in occupied territory is not that during peacetime. After asking rhetorically what law applied in invaded territory, the Court had answered, "It is military law,—the law of war,— and its supremacy for the protection of the officers and soldiers of the army, when in service in the field in the enemy's country, is as essential to the efficiency of the army as the supremacy of the civil law at home, and, in time of peace, is essential to the preservation of liberty."

The use of military tribunals in areas of the North remote from the fighting was much harder to justify. These trials were authorized by Secretary of War Stanton in the summer of 1862, and the procedures were supervised by the army advocate general. In the beginning, most arrests were initiated by state or local officials, but after a month, further requests required approval from Washington, a military commander, or the governor. The most defensible category of trials involved illegal combatants—Confederate soldiers operating out of uniform or otherwise violating the laws of war. But the use of military authority swept more broadly.

One example is the famous Vallandigham case. In the spring of 1863, antiwar sentiment was growing. It was fed by a series of Confederate victories and controversy (up to and including huge riots) over America's first military draft. Clement Vallandigham was an Ohio politician who had just been voted out of Congress and was anxious to restart his political career. He launched a series of inflammatory speeches attacking the war and Lincoln's emancipation of slaves. The speeches flew in the face of an order by General Ambrose Burnside banning expressions of sympathy with the enemy and "express or implied treason."

Burnside was an incompetent general who had been moved to Ohio after his troops were slaughtered at the Battle of Fredericksburg. He is best remembered today as the source of the term "sideburns," a term inspired by his name and facial hair. Appalled by Vallandigham's attacks on the war, Burnside declared martial law and issued an order that the "habit of declaring sympathies for the enemy will not be allowed in this Department." General Burnside had Vallandigham arrested in the middle of the night. Vallandigham was charged with "expressing sympathy for those in arms against the government of the United States" and "declaring disloyal sentiments and opinions with the object and purpose of weakening the power of the government." He was convicted by a military tribunal. When Vallandigham sought habeas, the judge declined because of the risk posed by "artful men, disguising their latent treason" and spreading "pestilent heresies among the masses of the people." Vallandigham's strategy was successful, however, in prompting his nomination as the Democratic candidate for governor.

Lincoln was under some pressure not only from Democrats but also from supporters in his own party. Two New York papers denounced Valladigham's conviction for making the mere expression of opinion a crime. Senator Lyman Trumbull from Illinois, a moderate Republican, said that the goal of the war was to protect liberty, not suppress it. Lincoln's cabinet considered Burnside's action a mistake, but Lincoln thought it would not be prudent to overrule the general. Lincoln stood by Burnside publicly, but he commuted Vallandigham's sentence to banishment to the Confederacy.

Lincoln defended his support for Burnside in an open letter. He argued that Vallandigham was not simply criticizing the administration but "attempting, with some success," to interfere with military recruiting and the draft. In the most famous line of the letter, Lincoln asked, "Must I shoot a simple-minded soldier boy who deserts, while I must not touch a hair of a wiley agitator who induces him to desert?" Since Lincoln was regularly confronted with requests that he pardon young soldiers who had attempted to desert and not infrequently did so, this must have seemed a rather poignant dilemma to him. Nevertheless, the arrest of Vallandigham was clearly a political mistake, making him a martyr for free speech despite Lincoln's commutation of his sentence.

So long as habeas was suspended, there was no way to challenge these military trials in the courts. It was only after the war that this became possible. When the issue reached the Supreme Court in a case called *Ex Parte Milligan,* the Court ruled that the military trials were unconstitutional in areas outside the war zone. Except for individuals connected with the US military, military trials were not allowed where "the courts are open, and in the proper and unobstructed exercise of their jurisprudence." Four justices agreed with the result but not the Court's reasoning. They argued that the Court should not have decided on the constitutionality of military trials. They thought Congress did have the power to authorize military trials of civilians even outside the theater of war. In this case, however, they believed Congress had not done so. All the justices agreed that the military trials of civilians in loyal areas of the North had been illegal.

World War II

The Civil War began a little more than eighty years after the Declaration of Independence—Lincoln's famous "four score and seven years ago." About four score and seven years later, the country again found itself engaged in a total national mobilization. Individual rights and national security again came into conflict.

As in the Civil War, there were issues regarding military tribunals in World War II. In a nearly forgotten episode early in the war, the Germans landed saboteurs on the East Coast. Two of them had been born in the United States and were therefore citizens. The saboteurs disposed of their German uniforms and then scattered. It is a violation of international laws of war for soldiers to operate out of uniform. (This is not just a matter of good sportsmanship. The other side is likely to mistakenly attack civilians if it cannot tell who is a soldier and who is not.) Consequently, the Germans were classified as unlawful combatants. That had two consequences under the laws of war. First, they were not entitled to prisoner-of-war status. Second, unlike ordinary soldiers, who cannot be punished for normal military actions such as shooting enemy troops, the German soldiers could be tried for espionage like any other spies.

There was a rather comic character to the efforts of these would-be saboteurs. None of them managed to commit any sabotage. Two of them turned themselves in to the FBI, with some difficulty since the FBI did not initially believe their story. The consequences for the captured soldiers, however, were far from humorous. They were tried by a military tribunal on the orders of President Franklin Roosevelt. The fact that two were American citizens, being tried on American soil, made the case even more fraught. The military lawyers for the soldiers went to the Supreme Court for redress. Notably, habeas corpus had not been suspended, so it was clear that they had a right of access to the courts.

The Court upheld the convictions on the theory that trial by military tribunal was legitimate for violation of the laws of war. The Court was under extremely heavy pressure to support the war effort at this point. It was thought that President Roosevelt might well execute the soldiers regardless of the Court's ruling. The pressure on the Court may have contributed to the speed of the decision, which upheld the convictions the day after oral argument but delayed formal opinions until later. Roosevelt commuted the sentences of the two who turned themselves in (which included one of the US citizens), but the others were executed before the Court had even had time to issue its written opinions in the case.

The federal courts were clearly in normal operation at the time, so the Supreme Court's post–Civil War ruling provides an argument that the soldiers had a right to be tried in civilian court. Although I was shocked when I first heard about this World War II military trial on American soil, I now think the decision was probably correct. As active members of a hostile military, the German soldiers were subject to the laws of war, not just civilian law. For that reason, they were properly tried by a military tribunal.

At least those German soldiers got access to the federal courts to determine whether the military had the right to try them. After the war, others were not so lucky. Some Germans captured by the US Army in China were tried for war crimes and transferred to Germany, where they were imprisoned by the army. They tried to get a federal court to review the legality of their treatment. The Supreme Court held that the federal courts had no jurisdiction over their claims. According to the Court, the prisoners were not entitled to seek habeas corpus. They lacked the connection with the United States needed for habeas because they were foreign citizens and outside our borders. Thus, they had no right to challenge the legality of their punishment.

These episodes are little known to anyone except a few historians and experts on national security law. What many people do know about, however, is the Japanese internment during World War II. In retrospect, the internment is generally considered one of the most shameful actions in US history.

After Pearl Harbor, President Roosevelt authorized the government to intern German, Japanese, and Italian citizens in the United States. Three months later, he issued an order allowing the secretary of war to designate exclusion zones from which "any or all persons" could be excluded. By the end of the year, the government had moved over a hundred thousand American citizens of Japanese descent to internment camps. Initially, the military had opposed mass evacuations of Japanese Americans. But by two months after Pearl Harbor, anti-Japanese feeling on the West Coast was at a fever pitch. A government report on Pearl Harbor mentioned in passing that some Japanese living in Hawaii had given information to the Japanese government. Officials in the War Department and J. Edgar Hoover, head of the FBI, were skeptical of any espionage threat. However, after Japanese victories in Singapore and elsewhere, the army general in charge of defending the West Coast decided to recommend the mass evacuation. Roosevelt deferred to the military's judgment, and Congress ratified the decision.

On Memorial Day in 1942, Fred Korematsu was arrested while walking with his Italian American girlfriend in San Leandro, California, a few miles from my house in Oakland. The charge was suspicion of being Japanese American. Korematsu had refused to report for relocation to an internment camp. He was moved first to San Francisco and then to an unused racetrack, where he was forced like many other detainees to live in a horse stall. Finally he was sent with his family to an internment camp in Utah. He was sentenced to five years of probation for failure to report for relocation. A federal appeals court upheld his conviction, and the case went to the Supreme Court.

The Supreme Court's opinion began on a high note, stating that "all legal restrictions which curtail the civil rights of a single racial group are immediately suspect." The opinion continued that such restrictions must be subjected to "the most rigid scrutiny" by courts and that "pressing public necessity may sometimes justify the existence of such restrictions" but that "racial antagonism never can." In the view of the majority, discrimination against a racial minority could only be allowed if it was necessary to achieve a compelling government interest.

But these fine words turned out not to mean much. The majority said that the Court could not make its own judgment about matters of military necessity and had to defer to the judgment of the military authorities that the evacuation was needed. In this, the Court had been misled by the Justice Department. Government lawyers did not inform the justices that there was actually considerable doubt within the government about whether these Japanese American citizens posed any national security threat.

Justice Frank Murphy wrote an impassioned dissent, accusing the government of having fallen into the "ugly abyss of racism." In his view—which is also the verdict of history—the detention order was based on an "assumption of racial guilt," a belief that "by reason of their descent all persons of Japanese ancestry may have a dangerous tendency to commit sabotage and espionage." Justice Murphy pointed to a statement by the commanding general referring to "all individuals of Japanese descent as 'subversive,' as belonging to 'an enemy race' whose 'racial strains are undiluted,' and as constituting 'over 112,000 potential enemies . . . at large today' along the Pacific Coast." Justice Murphy contended that "the exclusion order necessarily must rely for its reasonableness upon the assumption that all persons of Japanese ancestry may have a dangerous tendency . . . to aid our Japanese enemy." He doubted that "reason, logic or experience could be marshalled in support of such an assumption." Another dissenter referred to the relocation centers as concentration camps. There is little disagreement today with their view that the internment order was a shocking betrayal of American ideals.

Korematsu remains an ugly blot on the Court's record because it upheld the racist effort to sweep Japanese Americans out of the West Coast. What is less known, though, is that the Court in effect killed the internment program in another decision the same day. Essentially the Court's ruling meant that it had been constitutional to remove the Japanese Americans from the West Coast but not to keep them in detention camps. That case involved Mitsuye Endo, a Japanese American woman who was working at the Department of Motor Vehicles in Sacramento when the war broke out. She was first interned in California and then moved to a camp in Topaz, Utah. She sued to obtain her release. No one contested her claim that she was a loyal American citizen.

The Court distinguished between the initial order requiring Japanese Americans to leave the West Coast and the government continuing to confine them once they had been removed. This was a hairsplitting distinction. It upheld Roosevelt's order but interpreted it narrowly to allow only evacuation, not detention. This distinction allowed the Court to uphold Korematsu's conviction for refusing to turn himself in for evacuation but to reverse Endo's detention. While it did not directly rule on whether internment was unconstitutional, the Court said it was interpreting the president's order to avoid possible conflict with constitutional rights. Thus, the Court tactfully avoided having to say that Roosevelt had violated the Constitution but still managed to close the detention camps.

Roosevelt had been alerted that this decision was coming. He had responded with an order the previous day ending the internment and terminating the evacuation order itself. In the meantime, thousands of loyal Japanese Americans had been prisoners for more than two years.

Although the dissenters failed to persuade the majority in *Korematsu*, decades later a federal judge vacated Fred Korematsu's conviction because the government had concealed evidence directly undermining its claims. Ultimately, Congress acknowledged the "grave injustice" of the internments and provided reparations to the individuals involved. Of course, the past cannot be undone.

The War on Terror

Fast forward to the War on Terror in the early 2000s. World War II cases dealing with executive detention and trial by military tribunals, which had seemed like quaint relics of an earlier time, suddenly became relevant again. I was working on a book about Lincoln and the Constitution at the time. It was a shock to discover that what I had thought was an exercise in legal history was in fact tied to current events.

Although the warning signs were clear in retrospect, the government and the public were stunned when two airplanes crashed into the World Trade Center in New York City and a third smashed into the Pentagon. The planes had been hijacked by members of Al Qaeda. This organization was led by a Saudi, Osama bin Laden, and dedicated to ousting US influence from the Middle East and installing religiously "pure" regimes in Muslim countries. Al Qaeda had found a home base in Afghanistan under the friendly eyes of the Taliban. Agencies like the CIA were well aware of its threat to American interests, but efforts to counter Al Qaeda had stalled.

The last significant foreign attack on US soil had been during the War of 1812. Those who have grown up since 9/11 may find it hard to understand the shock and horror sparked by the attacks. Over three thousand Americans were killed, more than two-thirds of them civilians. President George W. Bush had taken office the preceding January. His relatively untested administration was caught off-guard by the attacks. He rallied the nation to respond to the attacks while also emphasizing the need for tolerance and respect toward Muslim Americans. In response to 9/11, Congress passed a resolution authorizing military action against these terrorists and their allies. This

Authorization for the Use of Military Force (AUMF) resolution remains in effect nearly twenty years later. Early steps in response to 9/11 included counterterrorism efforts by the CIA and the invasion of Afghanistan by a US-led coalition.

The Afghan invasion and US counterintelligence efforts resulted in the capture of Taliban and Al Qaeda fighters and their suspected supporters. The question was what to do with them. The administration was convinced that it was fighting a war, not tracking down criminals. Operationally, it wanted to interrogate detainees in ways that would not be allowed in a criminal investigation. It wanted to avoid the delays and risks of criminal trials in US courts. It also wanted the option of detaining prisoners indefinitely rather than face a choice of taking them to trial or releasing them. The small group of government lawyers involved in the decision all firmly believed that the decision on how to proceed was the president's alone as part of the executive power conveyed by the vesting clause. In other words, they believed fervently in the unitary executive theory in its most sweeping form.

In crafting the government's legal strategy, the World War II precedents suggested a path forward. By classifying the detainees as enemy combatants, the government would gain the right to detain them outside of the criminal justice system. It could try them in military tribunals for violating the laws of war. And, the World War II cases suggested, it could keep them from having any access to the US courts by detaining them outside the United States.

The Bush administration's decision was to house the detainees at the Guantánamo Naval Base in Cuba, technically foreign soil, although it was under total American control. The legal arguments were tricky, however: the United States wanted to classify the detainees as combatants (not criminal defendants) but did not want to treat them as prisoners of war under the Geneva Conventions. The argument was that they did not qualify for POW status because they were not fighting on behalf of functioning governments.

President Bush issued an order classifying Al Qaeda fighters as illegal combatants. The rationale was that they were guilty of targeting civilians and fighting out of uniform. Illegal combatants can be tried for war crimes, whereas lawful combatants can only be held as prisoners of war. Bush ordered their indefinite detention at Guantánamo (or Gitmo, as people learned to call it).

The first question to reach the Supreme Court was whether the detainees had any right to a hearing about their detention. *Hamdi v. Rumsfeld* involved a detainee who had been moved from Guantánamo Bay to a naval brig in South Carolina when the government discovered that he was a US citizen. Thus, he was clearly within the jurisdiction of the federal courts at the time a habeas petition was filed on his behalf. The Court held that the AUMF resolution authorized the president to indefinitely detain captured members of Al Qaeda. But it further held that the due process clause entitled Hamdi to notice of the allegations against him and a hearing before a neutral decision maker in which he could contest the government's charge that he was an illegal combatant.

Justice Sandra Day O'Connor wrote the lead opinion for four justices. Although that was not a majority, several other justices agreed with the result but wrote separate opinions. O'Connor's opinion held that the AUMF authorized detention by implication. She reasoned that detention of captured enemy combatants is "a fundamental and accepted incident to war." Hence, detention had to be considered part of the "necessary and appropriate force" authorized by Congress. But O'Connor was at pains to emphasize that the detainees were entitled to due process. "It is during our most challenging and uncertain moments," she said, "that our Nation's commitment to due process is most severely tested." And "it is in those times that we must preserve our commitment at home to the principles for which we fight abroad." She recognized that the government's national security interest and the individual's interest in freedom were both very strong. Consequently, she devised a compromise. Military tribunals could decide detention cases, but detainees were entitled to counsel. Four other justices would have gone even further and rejected the detentions entirely, at least as regarding American citizens like Hamdi.

Only Justice Clarence Thomas concluded that indefinite detentions of citizens without any hearings were valid. He agreed with O'Connor that the detention was authorized by the AUMF resolution but disagreed with the due process part of the Court's holding. In his view, Justice O'Connor's opinion underestimated "the breadth of the President's authority to detain enemy combatants, an authority that includes making virtually conclusive factual findings." His opinion came closest to the Bush administration's view of nearly unlimited presidential war powers.

Detention and trial are two separate issues, because a trial involves the potential imposition of punishment on individuals rather than merely holding them. In a subsequent decision involving the military trials of Guantánamo detainees, the Court held that any actual trials for violation of the laws of war must comply with the Geneva Conventions and normal court martial procedures. In another decision involving a challenge to the indefinite detention of the Guantánamo detainees, the Court held that Congress must allow access to the courts via habeas corpus or an equivalent process. It rejected the analogy to the post–World War II cases because Guantánamo, unlike occupied Germany, was for all practical purposes US territory.

In this series of cases, the Court took a much more active role than the World War II Court had done. This came as a very unhappy surprise to the Bush administration and its legal advisers. Why the difference? One reason may have been changes since the 1940s in the Court's role. In the intervening years, the Court had positioned itself as a vigorous defender of civil liberties. It had also become strong enough to be confident that the president would not defy its rulings. Moreover, partly as a result of World War II, the concept of universal human rights had taken hold, which seemed threatened by harsh treatment of detainees.

The circumstances were also different. World War II was a conflict that engaged the efforts of the entire nation, with overwhelming public support. After the first shock of 9/11 wore off, there was much more public opposition to the Bush administration than there had been to Roosevelt sixty years earlier. Moreover, World War II was a battle against specific enemies with a defined endpoint. The post-9/11 fight was against an amorphous network of terrorists that might potentially last for decades. There was no clear demarcation between the exceptional circumstances of war and the normal circumstances of peacetime. Many feared that a waiver of all constitutional protections could become an expanding threat to civil liberties.

Trump's Travel Ban

Although war provokes the sharpest clashes between individual rights and claims of national security, they can also arise in peacetime. That is the setting of my final example, which involves President Trump's efforts to halt travel from certain countries.

Trump's 2016 presidential campaign emphasized the issue of immigration. In a September 1, 2016, speech in Arizona, he accused President Obama of engaging in a "gross dereliction of duty by surrendering the safety of the American people to open borders." Trump promised a bevy of measures to deal with what he described as the dangers of immigration. He promised to build a wall along the US-Mexico border, impose sanctions on cities that refused to cooperate with immigration officials, and undertake mass deportations. He also promised to suspend immigration from countries like Syria, Iraq, and Afghanistan. He pledged to institute "extreme vetting" to ensure that "those we are admitting to our country share our values and love our people," including a check on "attitudes on radical Islam."

In the 2016 speech, Trump said that as soon as he took office, he would ask the State Department, the Justice Department, and the Department of Homeland Security to investigate cases of terrorism involving immigrants and give him a list of countries where vetting was inadequate. After he took office, however, things took a different course. Less than two weeks after Trump took the oath of office, he issued a ban on travel from seven predominantly Muslim countries. The ban was drafted by Stephen Miller, a thirty-year-old White House aide, with little input from agencies outside the White House. Career staff at the Department of Homeland Security did not see the final ban until the day it was issued. As a result, there was chaos at airports as authorities tried to figure out how to implement the ban. For instance, it was not clear whether the ban was supposed to apply to permanent US residents with green cards who were returning from trips outside the country. The ban itself said yes, but a "clarifying" statement said no.

The initial ban was enjoined by the courts. Trump then issued a revised version, banning travel from six majority-Muslim countries. The revised ban was also enjoined, and a third version was issued. The third version covered a somewhat different mix of countries (six Muslim, two others). It was accompanied by a more carefully drafted explanation for selecting those countries. All three orders cited poor security on the part of the countries involved and allegedly elevated risks to national security connected with visitors from these countries. The third version reached the Supreme Court in a case brought by the state of Hawaii and others.

In striking down various versions of the ban, the lower courts had relied on several arguments. The first and second orders were struck down by the lower federal courts as violations of either federal immigration law or the First Amendment's prohibition on discrimination against religions. The First Amendment argument was based on a finding that Trump's orders deliberately targeted members of a particular religion (Islam). The lower courts pointed to a series of public statements and tweets by Trump before and after his election and inauguration as president. The third version was also challenged for failure to provide an adequate factual grounding and for failure to comply with an immigration law regarding visas. But from beginning to end, the primary issue was whether the ban—which opponents called a Muslim ban—was based on religious bias.

For similar reasons, the lower courts also rejected the third travel ban. The Supreme Court, however, upheld the last of the three immigration orders by a vote of 5 to 4. The conservative majority made no effort to deny the existence of evidence of religious bias. The Court's opinion even recounted a series of statements by the President or his aides directed at Muslims or at Islam as a religion:

1. While a candidate on the campaign trail, the President published a "Statement on Preventing Muslim Immigration" that called for a "total and complete shutdown of Muslims entering the United States until our country's representatives can figure out what is going on."

2. Then-candidate Trump also stated that "Islam hates us" and asserted that the United States was "having problems with Muslims coming into the country."

3. Shortly after being elected, when asked whether violence in Europe had affected his plans to "ban Muslim immigration," the President replied, "You know my plans. All along, I've been proven to be right."

4. When the first version of the travel ban was issued, one of the President's campaign advisers explained that when the President "'first announced it, he said, 'Muslim ban.' He called me up. He said, 'Put a commission together. Show me the right way to do it legally.'"

5. After issuing the second version of the ban, "the President expressed regret that his prior order had been 'watered down' and called for a 'much tougher version' of his 'Travel Ban.'"

6. Shortly before the release of the final version of the ban, "he stated that the 'travel ban . . . should be far larger, tougher, and more specific,' but 'stupidly that would not be politically correct.'"

7. More recently, on November 29, 2017, the President retweeted links to three anti-Muslim propaganda videos.

In short, from beginning to end, Trump made it clear that the ban was aimed at Muslims.

Nevertheless, the Court upheld the third travel ban. The heart of the decision was the majority's tremendous deference to presidential actions in this sphere. The majority opinion by Chief Justice Roberts reviewed previous decisions that limited the ability of courts to review government decisions to exclude foreigners on the basis of national security. The majority focused on the language in the ban regarding national security and improved vetting of travelers. It said it would uphold the ban as long as there was some plausible connection with security, regardless of the president's actual reasons. Under this extremely deferential test, the Court would uphold a law unless its *only* purpose was a "bare . . . desire to harm a politically unpopular group."

Under this legal standard, it was not enough for the plaintiffs to show that religious bias motivated the travel ban. They had to show that bias was the sole reason for the ban. To defend the ban, the government merely had to show that the ban articulated some legitimate justification on its face. It is not clear whether the first two travel bans could have passed even this remarkably weak test, but by the third try, the government's lawyers had covered their bases. The third travel ban was "expressly premised on legitimate purposes," such as vetting travelers, and the text of the ban said nothing about religion.

Accordingly, the Court concluded that the executive order passed muster. While it might be clear to others—and maybe even to the justices in the majority—that the ban's targeting of Muslim countries was no accident, the Court felt compelled to accept the president's official explanation.

There were two dissenting opinions in the travel ban case. Justice Stephen Breyer, joined by Justice Elena Kagan, wrote a relatively low-key dissent, arguing that key portions of the evidence relied on by the majority to show a legitimate purpose were at least questionable and entitled to little weight. It seems fair to say that the majority did not so much disagree with the dissenters' view of the facts as refuse to consider the substance of the situation. The dissenters saw strong evidence that the ban would not in fact advance security, whereas the majority saw that as a question that only the president could decide.

Justice Sonia Sotomayor, joined by Justice Ruth Bader Ginsburg, was more outspoken in dissent. She complained strenuously that the majority was "ignoring the facts, misconstruing our legal precedent, and turning a blind eye to the pain and suffering the Proclamation inflicts upon countless families and individuals, many of whom are United States citizens." Emphasizing what she viewed as overwhelming evidence of anti-Muslim bias on the part of the president, she compared the Court's ruling to the *Korematsu* case. Justice Sotomayor saw the cases as similar examples of blatant discrimination, using manufactured national security claims as a screen for prejudice based on national origin (and in this case, religion). As in *Korematsu*, she said, the majority in the travel ban case was extremely deferential to the government and failed to acknowledge the ugly prejudices behind the order.

Apparently stung by Justice Sotomayor's charge, the majority opinion explicitly repudiated *Korematsu*, declaring that it "was gravely wrong the day it was decided, has been overruled in the court of history, and—to be clear—'has no place in law under the Constitution.'" Justice Sotomayor was unpersuaded by the effort to distinguish the earlier case. "By blindly accepting the Government's misguided invitation to sanction a discriminatory policy motivated by animosity toward a disfavored group," she said, "the Court redeploys the same dangerous logic underlying *Korematsu* and merely replaces one 'gravely wrong' decision with another."

In response, Chief Justice Roberts wrote that the "forcible relocation of U.S. citizens to concentration camps, solely and explicitly on the basis of race, is objectively unlawful and outside the scope of Presidential authority." In contrast, banning travel on the basis of national security was clearly within any president's power. The question was only whether "this President" had exercised the power improperly. In the end, the majority was as deferential to President Trump's claim of national security as the *Korematsu* Court had been to President Roosevelt's.

The fact that the case involved a presidential action based on national security was obviously key to this ruling. The same justices who upheld the travel ban had previously overturned an action of the Colorado Civil Rights Commission on far weaker evidence of religious bias. The commission had found a bakery owner guilty of anti-gay discrimination because he refused to sell a wedding cake to a same-sex couple. The baker claimed that he had done so because of his religious beliefs. The Supreme Court decided that the commission's ruling was tainted by antireligious bias.

The evidence that the commission was biased was less than overwhelming. The Court's main evidence of antireligious bias by the commission is this statement by one of the agency commissioners: "Freedom of religion and religion has been used to justify all kinds of discrimination throughout history, whether it be slavery, whether it be the holocaust. . . . To me it is one of the most despicable pieces of

rhetoric that people can use to—to use their religion to hurt others."
Only that commissioner said anything the Court's majority considered blatantly biased, and the other evidence of bias was circumstantial. The four dissenters in the bakery case sharply disputed the Court's interpretation of the facts.

It is fair to say that the evidence of antireligious bias on the part of the Colorado Civil Rights Commission was weaker by orders of magnitude than the evidence in the travel ban case. Even hints of bias were enough to lead the Court's majority to offer a stern lecture in the bakery case about respect and tolerance for all religious beliefs. But that case involved state government, not the president, and an antidiscrimination issue, not national security.

The majority in the travel ban case had some respectable arguments on its side. Earlier decisions had established that courts have very limited power to review national security-based bans on international travel. The challengers of the travel ban claimed an indirect constitutional violation, that a ban targeting Muslims in effect elevated other religions in violation of the Establishment Clause. The challengers were not the direct victims of the ban, who could not sue because as nonresidents outside our borders they had no enforceable rights of their own. And unlike the Japanese internment, the discriminatory nature of the ban was not present on its face. All these factors made the case less extreme than *Korematsu.*

All that being said, I think the dissenters were right. It is not so much that the national security justification was a pretext. Rather, it was based on a religious stereotype. Just as the author of the World War II detention order thought all Japanese Americans were presumptively security risks, Trump thought the same about all Muslims. The majority was right that the president's good faith should be presumed. It is another thing to maintain that presumption even when the president has proclaimed his true reasoning from the rooftops. The rule should not be, "The President cannot violate the Constitution unless, on the third try, government lawyers are able to get the paperwork right."

Overall, the Court's record provides mixed evidence about its willingness to check the president. The cases from the Civil War to the travel ban severely tested the Court's willingness to enforce individual rights. They involved claims of national security, where presidents get the most deference. It was only after the Civil War that the Supreme Court invalidated military tribunals in the North. In World War II, the Court folded completely in the *Korematsu* case, upholding the blatantly racist expulsion of Japanese Americans from the West Coast, though it did end the internments in a companion case. Over a half century later, the Court showed surprising vigor in the War on Terror, only to relapse into passivity a decade later in upholding the travel ban.

The dangerous combination of national security claims and presidential power pushes the Court on the defensive. Perhaps it is surprising that the courts stand up for individual rights in these circumstances as often as they do.

8   *The President and the Courts*

I have talked in previous chapters about the constitutional limits on presidential action. But those limits aren't self-enforcing. Some of the limits on presidents are purely political or involve the difficulty of getting a balky bureaucracy to execute policies it doesn't like. But many restraints involve pushback from the other two branches of the federal government. This chapter looks at the role of the courts—which are, after all, often thought of as existing in part to keep the other two branches within constitutional limits.

In some settings, the judicial role is relatively routine. With regard to typical domestic policies, such as regulations issued by agencies at the president's orders, the validity of presidential policy decisions can generally be tested in the courts without great difficulty. This creates a significant restraint on the president's control of domestic policy, as Presidents Obama and Trump both learned. Officials below the president are also subject to civil liability if their actions violate clear constitutional rules, and they are subject to criminal prosecution even while they are in office. But there are several less routine situations in which the relationship between the president and the courts can raise serious constitutional questions.

Those constitutional questions can take several forms. In the international sphere, courts may lack authority to review presidential decisions under what is called the "political question doctrine." That may allow the president's decisions to go unchecked, even if the president is quite clearly violating the law. Also, in litigation of various kinds involving the federal government, the president may be entitled to keep some information out of the hands of the courts by claiming executive privilege. Neither Congress nor the courts can exercise much control if they can't get information. Finally, there is the question whether the president can be sued for damages or subjected to criminal prosecution while in office. Under the Constitution, although the president may be considered merely an ordinary citizen rather than royalty, it remains true that rank has its privilege.

In short, the courts do not offer a complete answer to potential abuses of power by a president. They can hem in certain kinds of abuses but do less about others. The fundamental problem is that giving them the power to deal with abuses more efficiently could at the same time hinder bold exercise of presidential power when it is really needed. In this chapter, we will see how the courts have tried to navigate this dilemma, a dilemma that the Framers of the Constitution were themselves aware of.

The Political Question Doctrine

Issues about presidential power over foreign affairs have largely been fought out in the political arena. There has been little input from the courts. This has largely been true in the modern era in terms of the president's use of the military. Much of the reason for this hands-off attitude is a constitutional principle referred to as the political question doctrine, which holds that certain constitutional issues can only be decided by the president and Congress, not the courts.

The political question doctrine stems from the *Luther v. Borden* case, which involved what amounted to a civil war in Rhode Island. Some citizens who were disenfranchised under the original colonial charter rebelled, seeking a new and more democratic state constitution. They organized an alternative government. The issue in the case was whether the original colonial charter government was still in power or whether the insurgents had created a legitimate new government. The president had treated the old government as the legitimate authority in responding to a request that he help quell the rebellion. The supporters of the rebellion argued that the old government, because of its undemocratic features, violated the constitutional guarantee of a "republican form of government." Thus, in the end, the case turned on which of the contending "governments" had been legitimate.

The Supreme Court ducked the issue. It held that a federal court could not determine which of two competing state governments was legally authorized or whether a state government was "republican" in nature. Only Congress and the president could make that decision. The upshot of the case was that the old government, which had been recognized by the president, was considered the legitimate one.

The leading modern case interpreting the political question doctrine is *Baker v. Carr*, which paved the way for the one-person, one-vote doctrine. The case involved the severely malapportioned Tennessee legislature. The issue in the case was whether malapportionment issues were outside the jurisdiction of the courts due to the political question doctrine. The opinion has significance far outside the redistricting question because the Court used the case to reformulate the doctrine.

Justice William Brennan, author of the majority opinion, carefully sifted through the precedents. He distilled from his analysis a set of guiding principles governing application of the doctrine: (1) whether the Constitution expressly assigned an issue to another branch of government, (2) whether there were judicially manageable standards for deciding an issue, (3) the need for the government to speak with a single voice as in foreign affairs, and (4) whether courts could provide an effective remedy. Applying these principles,

Brennan concluded that the political question doctrine did not apply to the reapportionment case. Those guiding principles are relevant to judicial review of presidential power. One of the areas Justice Brennan flagged for application of the political question doctrine in *Baker v. Carr* was foreign affairs.

More recently, the Court narrowed the application of the political question doctrine even in foreign affairs cases. The case is confusing because there were two Supreme Court opinions at different stages of the litigation. The ruling on the political question doctrine was part of the Jerusalem passport litigation I discussed earlier in the book. The underlying issue in the case was the constitutionality of a statute allowing Americans born in Jerusalem to have Israel listed as their place of birth on their passports. This was contrary to a long-standing executive branch decision by presidents of both political parties. The Court ultimately ruled that the president, not Congress, had the final word. It had considered in an earlier opinion whether the case should be dismissed because of the political question doctrine. The Court held in that earlier opinion that there was no political question. It reasoned that the only issue in the case was a purely legal one regarding the constitutionality of the statute, giving the Court clear standards to apply.

This ruling seems to significantly restrict the political question doctrine as applied to foreign affairs. This outcome could eventually involve the Court in other disputes between the president and Congress. For instance, if Congress passes a law forbidding the use of the US military in a conflict, the same reasoning implies that the Court would decide if the statute infringed the president's war power. That could land the Court on the political hot seat.

The concerns underlying the political question doctrine pop up in cases involving other issues of federal jurisdiction. Those concerns include respecting the proper roles of other branches of government and avoiding cases in which there are no legal standards. Thus, in determining whether individual members of Congress or the House of Representatives as a body has standing to sue the president, the courts express similar worries about being drawn into issues that more properly belong to the other branches of government. Even when the political question doctrine may not apply, the courts can use other doctrines to dodge highly sensitive cases. For example, during the Vietnam War, the courts used a variety of legal doctrines to avoid having to decide on the legality of the war. As a result, there was never a definitive judicial ruling.

Immunity from Court Orders

Often, challenges to a presidential decision can be brought against the government officials who are implementing the decision. But sometimes there is no practical alternative to suing the president. Presidents have claimed immunity from such suits. That argument succeeded in a post–Civil War case, *Mississippi v. Johnson.* After the war, Congress passed laws governing the restoration of state governments in the South. One law gave the military the task of governing the South until civilian government could be restored. Another law provided for registering voters to vote on the adoption of new state constitutions. The State of Mississippi asked the Supreme Court for an injunction against President Andrew Johnson to prohibit him from enforcing the two laws. The Court pointed out that it would have no power to enforce the injunction if the president refused to comply. On the other hand, if he did comply, defying Congress, he might well be impeached, putting the Court directly in the middle of an impeachment dispute. (Of course, Johnson was ultimately impeached and nearly convicted but on different grounds.)

In modern times, the Court has not taken that case to mean the president has blanket immunity from judicial orders. The Supreme Court squarely rejected that view in *United States v. Nixon,* a decision that led to the president's resignation under threat of impeachment. The case arose from the Watergate scandal and involved allegations that the president had been part of a conspiracy to cover up the burglary of the Democratic Party's campaign headquarters.

On the night of June 16, 1972, five men had broken into the Democratic National Committee offices at the Watergate building complex in Washington, DC. Four of the burglars were from the Special Investigations Unit in the White House, and one was from Nixon's reelection committee. They were unlucky: a building guard called the police, and they were arrested. At the time of the arrests, the burglary did not receive widespread attention. But Nixon and his top aides were deeply worried and began to look for ways to fend off a criminal investigation. They decided to cover up the White House's involvement, which they were able to keep under wraps until after the election. All but two of the defendants pled guilty in federal court, and the other two were convicted after short trials.

Then the cover-up began to fall apart. A Senate committee launched an investigation. One defendant, James McCord, wrote to the trial judge in the burglary case, alleging that there had been perjury during his trial. The trial judge postponed sentencing and told the defendants that their cooperation with congressional investigators would be an important consideration in setting their sentences. Evidence of a White House cover-up kept mounting. McCord, who had written the judge about perjury, began cooperating with the Senate investigation, giving information that implicated the attorney general and several top White House aides. Others were implicated, and they in turn provided information implicating still others. A White House staffer let slip in testimony before the Senate committee that a taping system had been installed in the Oval Office to preserve conversations there for posterity.

In the meantime, a special prosecutor had been appointed by the Justice Department. Prior to the trial of some members of the Nixon administration, the special prosecutor got a subpoena to obtain tapes of conversations regarding the break-in and the cover-up. The plan was for the judge in charge of the proceedings to examine these materials privately and determine whether they should be disclosed. Nixon claimed that he could not be subpoenaed or subjected to any other court order. He cited the Andrew Johnson case in which the Supreme Court held that courts lack the power to issue injunctions against the president. Even if the courts did have the power to issue a subpoena, the president argued, conversations involving the president were exempt from disclosure. The case quickly reached the Supreme Court.

Then-Justice Rehnquist did not participate, presumably because of his own prior role in the Nixon Justice Department before joining the bench. The other eight justices, in an opinion written by Chief Justice Warren Burger, held that the president is not completely immune from court orders, at least in federal criminal proceedings. Nixon had argued that "the separation of powers doctrine precludes judicial review of a President's claim of privilege." The Court held, however, that giving the president an absolute privilege against subpoenas in criminal cases would upset the constitutional balance of "a workable government" and "gravely impair" the constitutional role of the courts in overseeing grand juries and ensuring fair criminal trials.

Once the Court ruled that Nixon was subject to subpoena, the question was whether the particular material covered by the subpoena was subject to disclosure. I will return later to the question of whether Nixon could claim the right to keep the tapes confidential in response to the subpoena. For now, the point is that the president cannot simply issue a blanket rejection of all subpoenas. To resist answering questions or providing documents, the president would have to show some specific reason why that particular evidence was not subject to disclosure.

In more recent events, the Mueller investigation of President Trump had the potential to raise similar questions about presidential prerogatives. Trump's lawyers, however, adopted a strategy of providing a great deal of voluntary compliance with Mueller's investigation while resisting on key points. By this means, they were able to fend off Mueller's desire to interview Trump directly. Instead, Trump supplied written answers to questions.

Nevertheless, another investigation of Trump did result in federal litigation. The issue of presidential immunity from judicial process in criminal cases returned to the Supreme Court in 2020. This time, the investigation involved a state criminal investigation, not a federal one. In the summer of 2018, the State of New York's district attorney in Manhattan began an investigation into business transactions of President Trump and others within the president's company, the Trump Organization. The investigation targeted payments allegedly made to a woman in exchange for an agreement to stay silent about a sexual encounter with Trump. The subpoena was based on information derived from public sources, confidential informants, and the grand jury process. The investigation paused for around a year at the request of federal prosecutors who were also conducting an investigation. After that pause, the Manhattan district attorney, Cyrus Vance, resumed his investigation.

On August 1, 2019, Vance served the Trump Organization with a grand jury subpoena seeking financial statements and tax returns. The Trump Organization complied with part of the subpoena, furnishing thousands of pages of financial records. It did not release the president's tax returns, claiming they were outside the scope of the subpoena. At the end of the month, Vance served Mazars USA, Trump's accounting firm, with a subpoena seeking financial records and tax returns from 2011 to 2019. Trump sued to stop Mazars from delivering the information.

On September 19, 2019, the president challenged the Mazars subpoena as a violation of presidential immunity. Mazars said it would obey the subpoena unless told otherwise, but it had no interest in either defending or challenging the subpoena. The district attorney stepped into the case in defense of the subpoena. The federal trial court dismissed Trump's challenge to the subpoena on the ground that his challenge belonged in state court. The federal appeals court rejected that argument but held that the subpoena was valid. According to the appeals court, "Any presidential immunity from state criminal process does not extend to investigative steps like the [state] grand jury." The appeals court used *United States v. Nixon* to guide its holding that the president is subject to the subpoena power. Although the appeals court said it "had no occasion to decide the precise contours and limitations of presidential immunity from prosecution," it found that the subpoena was clearly valid in this case. The federal appeals court left open the possibility that the State of New York could investigate the president while he was still in office but not bring charges until after he left office. This set the stage for the Supreme Court's entry into the case.

Chief Justice Roberts wrote the majority opinion. He began by rejecting Trump's argument that presidents are absolutely immune from state subpoenas. Roberts cited examples going back to Thomas Jefferson in which presidents had responded to subpoenas. Based on this unbroken tradition combined with evidence of original intent, he found no basis for absolute immunity. Every member of the Court agreed on that point.

The Court was divided only on what safeguards were appropriate to prevent abuse of the subpoena power by state prosecutors. Roberts's majority opinion found that no special legal restrictions were necessary. The majority pointed to a variety of generally available objections to a subpoena, including improper motives by the prosecutor, harassment, or excessive burden. The safeguard for the president, compared to other recipients of state grand jury proceedings, was the ability to make such claims in federal court because of the national interest in protecting the effective functioning of the presidency.

Of the other four justices, only Justice Alito adopted the government's proposed "heightened standard" for subpoenas against the president. The other three had proposals of their own. While these various proposals differed in detail from the majority's approach, Chief Justice Roberts suggested in a footnote that the practical importance of these differences might not be dramatic. The upshot of the case, in any event, is that a president can indeed be subpoenaed but has a greater ability to contest the subpoena and delay the proceedings than an ordinary citizen.

Executive Privilege

The *Mazars* case involved personal documents of the president rather than material relating to his official duties. Confidential documents within the executive branch raise different questions. Even if a subpoena is issued, the government may argue that those particular documents cannot be disclosed. It is time to return to the Watergate tapes case to see how those arguments are handled.

After the Supreme Court held that President Nixon was not entirely immune from subpoenas, the question was whether the tapes themselves were privileged. The law of evidence is complicated, but most of us have seen dramas in which lawyers jump to their feet and object to a question from the other side. There are various grounds of objection, but one of them is that the information involves a privileged communication. Some background about evidence privileges may be helpful in understanding the Court's ruling.

There are two kinds of evidentiary privilege. With a few exceptions, communications from a client to a lawyer are subject to an "absolute" privilege. That means that no matter how much the evidence is needed, a court cannot require its disclosure. The reason for the privilege is to ensure that people are not afraid to give complete, honest information to their lawyers. Criminal defendants might be unwilling to fully disclose the facts to their lawyers if they thought their lawyers could be forced to disclose the information. That could impair their right to a full defense. Other privileges are "qualified," which means that disclosure *can* be required if there is an especially strong need for the information. That applies to evidence that a lawyer might uncover while investigating a case. Lawyers should not be afraid to investigate a case fully for fear that they might find evidence that would help the other side. But that does not seem as crucial as protecting lawyer-client conversations. That is why this evidence is not protected as strongly.

Nixon argued that just as lawyers and clients need to have completely open, honest discussions, the same is true of a president and the president's advisers. Advisers might hold back if they thought their advice might later have to be disclosed to a court (or even worse, a congressional committee). So the Supreme Court in the Nixon tapes case was faced with two questions. First, does the Constitution recognize executive privilege at all, or are communications involving the president open to disclosure like those of other organizations? Second, if executive privilege does exist, is it an absolute privilege or a qualified one?

The Court first held that executive privilege does exist. Chief Justice Burger reasoned that the president's need for confidentiality "has all the values to which we accord deference for the privacy of all citizens and, added to those values, is the necessity for protection of the public interest in candid, objective, and even blunt or harsh opinions in Presidential decision-making."

Furthermore, Burger said, the president and those who assist the president must be free to explore every alternative in the process of shaping policies and making decisions and to do so with "a brutal honesty" that might be hampered by the possibility of disclosure. Thus, the Court accepted that some type of executive privilege was necessary for the president to effectively carry out the duties of office.

The Court then rejected Nixon's argument for absolute privilege. Except when national security secrets are involved, it said, the need for confidentiality would not be seriously compromised by having a judge privately examine the materials. Moreover, the Court continued, "an absolute, unqualified privilege" would "plainly conflict" with the constitutional duties of the courts. "To ensure that justice is done," Burger wrote, "it is imperative to the function of courts" that subpoenas be available for the production of evidence needed by prosecutors or defendants. Thus, an absolute privilege was not acceptable.

Instead, the Court settled on a more limited version of executive privilege. The burden was on the special prosecutor to demonstrate that the presidential material at issue was "essential to the justice of the (pending criminal) case." In ordering the subpoena to produce the tapes, the trial judge had already made this determination. Thus, the president was obligated to turn over the tapes. Nixon apparently toyed with the idea of refusing to comply with the subpoena but was told by subordinates that doing so was untenable. He did turn over the tapes to the court, and the conversations in the tapes left no doubt that Nixon was directing the cover-up. He was forced out of office soon afterward.

Although the Watergate tapes case involved a criminal subpoena against the president, its test for applying executive privilege has been used more broadly. For instance, when Congress seeks to subpoena documents from the executive branch, presidents not uncommonly claim executive privilege. If Congress holds the custodian of the documents in contempt, a court will apply qualified privilege to determine if the subpoena can be enforced.

The Watergate tapes case was decided in an era before original-ism loomed so large in the Court's interpretation of the Constitution. Today, however, it is natural to ask how well the Nixon tapes decision accorded with the original understanding. The history suggests that, if anything, the Court in the Nixon case may have been too deferen-tial to the president's claim of privilege.

The term "executive privilege" was not in use until the mid-twenti-eth century. At the time the Constitution was written, the English king could not be personally subpoenaed because as the sovereign he was exempt from any judicial oversight in his own courts. But in terms of government documents, subpoenas against the king's ministers were not uncommon. No privilege to withhold documents or testimony from Parliament was recognized in England. The issue was not discussed at the Constitutional Convention or in the ratification debates.

After the Constitution went into effect, however, there were sev-eral incidents involving the president's power to withhold informa-tion based on something akin to executive privilege. Most of these incidents involved information requests from Congress, but they are relevant since the issues are very similar.

In one incident, Congress was investigating the massacre of an army division during a frontier battle. A House committee requested documents from the secretary of state relevant to the investigation. George Washington's cabinet apparently thought he had discretion to withhold some of the documents if that was necessary to protect the public interest. But eventually a decision was reached to turn over the documents. In the meantime, the House had passed a formal res-olution requesting "papers of a public nature" bearing on the massa-cre. The reference to "papers of a public nature" might be considered an acknowledgment of Washington's power to withhold confidential documents.

The second incident involved papers relating to diplomacy with France. The Senate requested papers from President Washington.

He sent them the papers but said he was not including material that he thought should not be communicated. The material in question related to confidential informants and some embarrassing commentary on the French government. The Senate did not challenge these deletions.

In the third incident involving Congress, the papers related to Washington's request for funding to implement a controversial treaty with England. The House requested documents relating to the directions given the diplomat who negotiated the treaty. The president refused to turn over the papers, saying that doing so would undermine future negotiations. He also said that the papers did not seem to relate to any legitimate legislative purpose except impeachment, which had not been referenced. The House then reaffirmed its right to get the documents and to deny appropriations to carry out the treaty if it did not get them. Washington never delivered the documents. But denying the appropriations turned out to be politically untenable, so the House ended up voting in favor of the appropriations anyway. Taking the three incidents involving Congress as a whole, there is not much evidence that Congress ever accepted a presidential right to withhold confidential information.

The final case involved a subpoena issued by a court rather than a document demand from Congress. The subpoena involved the unscrupulous and ambitious Aaron Burr. Burr was Jefferson's vice president because of a quirk in the way the Constitution originally structured presidential elections. He is best known today for shooting Alexander Hamilton in a duel. Burr was never prosecuted for killing Hamilton, but revulsion at his action ended his political career.

In an effort to regain his stature, he planned a bold move to seize Texas and parts of Florida from Spain, hoping to take advantage of a war with Spain that seemed at the time to be on the horizon. After many discussions with the commanding general and governor of the Louisiana Territory to win the general's cooperation, Burr made a foray down the Ohio and Mississippi Rivers, conferring with various people. In the summer of 1806, he led sixty men down the Mississippi to New Orleans. Perhaps he merely meant to take Florida or Texas from Spain (either to hand to the United States or to rule himself). Or perhaps he had an even bolder plan to separate *all* of what was then considered the "West" from the United States and set himself up as its ruler. Whatever his goals, Burr's conspiracy was betrayed to the government. The commanding general warned President Jefferson of a "deep, dark, and wide-spread conspiracy." Jefferson went to Congress for authority to send the army after Burr, which he received. Burr was then arrested for treason and conspiracy.

The charges were heard by two judges. In those days, Supreme Court justices "rode circuit," traveling around to assist in trials. One of the judges in the trial was Chief Justice John Marshall. Marshall is generally credited with shaping the Supreme Court into the form we know it today, so his views are given special weight. The commanding general was expected to be a witness against Burr. Burr demanded a copy of a letter the general had written to Jefferson about the conspiracy, so that any inconsistencies in the general's testimony could be brought before the jury. The prosecutor objected. He argued that the president could not be subpoenaed and that the letter might contain confidential information.

Chief Justice Marshall ruled in favor of Burr. He admitted that in English law the king could not be the subject of a subpoena. But the president was no king. The United States did not adopt the maxim that the king can do no wrong as applied to the president. And no one had ever claimed a state governor—or for that matter, a British cabinet minister—was immune from a subpoena. Regarding the content of the letter, Marshall wrote, "There is certainly nothing before the court which shows that the letter in question contains any matter the disclosure of which would endanger the public safety." After the subpoena was issued, Jefferson had the papers "voluntarily" sent to the prosecutor for presentation to the court. When presenting them, the prosecutor asked that portions "which it would be improper to exhibit in public" be deleted. The court did not press the matter further. That could be interpreted as accepting Jefferson's argument that he was entitled to hold some information back, although there are other possible explanations.

These incidents fall far short of establishing that executive privilege was endorsed by the Founding Fathers. Washington seemed to think that he could hold back papers under some circumstances, but there is thin evidence that anyone outside of his own cabinet agreed. Jefferson also declared the power to withhold some portions of documents, but again it is not clear that the court agreed. Chief Justice Marshall clearly did not agree with Jefferson's claim that he was immune from providing any evidence at all. This is thin evidence that any form of executive privilege was part of the original understanding. At a minimum, the evidence suggests that an absolute executive privilege was never part of the original understanding. Even the existence of a qualified privilege seems questionable in terms of the original understanding, although the historical record is ambiguous.

Rather than being based in the constitutional text or the original understanding, the argument for executive privilege seems to be much more a practical one. Some material communicated to the president is legitimately considered secret or confidential. This is particularly clear in areas involving national security or foreign affairs. Similarly, releasing discussions about legislative strategy might undermine the president's ability to work with the legislature in the future. The same might be true of some lower-level communications within the executive branch. Making all of that material public could be problematic.

The Court in the Watergate tapes case stressed the possible chilling effect on advisers who might worry about giving advice that could be made public. It is not clear to me how persuasive this argument is.

One would hope that presidential advisers would have the integrity to speak out when the national interest is at stake, even if they thought there was a risk that their own reputations would someday be harmed. In any event, given the frequency of leaking these days, such advisers would be foolhardy to assume their remarks would be kept secret. A better argument for executive privilege might be that otherwise presidents might discourage candid discussions for fear of creating evidence that could be used against them. Whatever the arguments pro or con, however, executive privilege seems to be firmly embedded in constitutional doctrine today.

Civil and Criminal Liability

In contrast to subpoenas, whether the president would be immune from prosecution or damage actions actually was discussed when the Constitution was under consideration. Again, the evidence does not give strong support to presidential claims of immunity and, if anything, leans the other way.

Toward the end of the Constitutional Convention, James Madison asked whether it would not be wise to consider what privileges were linked to the presidency. The suggestion apparently went nowhere. In contrast, the Constitution does explicitly recognize congressional immunity. It provides that members of Congress "shall not be questioned in any other Place" regarding any "speech or debate." This means that nothing said on the floor of Congress or in committee can be subject to a lawsuit or criminal proceeding. Only Congress itself can discipline its members.

Perhaps Madison wanted to make some similar provision for the president. If so, he was unsuccessful, since nothing was added to the Constitution on this topic.

The issue also came up in the ratification debates. Views were divided. James Wilson, a delegate at the Constitutional Convention and future Supreme Court justice, said that "not a single privilege is annexed" to the presidency. "Far from being above the laws," the president is "amenable to them in his private character as a citizen, and in his public character by impeachment." Later, in speaking of the president, Wilson asked rhetorically, "Is there a single distinction attached to him more than there is to the lowest officer in the republic?" Another future Supreme Court justice said that "if the President does a single act by which the people are prejudiced [harmed], he is punishable himself." If the president commits a crime, the future justice continued, "he is punishable by the laws of his country, and in capital cases may be deprived of his life." Another speaker stated that if the president gave illegal instructions to subordinates, citizens "would have redress in the ordinary courts of the common law." One supporter of the Constitution wrote that the president is "not so much protected . . . as a member of the House of Representatives," because "he may be proceeded against like any other man in the ordinary course of law." With some work, it is possible to explain away these statements, but on their face, they seem to squarely reject any immunity of the president from legal redress.

The issue lay dormant for nearly two centuries. When the president's immunity from damages finally came before the Supreme Court, it was in a case that also involved President Nixon. This case did not, however, involve the Watergate scandal. A senior air force civilian employee claimed that he was fired from his position in retaliation for his testimony to Congress disclosing a $2 billion cost overrun. He sued the president and others for damages. There was no question that Nixon was responsible for the firing decision. Nixon had said at a press conference, "I was totally aware that Mr. Fitzgerald would be fired or discharged or asked to resign. No, this was not a case of some person down the line deciding he should go. It was a decision that was submitted to me. I made it, and I stick by it." The lower court held that these facts, if proven, would establish violations of statutes as well as the First Amendment right of free speech.

The Supreme Court dismissed the case against Nixon. It held that a president is absolutely immune from civil liability for conduct within the "outer perimeter" of the president's official duties. The Court said that like prosecutors and judges—for whom absolute immunity now is established—a president is constantly involved in issues that "arouse the most intense feelings." But it is in these very cases, the Court contended, that an official's judgment must be unaffected by fear of personal consequences. In the Court's view, this concern is especially compelling in terms of the presidency, an office "where the officeholder must make the most sensitive and far-reaching decisions entrusted to any official under our constitutional system." In addition, the Court said, the prominence of the office makes it especially likely to prompt litigation against the president, and such litigation could distract from the performance of vital duties. Thus, the Court concluded, the president must enjoy absolute immunity from suit for official acts, unlike lower-level government officials, who receive only qualified immunity. Note that this was purely a pragmatic argument, not one based on the text or original understanding of the Constitution.

The dissenters argued that absolute immunity "places the President above the law" and "is a reversion to the old notion that the King can do no wrong." The dissent also raised the question of whether other legal actions against the president can be taken. "Taken at face value," the dissent observed, "the Court's position that as a matter of constitutional law the President is absolutely immune should mean that he is immune not only from damages actions but also from suits for injunctive relief, criminal prosecutions and, indeed, from any kind of judicial process." The dissent held that there was no contention that the president was immune from criminal prosecution under state or federal law—"nor," the dissent said, "would such a claim be credible."

The fired air force employee had also sued senior members of the White House staff. He accused them of being part of a conspiracy with the president to get rid of him. The Court came to a different conclusion regarding these subordinates. It said that the senior aides were entitled only to qualified immunity. That meant that they could be sued for damages but that they could defend themselves by showing that their actions did not violate any clearly established constitutional rule. The Court relied on a previous case in which it had held that cabinet officers were only entitled to partial immunity. The Justice Department continues to claim that senior White House aides are "alter egos" of the president and therefore entitled to the same immunity from subpoenas. This seems hard to square with the Court's rejection of the same argument regarding civil liability.

The practical downside of allowing damage suits over presidential decisions is real. It is easy to imagine former presidents being deluged with litigation. The Court seems to have given short shrift, however, to maintaining the principle that no one is above the law. It seems unfair to make underlings liable for carrying out the president's orders while the president, who gave the orders, pays no penalty. A more defensible solution would be to limit the president's liability to cases involving an undeniable constitutional violation. This would prevent the president from being inhibited in cases where an action is supported by a reasonable legal argument but would deter blatantly unconstitutional actions by a president.

The case of the air force employee involved a lawsuit against a president for official acts. What about suing a president for damages from personal actions or actions that took place before taking office? In *Clinton v. Jones,* that issue came to the Supreme Court in a lurid case that ultimately led to Bill Clinton's impeachment. Paula Jones alleged that Clinton had sexually harassed her when she was an Arkansas government worker and he was governor. He allegedly had a state trooper invite her to a hotel room where he exposed himself and asked for sex. She refused. Everyone agreed that he could be sued for damages for such actions since any other person could be sued for similar conduct. Becoming president does not wipe the slate clean of prior wrongdoing. The question was whether he could be sued while he was still president or whether the case would have to wait until he was out of office.

The Court held that sitting presidents are not immune from civil suits for nonofficial conduct prior to becoming president. In contrast to the case against Nixon, this case did not even remotely involve the president's official duties; the alleged harassment took place much earlier. The Court unanimously rejected President Clinton's argument that the suit could not proceed until after he had left the presidency. The Court concluded, perhaps overoptimistically, that the federal trial judge could manage the litigation so as to limit demands on the president's time and interference with his ability to conduct his duties.

As the litigation moved forward, Clinton gave testimony in a deposition at odds with information that came out regarding another relationship. This time it involved a White House intern, Monica Lewinsky. Whether his testimony was technically perjury was disputed. The matter was investigated by an independent counsel who had originally been appointed to investigate unrelated matters, none of which resulted in charges. The independent counsel reported his findings to Congress. The House voted to impeach the president, but the Senate did not convict. In the end, there was a great deal of disruption to Clinton's presidency, though whether he brought it on himself is subject to debate.

Some key issues regarding checks on the president remain unresolved to this day. It is uncertain and debated by scholars whether impeachment provides the only redress for serious presidential misconduct and whether criminal prosecution must wait until the defendant is no longer president. The main argument for temporary criminal immunity is that criminal proceedings would interfere drastically with the performance of presidential duties. The primary argument on the other side is that no one should be above the law.

In all the cases discussed in this chapter, the courts seem torn in two directions. On the one hand, the president is a person of singular importance in our system of government, charged with enormous responsibilities that have an impact on all of us. That argues in favor of giving the president some safe space within which to operate. On the other hand, we are strongly committed to the idea that no one is above the law. That argues for subjecting presidents to the same redress as other citizens. The Supreme Court has tried to navigate a middle course. This is one area where the "living Constitution" seems alive and well, since consideration of the original understanding has been decidedly secondary.

9   Congressional Checks and Balances

Short of the ballot box—which is not an available remedy for second-term presidents—the most effective checks on the president come from Congress. Many powers exercised by the president or subordinates derive from statutes. When it passes those statutes, or in later amendments, Congress can limit the amount of executive discretion, leaving it to the courts to ensure that those limits are respected. This approach has limits, however. It is not practical to write statutes in such detail that they leave no leeway for the president to exercise discretion. Moreover, it may be difficult for Congress to overturn a presidential action after the fact, since doing so invites a presidential veto. Finally, in some areas, like foreign affairs, the president does not need congressional permission to act.

Congress has other tools that can be more effective. It can refuse to fund activities that it disagrees with and bring executive officials before investigating committees. The ultimate—but rarely used—tool is impeachment, a method of control that is subject to large unsettled constitutional issues. None of these tools is effective in the absence of congressional will to use them, meaning that these limits on the presidency are inevitably intertwined with politics.

The Power of the Purse

The president has no independent source of funding, which gives Congress considerable leverage, since most things a president wants to do involve spending money or using paid staff. It is no accident that the Constitution gives Congress, not the president, the power to raise money. Control of revenue was the key lever that the English Parliament used to limit the power of the king. For instance, Parliament blocked unpopular military ventures by refusing to finance them. The Framers were well aware of that history. The president may have considerable power to begin military actions, but he has no power to raise taxes to finance them.

In addition to having the exclusive power to raise money, Congress has exclusive constitutional power to control spending. The appropriations clause provides that "no Money shall be drawn from the Treasury but in Consequence of Law." This requirement by itself is a significant restraint on the president, since every penny spent must somehow be tied to a specific appropriation law. The requirement gives Congress the ability to pull the plug on nearly any presidential activity, if Congress has sufficient political will to do so, simply by refusing to appropriate funds to support the activity. In fact, under the Antideficiency Act, it is a criminal offense to spend federal funds without a valid appropriation. The act also provides administrative sanctions. No one has ever been prosecuted criminally, but a number of federal officials have lost their jobs for violating this law. Even the most devoted advocates of presidential powers concede that Congress can end a war or prevent one simply by refusing to fund it.

A dramatic illustration of the power of spending restrictions occurred during the Vietnam War era. Although I was a college student then, I had completely forgotten the role of Congress in ending that war. In fact, Congress gave Presidents Nixon and Ford very little maneuvering room. Although Nixon remained firmly committed to military action, Congress voted in 1969 and 1970 to bar the use of funds for ground troops in Laos, Thailand, and Cambodia. Starting in 1973, Congress prohibited the use of funds for any combat operations in Southeast Asia.

These funding restrictions were taken seriously by the executive branch. In the spring of 1975, Gerald Ford had just taken over from Richard Nixon. He was faced with the need to evacuate Americans from Cambodia and Vietnam as the fighting wound down. The task was greatly complicated by restrictions imposed by Congress. Ford felt compelled to comply with the restrictions. He went to Congress to get special funding for evacuating Americans. Cambodia presented a special problem. Ford maintained that military evacuation from that country was to protect American citizens, that any fighting would only be in support of that mission, and that evacuation of any Cambodians would be incidental. Donald Rumsfeld—the future Iraq War advocate and secretary of defense—felt that calling the Cambodians' evacuation incidental was a stretch, since they greatly outnumbered the Americans who would be evacuated. Ford reported the evacuation effort to Congress under the War Powers Act. In the end, there was no fighting, and the evacuation was conducted with civilian aircraft. The takeaway from this episode is that even in the national security area, where presidents claim the most power, funding restrictions can override their desires.

Congress can also overrule presidential policy decisions by requiring the government to spend money on programs against the president's wishes. The Supreme Court reinforced this principle in another case from the Nixon administration. Nixon had vetoed the 1972 Clean Water Act because it called for massive funding to upgrade municipal sewage treatment, but Congress overrode the veto. He tried to achieve the same result by "impounding" about half the funding after it was appropriated. The Supreme Court held that this was unauthorized by law and therefore illegal.

Control of funding is probably the most powerful tool available to Congress to restrict presidential action even in areas like national security where presidential power is at its peak. It offers Congress the option to kill presidential programs by defunding them or of limiting how they are implemented. Thus, the power of the purse is a potent tool for control of the executive branch. Congress might need to stop short of using funding restrictions to control the very core of presidential powers. But that limit on congressional power would apply only in a few extreme cases such as the use of funding conditions to try to control the president's communications with foreign leaders.

Investigation and Oversight

Oversight hearings are another powerful means for Congress to influence administration officials. Hearings attract public attention to controversial actions and uncover misconduct. Congress may unearth damaging information about an administration. Such hearings can have political consequences. Hillary Clinton's presidential campaign was seriously weakened by the congressional hearings targeting her work as secretary of state during the Obama administration, particularly with respect to the killing of a US ambassador in Benghazi, Libya. Hearings can also be unpleasant experiences for powerful members of the executive branch, who must put up with aggressive cross-examination and hostile harangues by members of congressional committees. The Benghazi hearings illustrate this, with Secretary Clinton undergoing an eleven-hour grilling at one point.

Investigations can also produce information providing the basis for other congressional actions, such as statutory amendments, budget restrictions, or, in rare cases, impeachment of executive branch officials. Most important legislation is preceded by lengthy hearings. Impeachment is also generally preceded by hearings. For instance, the (first) impeachment of President Trump was an outgrowth of hearings held by the House Intelligence Committee. But impeachment is a rare outcome: more commonly used tools to block a president's actions are changes in appropriations or amendments to existing statutes.

The Constitution does not expressly provide Congress with the power to compel witnesses to testify in hearings. Nevertheless, the Supreme Court has held that this investigative power is inherent in Congress's legislative powers, pointing to a long history of such investigations. The Court observed that securing information through hearings "has long been treated as an attribute of the power to legislate." This was true "in the British Parliament and in the colonial Legislatures before the American Revolution, and a like view has prevailed and been carried into effect in both houses of Congress and in most of the state Legislatures." In addition, the Court emphasized, congressional practice since 1798 constituted a "practical construction" of Congress's constitutional powers and "therefore should be taken as fixing the meaning of those provisions, if otherwise doubtful." The Court concluded that by vesting the legislative power in Congress, the Constitution implicitly gave Congress the power to conduct investigations and compel testimony. Indeed, Congress has sometimes exercised that power by arresting recalcitrant witnesses until they agree to cooperate.

The Court was right about the historical roots of congressional investigation. By 1600, the English Parliament was already conducting investigations and claiming the power to hold witnesses in contempt in order to compel testimony. Some early state constitutions explicitly gave legislatures the contempt power. Soon after the Constitution was ratified, Congress began to exercise its power to investigate. I have already discussed some of those incidents involving the Washington administration.

Historically, executive privilege has been the primary focus of disputes between the president and Congress over investigations.

The Watergate tapes case provides the basic framework: executive privilege presumptively applies but can be overcome by a strong showing of need.

Presidents have frequently claimed privilege, which typically leads to negotiations with the relevant congressional committee over what information will be provided. More recently, broader issues regarding congressional investigations have surfaced. The courts were confronted with those issues in three lawsuits involving President Trump. In none of the cases was executive privilege an issue, because none of the cases involved communications within the government. Rather than involve government documents, they related to Trump's personal finances, and the documents in question were held by private parties rather than the government. Trump's personal finances were complicated because while serving as president he continued to hold a financial stake in his far-flung business organization.

In response to several news reports of questionable financial practices involving Trump and large banks, the House Financial Services Committee issued subpoenas to eleven financial institutions to investigate "compliance with banking laws [and] to determine whether current law and banking practices adequately guard against foreign money laundering and high-risk loans." Two of the congressional subpoenas, to Deutsche Bank and Capital One, specifically asked for records of accounts associated with the president and his family. Trump challenged those subpoenas.

The House Intelligence Committee also issued a subpoena to Deutsche Bank to secure President Trump's financial records. The subpoena was part of an investigation of possible foreign financial leverage over the president. It was also intended to provide information relevant to future legislation regulating "presidential transitions and inaugurations to prevent foreign powers from exercising influence," including whether or not the US intelligence community needs additional funding to do so.

At around the same time, a third House committee launched its own investigation. The House Oversight Committee issued a subpoena to Mazars USA, Trump's primary private accounting firm. This was separate from the subpoena by the Manhattan prosecutor discussed in the previous chapter. The Oversight Committee was investigating possible conflicts of interest, violations of federal laws, and undue influence by foreign powers. Trump also challenged that subpoena in court.

The litigation took place on two tracks. The Deutsche Bank litigation was filed in New York City. There, the federal district court denied Trump's request for an injunction against enforcing the subpoenas. The court of appeals affirmed, finding that the committees had a "valid legislative purpose" and that the subpoenas "easily pass" any judicial scrutiny.

The Mazars litigation was filed in Washington, DC. As in the New York case, the district court ruled against Trump. The court of appeals agreed, finding the authority "under both House Rules and the Constitution to issue the subpoena." As in the New York case, Trump's argument that the subpoenas were issued for an "illegitimate law-enforcement purpose" was rejected. Two judges on the appeals court panel in Washington joined the majority opinion; one dissented. The dissenter argued that Congress can investigate misconduct by officials only through the impeachment process.

The Justice Department filed separately and took a narrower position than did Trump. It argued that the Court should allow some congressional investigations of the president's personal affairs but only under limited circumstances. Under the Justice Department's proposed approach, a subpoena could only be issued if the full House or the Senate "set forth with particularity its legislative purpose" before issuing a subpoena. The proposal further added that the stated purpose should be carefully scrutinized by the courts, to ensure that it is not merely a pretext for political harassment. Moreover, the president should be allowed to block the subpoena unless the information sought is "demonstrably critical" to the congressional investigation.

The Supreme Court gave partial victories to both sides. In a 7–2 ruling, Chief Justice Roberts firmly upheld the general legislative power of investigation. In cases involving the president's papers, however, the Court adopted a more cautious approach. Roberts stressed that disputes about presidential papers had always been settled by negotiation between the parties in the past. Because demands for such papers—even those relating to the president's private affairs—can function as tools for struggle between the two branches, they require special judicial scrutiny. Roberts directed the lower courts to apply a multifactor test. He required Congress to show that other sources of information would not suffice and that the subpoena was no broader than necessary to serve Congress's legislative purpose, which Congress should describe as specifically as possible. The judge should also consider the burdensomeness of the subpoena. Clearly, the intent was to make litigation a last resort for Congress but to leave the door open if negotiations failed.

There were two dissenters. Justice Thomas argued that except in connection with impeachment, Congress had no power to subpoena private papers from anyone, least of all the president. He applied a very narrow test for implied congressional powers—far narrower than the test he has applied to implied presidential powers. The other dissenter, Justice Alito, also signaled partiality to the presidency, casting aspersions on Congress's motivations, whereas in other cases he had indignantly rejected such evidence regarding the president.

In the *Mazur* and *Deutsche Bank* litigation, the president sued to block a congressional subpoena because the subjects of the subpoena were willing to comply. Subpoena cases can also reach the courts if subjects of the subpoena refuse to comply and Congress sues to enforce the subpoena. There is an important procedural difference between those cases and the ones I just discussed. In *Mazur* and *Deutsche Bank,* the president was asking for the help of the courts to stop third parties from complying with subpoenas. But the issue I am discussing now is whether Congress can ask for the help of the courts to enforce its subpoenas. The Supreme Court has not yet addressed this issue.

In a February 2020 ruling, however, the federal court of appeals in Washington, DC, ruled on the authority of federal courts to enforce a congressional subpoena. The case involved former White House counsel Don McGahn. He had been subpoenaed in connection with an investigation of Trump's alleged abuse of power and obstruction of earlier congressional inquiries. McGahn made two arguments: first, that the courts had no jurisdiction to enforce the subpoena; and second, that senior White House staff were absolutely immune from congressional subpoenas. The second argument corresponds with a view held by the Justice Department that senior staff are "alter egos" of the president and therefore immune from compelled testimony.

The three-judge panel of the appeals court dismissed the case without deciding the question of McGahn's immunity. Two of the judges agreed that there was no jurisdiction and that the courts therefore could not enforce a congressional subpoena against the executive branch. They argued that the courts should not get in the middle of disputes between the other two branches. The third judge dissented. She argued that the court did have jurisdiction and poohpoohed the majority's worries about getting between the other two branches. She was also skeptical of McGahn's second argument, which was that White House aides are immune from subpoena. One of the majority judges also seemed skeptical of that second argument. Thus, two of the three judges seemed to think that McGahn's claim of blanket immunity for White House aides was weak. The language in their opinion could someday be helpful to Congress.

The full DC Circuit Court of Appeals overturned the three-judge panel's ruling on standing. Instead, it held that Congress clearly had a sufficient legal interest to give it constitutional standing to enforce its subpoenas. The case was then sent back to the three-judge panel, which ruled against the House on different grounds. The panel pointed out that a statute empowers the Senate to bring lawsuits to enforce subpoenas, but there is no such statutory authorization for the House to sue. Hence, the panel said, the House lacked the ability to bring such suits. The full court vacated the panel ruling as a prelude to rehearing the case, but then the House subpoena expired when the new Congress was sworn in. The House committee had previously notified the court of its intention to reissue the subpoena, but the dispute was later resolved after Trump left office.

Although the Supreme Court has upheld the validity of congressional subpoenas, it has not yet ruled on whether the subpoenas can be enforced in court. Without the help of the courts, Congress would have an uphill battle in obtaining evidence from the executive branch. Currently, the executive branch seems to feel legally free to withhold evidence at will. Depriving Congress of access to the courts to enforce subpoenas in reality prioritizes presidential claims of privilege over the congressional power to investigate. Neither executive branch privilege nor the power to investigate is expressly granted by the Constitution. Rather, both are implied on the basis that they are required for the effective functioning of Congress or the president. Unless we think that presidential powers are simply more important than congressional powers, it is difficult to see the argument for giving one complete priority over the other.

The Legislative Veto

The Supreme Court has eliminated legislative vetoes. When they existed, however, they were a way to curb some of the power that Congress delegated to the president and to administrative agencies (which are mostly under the president's control). Legislative vetoes gave legislators the ability to nullify administrative actions. Depending on the statute involved, the veto sometimes required both houses of Congress to agree, but sometimes a vote by a single house was all that was required. Note that the president was not given the power to veto these congressional decisions.

As an example of why this was a useful tool, consider the National Emergencies Act. Under this law, the president can declare national emergencies, which then triggers emergency powers under other laws. President Trump used this mechanism, for example, to reallocate construction funds from military projects to build his wall at the US-Mexico border. At that point, if we were still in the era of the legislative veto, congressional disapproval would have been enough to overturn the emergency declaration.

We are not, however, still in the era of the legislative veto. In 1983, after the passage of the National Emergencies Act, the Supreme Court invalidated all legislative vetoes. The House and the Senate did pass a joint resolution disapproving Trump's emergency declaration. Since the legislative veto no longer exists, the joint resolution was treated legally as if the House and the Senate were passing a completely new law to prohibit Trump's transfer of funds. Like any new legislation, it went to Trump's desk. He promptly vetoed it. There were not enough votes in Congress to override Trump's veto. So Trump's emergency declaration, which would have been invalidated if Congress still had a legislative veto, emerged unscathed. (The emergency declaration was terminated by President Biden soon after taking office.)

Legislative vetoes met their downfall in an immigration case, *Immigration and Naturalization Service v. Chadha*. A deportation proceeding was undertaken against Jagdish Chadha for long overstaying his visa. He conceded that he was deportable but asked the US attorney general to suspend his deportation. He had a sympathetic case: he had been born in Kenya of Indian parents and traveled under a British passport, but as it turned out, none of those countries recognized him as a citizen. Thus, if he were deported, he might have nowhere to go. The attorney general granted him a suspension of his deportation. But the story doesn't end there. The immigration law that gave the attorney general this power also empowered either house of Congress to veto the suspension of deportation. For reasons that were unexplained, the House of Representatives overturned Chadha's deportation suspension. The case ultimately went to the Supreme Court.

The Supreme Court might have decided the case on narrower grounds, but it instead took the occasion to rule on the general constitutionality of legislative vetoes. Congress had often included the legislative veto provision when passing new laws. But presidents had often protested the validity of such veto provisions. In a victory for the executive branch, the Court held that legislative vetoes are unconstitutional because they are not subject to presidential veto. In addition, they went further and declared that one-house vetoes like the kind involved in *Chadha* are also unconstitutional because they violate the requirement that all legislative acts pass both houses of Congress. The effect of the ruling was to invalidate scores of legislative veto provisions that had been part of many statutes over the decades.

Chief Justice Warren Burger's opinion for the Court dismissed the relevance of historical practice and instead viewed the case as a straightforward application of logic:

1. The Constitution says a bill cannot become law until it has been passed by both houses of Congress and presented to the president for veto or signature.
2. The legislative veto in *Chadha* was a new law (in Burger's view), but it had not been passed by both houses, nor was it ever presented to the president.
3. Ergo, the legislative veto was unconstitutional. Q.E.D.

The key to the Court's logic was the assumption that the legislative veto was a new law. But one could also argue that the legislative veto was not a new law; it was simply a mechanism built into the existing immigration law along with the attorney general's power to issue suspensions. This may seem like a purely semantic issue, but it is the entire basis of the Court's reasoning.

In dissent, Justice Byron White pointed out the existence of legislative vetoes in two hundred statutes, all of them presumably invalid after the Court's decision. He argued that the legislative veto had "become a central means by which Congress secures the accountability of executive and independent agencies." Without the option of the legislative veto, he argued, Congress was "faced with a Hobson's choice: either to refrain from delegating the necessary authority, leaving itself with a hopeless task of writing laws with the requisite specificity to cover endless special circumstances across the entire policy landscape, or in the alternative, to abdicate its lawmaking function to the executive branch and independent agencies." Justice White regarded neither choice as satisfactory: refusing to delegate "leaves major national problems unresolved"; delegating without the legislative veto "risks unaccountable policymaking by those not elected to fill that role."

Moreover, in White's view, the legislative veto strengthened the separation of powers; it did not undermine it. It provided a way of maintaining checks and balances in an ever more complex world where much authority has to be delegated to the executive branch. From White's perspective, if the goal of the separation of powers is to prevent any branch of government from acquiring too much power at the expense of the other branches, the legislative veto in *Chadha* actually advanced this goal by giving Congress a check on the attorney general's discretion.

The National Emergencies Act illustrates Justice White's point. As originally written, the act gave the president the right to use emergency powers quickly and flexibly while retaining a congressional check if this power was abused. Once the legislative veto was eliminated, Congress's only option was to pass a new law overturning a specific emergency declaration. But that was pretty much an exercise in futility, since in the absence of a two-thirds supermajority opposition in Congress, the president would obviously veto such an attempt to overturn the president's own action. The upshot was that the elimination of the legislative veto left the president with tremendous discretion but eliminated any realistic check on that discretion.

The majority opinion in *Chadha* and the dissent exemplify two different forms of constitutional reasoning. The majority of the Court viewed its task as logic: simply apply the rules written in the Constitution to the subject of the legislative veto. To the Court's majority, the consequences of the decision were not relevant to the logical analysis. Justice White, on the other hand, applied a pragmatic analysis, attempting to determine whether the legislative veto furthered the goals of accountability and effective government.

In legislation enacted after *Chadha,* Congress has attempted to use means other than the legislative veto to retain some control over how a president implements a statute. For instance, Congress established a special mechanism for imposing budget cuts in order to balance the budget. The mechanism was complex, but the key decisions on where to cut would be made by the comptroller general. The comptroller general's role created a constitutional issue. The comptroller general is appointed by the president but removable by Congress. Is that constitutional?

In a case challenging the statute, the Court held that the comptroller general was performing an executive function in implementing this statute and that such a function could not be performed by an official removable by Congress: "As *Chadha* makes clear, once Congress makes its choice in enacting legislation, its participation ends. Congress can thereafter control the execution of its enactment only indirectly—by passing new legislation." So the Court held the budget-cutting provisions involving the comptroller general unconstitutional. This is actually a broader ruling than *Chadha*, since it announces a broad principle that reaches beyond the specific constitutional language involved in *Chadha*.

The decisions discussed in this section express concern about Congress's use of legislation to aggrandize its own power at the expense of the executive branch. But the difference between aggrandizing power and attempting to maintain a balance of power may be in the eyes of the beholder. From a different perspective, these decisions, by invalidating Congress's efforts to check executive power, may have contributed to a long-term shift of power into the hands of the president.

Impeachment: The Nuclear Option

When all else fails, Article II of the Constitution creates the mechanism for removing a president or other official from office. It provides that "the President, Vice President and all civil Officers of the United States, shall be removed from Office on Impeachment for, and Conviction of, Treason, Bribery, or other high Crimes and Misdemeanors." The most disputed issue is the meaning of "high Crimes and Misdemeanors." Do they have to be criminal offenses? Or can the president or a federal judge be impeached for conduct that does not violate criminal law? If a criminal offense is required, do only some criminal offenses qualify, or do all of them? These questions ask us to find the line between garden variety misconduct or policy disagreement and impeachable offenses.

Let's begin with the text of the Constitution itself. The Constitution has a good deal to say about impeachment. Unfortunately, it devotes more attention to the procedures and consequences of impeachment than to defining its scope. The House of Representatives has the "sole Power of impeachment," and the Senate has the "sole Power to try all impeachments." Under Article II, removal requires a two-thirds vote in the Senate. The Senate may also ban a removed official from holding any future office, but it may not impose any further punishment. (In England, impeachment could be accompanied by prison or other penalties.) However, the former official remains "subject to Indictment, Trial, Judgment and Punishment, according to Law," and the president's power to pardon offenses does not apply "in cases of impeachment." Thus, the president cannot free an impeached individual of later criminal punishment. Article III provides the final mention of impeachment, stating that the "trial of all Crimes, except in Cases of Impeachment, shall be by Jury."

The Framers did not invent impeachment. It has a long history, going back four centuries before they wrote the Constitution. The first impeachments in England occurred in the late 1300s. The charges involved military failures, corruption, and wasting government money. It was in 1386 that the phrase "high Crimes and Misdemeanors" was first used. That phrase was used again in 1450. In that case, some of the charges against the defendant involved criminal offenses. Other charges were that the defendant procured offices for people who were unfit and squandered public funds. Impeachment had an on-again off-again history as a tool for Parliament to get rid of unpopular royal officials. After falling out of use for a long period, impeachment became prominent again under the Stuart kings, who ruled after Queen Elizabeth I's death. The charges against officials in that period included noncriminal conduct such as mismanagement, subverting the law, promoting tyrannical government, and giving bad foreign policy advice. One judge was impeached for browbeating witnesses and getting drunk.

The Framers may not have known all the details of British history, but they would have been well aware of the general practices. At the same time the Constitution was being written in Philadelphia, impeachment was again a subject of lively interest in England. Parliament was immersed in impeachment proceedings against Warren Hastings. He was charged with abusing his power in managing India on behalf of the English. Edmund Burke, the leading advocate for impeachment, made it clear that no criminal charges were involved.

That was the last major impeachment proceeding in England. Impeachment became obsolete soon afterward because changes in the English government allowed Parliament to throw out ministers through a vote of no confidence. But while impeachment was in use, it had not been limited to criminal offenses. Charges of high crimes and misdemeanors frequently included corruption, incompetence or neglect of duty, betrayal of the national interest, and subversion of constitutional norms.

Impeachment was familiar to Americans, not only because they had read about its use in England, but also because they had used it themselves. A century before independence, Maryland impeached a colonial officer for bungling a military expedition, sabotaging the colony's policy on Indians, and murdering hostages. In Pennsylvania, a colonial official was impeached for legislative contempt. Closer to independence, a judge was impeached after agreeing to receive a salary from the king rather than the colonial government, which the Massachusetts legislature viewed as a case of undue royal influence.

At the Constitutional Convention, there was initial disagreement about whether impeachment was necessary or whether the desire for reelection was a sufficient restraint on misbehaving presidents. Once that was resolved, there was protracted discussion of who should judge impeachments—the Senate, the Supreme Court, or some other body? And finally, the convention delegates had a hard time finding the right description of the grounds for impeachment. They began with "mal-practice or neglect of duty," changed that to "treason, bribery, or corruption," then hit on "treason, bribery, or high crimes and misdemeanors against the state." "Against the state" got changed to "against the United States" before being dropped entirely, leaving us with the final constitutional phrasing, "high Crimes and Misdemeanors."

Madison's terse notes have been plumbed for clues to what the delegates had in mind. He and some other delegates were clearly concerned about presidential abuse of power going beyond criminal conduct. Among the grounds for impeachment mentioned during the debates were corruption, loss of capacity, bribery, treachery, negligence, and "perfidy." Preelection misconduct was also discussed, including the risk that a president might gain office by corrupting the members of the electoral college.

The discussion relating most directly to the meaning of high crimes and misdemeanors took place on September 8, 1787. A committee proposed a draft that made treason and bribery the only grounds for impeachment. George Mason pointed out that this formulation would not include a case like that of Warren Hastings. (Recall that the convention took place during Hastings's impeachment trial in England for abusing his power as a colonial administrator.) Nor, Mason complained, did the committee's proposal include "attempts to subvert the Constitution." He moved to add "maladministration" as an additional ground for impeachment.

Madison responded that this term was too vague. He had earlier favored making the president impeachable in order to address the risks that a president "might betray his trust to foreign powers" or "pervert his administration into a scheme of peculation or oppression." This suggests that Madison did not mean to suggest limiting the grounds for impeachment entirely to criminal conduct when he criticized Mason's proposal. In response to Madison's criticism, Mason then proposed new language: "other high Crimes and Misdemeanors against the state." That proposal passed. It remains the operative constitutional language, with only the removal of the final phrase ("against the state").

This was the only direct discussion of the current constitutional language. As with other crucial passages in Madison's notes, our knowledge of what was said is frustratingly limited. Presumably the reference to "high Crimes and Misdemeanors" was chosen with reference to the historical use of that term in impeachments, with which the delegates were at least generally familiar. Unfortunately, none of them thought to explain what they understood to be the meaning of the language, or if they did, Madison did not write it down.

Impeachment also received some discussion during the ratification of the Constitution. It got a few mentions in the Federalist Papers. In frequently quoted language from Federalist No. 65, Hamilton said that "the subjects of impeachment are those offenses which proceed from the misconduct of public men, or, in other words, from the abuse or violation of some public trust." He continued that those offenses "are of a nature which may . . . be denominated POLITICAL"—his emphasis—"as they relate chiefly to injuries done immediately to the public." This language suggests a focus on abuse of power rather than criminality. In discussing the judicial branch in Federalist No. 79, Hamilton said that judges were subject to removal for "misconduct." He also discussed whether judges should be removable if they were unable to function in that role. He opposed this as a general matter but described "insanity" as a "virtual disqualification." Later, in Federalist No. 81, Hamilton said that judges would not dare undermine legitimate legislative prerogatives because Congress "was possessed of the means of punishing their presumption" through impeachment. The most natural reading of Hamilton's language seems to be that commission of a crime was not the only basis for impeachment. Someone so inclined could read his language more narrowly, however.

What about impeachment experience under the Constitution? There have been many proposed impeachments, but comparatively few have gone forward. There have been only a couple of impeachments of officials other than presidents and judges. Nine years after the Constitution went into effect, the House impeached a senator who had been part of a scheme to give the English control of Louisiana and Florida, which were then under Spanish rule. The House did not accuse him of a crime. The Senate decided that its members were not "civil officers" subject to impeachment, although its members are subject to expulsion by their peers for misconduct. There has been only one case involving impeachment of an executive officer below the president. In 1876, the House impeached the secretary of war for forcing an official running a trading post to give kickbacks to a third party, some of which found their way back to him. The defendant had resigned his post, and while a majority of the Senate ruled that it had jurisdiction, there were apparently enough with the contrary view to prevent a two-thirds majority for conviction.

All the successful impeachments, and nearly all the others, involved federal judges. Since federal judges have life tenure, impeachment is the only way to remove them. Corruption has been the primary justification. One judge was removed for treason, having gone over to the Confederacy during the Civil War. Others were removed for incapacity (such as being mentally incapable or drunk on the bench), committing crimes while serving as judges (such as tax evasion), or abusive behavior during trials. The cases involving abusive behavior and incapacity suggest that noncriminal behavior can qualify as high crimes and misdemeanors.

Presidential impeachments, none of which has been successful, have covered a range of offenses. Andrew Johnson was charged with criminal violations of a law governing removal of government officials, which had been passed with impeachment in mind. He was also charged with failing to "take care that the laws be faithfully executed" and with undermining Congress through false criticisms. In the proposed impeachment resolution, Nixon was charged with several criminal offenses, along with more general charges of undermining the Constitution. Although he resigned before the House could vote on the resolution, it seems clear that the vote would have gone against him. Bill Clinton was charged with purely criminal offenses, perjury and obstruction of justice.

In his first impeachment, Donald Trump was charged with "corruptly" soliciting the assistance of Ukraine to obtain negative information about a possible political opponent (Joe Biden) in exchange for financial aid to Ukraine and with blocking the House investigation by withholding evidence "without cause or excuse." The first charge arguably involved a violation of campaign finance laws and might be classified as "bribery" by Trump of the Ukrainians, under the impeachment clause. The second charge also might constitute a criminal offense, obstruction of Congress. However, the House chose not to allege criminal violations in order to avoid getting bogged down in issues of criminal law, such as whether information about a political opponent constituted a "thing of value" as required for a violation of the campaign finance laws. Some Republican senators voting against conviction argued that a criminal violation had to be charged by the House; others simply denied that the president had done anything improper.

The charge against Trump in his second impeachment involved conduct that would be considered criminal but also involved failure to enforce the law and undermining the electoral process. Trump's second impeachment took place after the final manuscript of this book was completed. It raises some broader issues that merit separate discussion, and for that reason, I've added an afterword rather than try to shoehorn the discussion into this chapter.

It seems clear from history that the core of the impeachment clause covers criminal offenses, which are the most frequent charges, but it also most likely covers serious, noncriminal abuses of power. That seems true whether we consider the history of impeachment in England or its use in America prior to the Constitution, at the adoption of the Constitution, or in later impeachment proceedings.

Based on this history, it seems to me that the House's accusations against Trump in his first impeachment, if proven, would qualify as "high Crimes and Misdemeanors." The House alleged that Trump had used the powers of his office to investigate the family of a likely political opponent, not as part of a legitimate effort to deal with foreign corruption, but instead for his own political advantage. The House also alleged that Trump had instructed subordinates to stonewall the House impeachment investigation, again in the pursuit of self-interest rather than any legitimate governmental purpose. If those charges were proved, they seem sufficiently grave to qualify as impeachable offenses. The Clinton impeachment presents a closer case. Perjury, if in fact Clinton intentionally lied, is a serious criminal offense, but the context was an investigation into a sexual affair that might be regarded as tangential to his fitness as president. There is room for reasonable disagreement, but my own view is that this incident was not enough for the Senate to remove Clinton from office. Given the lack of any definitive resolution of the meaning of "high Crimes and Misdemeanors," however, there will always be room for disagreement.

You might think that the Supreme Court must have ruled on such an important issue of constitutional law at some point in the two centuries since the Constitution was ratified. But you would be wrong. In fact, there are no rulings by any federal court about the meaning of "high Crimes and Misdemeanors."

Most likely, there never will be a court ruling on the issue. The Supreme Court has signaled that it does not want to be involved in anything to do with impeachment, apart from the Chief Justice's largely ceremonial role at Senate trials. Indeed, it has indicated that federal courts lack jurisdiction to intervene. In 1993, in a case involving the impeachment and conviction of a federal judge, the Court refused to consider whether the streamlined procedure used by the Senate was unconstitutional. The Senate had delegated the task of hearing evidence to a committee, and the judge who was impeached argued that this was inconsistent with the constitutional requirement that the Senate conduct a trial. It was not a silly argument: a jury cannot delegate the work of listening to witnesses to a few jurors while the others go about their business. But the Court refused to consider the claim. Applying the political question doctrine, discussed in the previous chapter, the Court denied that it had jurisdiction to consider that claim. It relied primarily on the Constitution's grant of the "sole power" of impeachment to the Senate as precluding a role for the judiciary.

In addition, the Court saw important reasons to make the Senate's conviction final in impeachment cases. For instance, an appeal by an impeached president to the courts would leave a cloud over the legitimacy of a successor. The Court feared the possibility of political chaos while a lawsuit over the president's removal was pending. Although the judge's lawsuit in the 1993 case involved a challenge to the procedure used by the Senate, the Court's reasoning would seem to apply just as much to an appeal of whether the charges actually constituted high crimes or misdemeanors. This case suggests that all challenges in the courts to conviction and removal by the Senate are precluded.

Thus, it is up to the House and the Senate to decide what constitutes an impeachable offense. Historically, this has included serious abuses of power even if they do not violate any criminal statute. This also seems to be a sensible interpretation of the Constitution. For instance, suppose the president announced a policy of pardoning only members of a favored racial group or religion or political party. That would not violate any criminal law. Or suppose a president announced that US foreign policy would be dictated by the leader of a foreign country and that that country's interests would be placed above our own. Unless we are at war with that country, that is not treason, bribery, or a criminal offense. Yet it seems intolerable that a president who does such things should be allowed to remain in office.

The argument on the other side is that such extreme cases are very unlikely and that it is dangerous to give Congress too much discretion in what constitutes an impeachable offense. Hence, the argument goes, it is better to confine impeachment to criminal offenses. That argument is not negligible. On the other hand, limiting impeachment to criminal offenses may not do that much to narrow Congress's discretion. The federal criminal code covers a wide swath of conduct these days, as illustrated by the possibility that the charges against Trump could have been rephrased as criminal violations.

Moreover, there is another powerful constraint on abuse of the impeachment power. That is the requirement of a two-thirds majority in the Senate for conviction. That requirement, combined with the prior need for a majority in the House, requires a very strong consensus that a judge or a president has violated the public trust. If such a consensus exists, it is unlikely that nitpicking over the fine points of criminal law will make any difference. And if such a consensus exists, it is unlikely that a president could continue to function successfully in any event.

Despite the enormous difficulty of removing a president from office, even the small risk of removal from office may have some disciplining effect. And while no president has ever been formally removed, Nixon's resignation seems to indicate that he thought it was a serious prospect. Still, as a practical matter, investigations and funding restrictions are clearly Congress's main tools for restraining presidential power.

This marks the end of my tour of the constitutional issues relating to presidential power. It is time to see what themes we can distill from that tour.

10 *Concluding Thoughts*

I have covered a broad array of topics, ranging from war powers and foreign policy to impeachment and civil liability. Each has its own history and intricacies. The issues in these areas are not completely disconnected, though. Certain themes and arguments crop up over and over again.

One constant is the amount of disagreement over presidential powers. The presidency is a work in progress—at least as a matter of institutional and political reality, if not according to some constitutional theories. Many of the constitutional issues surrounding the presidency have been contested for much of US history. The shifting politics surrounding debates on presidential power will come to rest only when presidents stop taking major controversial actions on vital national issues. This is another way of saying that we can expect the scope of presidential power to remain contested as long as the office endures.

Not everything is up for grabs. Supreme Court precedents have settled some issues. Congress and the president have informally resolved some others. It seems clear, for instance, that Congress does not object to short-term military actions that are unlikely to spark broader conflicts but that presidents face considerable pressure to get congressional authorization for large-scale use of the military. We can point to fairly broad areas where presidents are free to act and others that seem off-limits. But the boundaries are constantly contested.

The contesting viewpoints have crystallized into two competing constitutional visions, which have made an appearance in almost every chapter of this book. One model of the presidency seeks to define a clear field for presidential action with little or no restraint from Congress or the courts. This presidentialist model of government has been championed by presidents, their lawyers, and some judges. It seeks clearly separated powers, with a high wall surrounding each of the branches. The other model gives presidents considerable power but envisions strong checks and balances to keep that power under control. This model of balanced government has had support from advocates of congressional power, civil libertarians, and, in many cases, the Supreme Court.

It is time to put the pieces together and show how each model resolves the constitutional issues surrounding presidential power. Then it will be time to think about how this conflict is likely to play out in the future.

Organizing Frameworks: The Two Models and the Court

In laying out two models of presidential power, I do not mean to imply that scholars, judges, or even presidents fall neatly into two camps. These are complex issues, and the views held by individuals may incorporate elements of both models. But the two models provide the focal points around which the debates are organized. I have referred to these models throughout the book, but it may be helpful to recap now that I have covered the application of these models to major areas of presidential power. Keep in mind that these models represent clusters of legal positions.

Let us begin with the model that celebrates presidential power and downplays restraints from the other branches. In terms of the original understanding, the canonical texts for this presidentialist model are Hamilton's essays about the critical importance of energetic, decisive executive action. Looking to an earlier period, the advocates of presidentialist governance seek support in the writings of authors like the philosopher John Locke that define the "executive power" expansively. Stressing the desire of the Framers for a much stronger executive than most state governors enjoyed, presidentialists focus on a single clause of the Constitution. For them, the clause vesting the executive power in the president eclipses any of the more specific grants of presidential power in the Constitution. In particular, they view the president as having inherent power to conduct foreign policy free from interference and to deploy the military unilaterally.

There is an old map from the *New Yorker* showing the New York perspective on the rest of the country. New York City and the East Coast are huge, along with a fairly large West Coast, while the rest of the country is compressed into a few inches. The presidentialist vision of Article II would show the vesting clause in huge letters, with the other provisions in fine print.

In terms of control of the bureaucracy, presidentialists view the entire executive branch as essentially an extension of the president's will. From top to bottom, the officials are merely the president's alter egos. (I'm tempted to say "sock puppets," but that's a little unfair. Presidentialists do recognize that as a practical matter many subordinate officials, like good butlers in historical dramas, will be required to exercise some independent judgment.) Presidentialists see the president as having unlimited power to fire any member of the executive branch, and they believe that anyone exercising any significant executive power must be appointed by the president or one of the president's underlings.

This is not to say that presidentialists view presidential power as unlimited. They agree that Congress can use the power of the purse for purposes such as ending unpopular wars. They also agree that the courts can sometimes play a role in limiting presidential powers. But in both cases, the available tools for checking the president are limited. In their view, presidents are immune from lawsuits and from criminal prosecution. Their robust version of executive privilege prevents Congress or the courts from probing the inner workings of government. In the view of many presidentialists, the power of impeachment may be limited to serious criminal offenses rather than encompass abuses of power. (This became a contentious issue in the first Trump impeachment.)

There is one respect in which members of the presidentialist school currently seem intent on limiting presidential power. That is their effort to limit the president's role in domestic policy by requiring Congress to give detailed instructions regarding government regulations. This deviation may simply reflect the fact that many presidentialists are conservatives and prone to distrust government regulation. It may also reflect their failure to realize that government regulation these days is no longer decided by bureaucrats; rather, it is steered by the president. Or perhaps they are willing to reduce presidential power over regulations as part of their general commitment to a wall of separation between the branches of government—letting only the president control some things like warfare and only Congress control others like domestic policy.

Although there are certainly refined analytic arguments for the presidentialist view, I do not think that is where the real persuasive power of this position comes from. Instead, I think it comes from the veneration that many of us feel for the strong presidents who have made the office what it is today. In times of national crisis, presidents such as George Washington, Abraham Lincoln, and Franklin Roosevelt took bold actions, providing leadership and shaping the society we have become. Surely, the presidentialists remind us, the Constitution should make room for the actions of these great historical figures. The presidentialist model takes these presidents and their actions as the paradigms of presidential authority. Among the Founders, Alexander Hamilton would have been most in sympathy with this model.

The other major model of presidential power does not come with a handy label such as "presidentialist." I considered calling this the Madisonian model, because it resonates with his general emphasis on checks and balances rather than on clean boundaries between different branches of government. Madison agreed with many, though not all, of the specifics of the balanced power model. But he did have presidentialist views on a few issues, so giving the nonpresidentialist model his name could be confusing. The model could also be named after the *Steel Seizure* approach (derived from the decision overturning Truman's seizure of the steel mills during the Korean conflict). That case has figured heavily in this book, but naming a presidential power model for a judicial decision seems a bit too lawyerly. I have called this the balanced government model, since it emphasizes the dangers of letting too much power fall into the hands of any one branch of government.

In terms of the constitutional text, the balanced government model downplays the significance of the vesting clause. Rather than base the president's powers in foreign affairs on some broad conception of the "executive power" vested in the president, it looks to the more specific constitutional powers to negotiate treaties and receive ambassadors as the foundation of the president's lead role in international affairs. In terms of war powers, the balanced government model acknowledges the need for the president to take unilateral action when required by emergencies but favors congressional authorization as a prerequisite for major military actions.

In terms of domestic powers, balanced government thinkers believe Congress should have the ability to limit the president's power to remove certain government officials. They believe that requiring good cause to fire certain officials provides a check on some potential abuses of power by the president. For instance, they believe, the independence of the Federal Reserve limits the president's power to manipulate the economy to obtain a partisan electoral advantage. They also believe that broad delegations of power to the president and executive agencies can be a practical necessity, which has been consistent with balanced government because so many safeguards are provided by administrative law.

As with presidentialism, there is no lack of analytic arguments supporting this position. But again, I think that much of the persuasive force of this model comes from elsewhere. It comes from the American distrust of unrestrained power and fear of the perils of authoritarian government. Those who downplay these concerns may consider them irrational phobias rather than realistic assessments of risk.

Congressional and judicial oversight are a key part of the modern vision of checks and balances. This means a narrower interpretation of executive privilege and a rejection of presidential immunity from investigation. It also means interpreting "high Crimes and Misdemeanors" broadly. Under this view, serious abuses of power are impeachable offenses regardless of whether they also violate the criminal laws. Congress's power of the purse also stands as a key restraint on the presidency.

The Supreme Court has never adopted either theory in pure form. A few of the Court's early twentieth-century opinions on foreign affairs and on removal of executive officers come closest to articulating the presidentialist theory. Some individual justices such as Antonin Scalia and Clarence Thomas have also adopted this basic framework. The Court has also come to presidentialist conclusions in other areas, such as granting the president absolute immunity from civil liability for official acts, eliminating the legislative veto, and supporting Lincoln's use of force at the start of the Civil War. And the presidentialist approach may have picked up some supporters from Trump's recent Supreme Court appointees, so perhaps it represents the wave of the future. This is a trend to keep an eye on.

Nevertheless, at least up until now, the balanced government approach has made a larger mark on the Court's decisions. No one on the modern Supreme Court denies the central importance of the president to modern American government. And the Court rarely tries to put absolute limits on presidential power, leaving some flexibility for itself in future cases. Still, the Court's rulings have more often sought to maintain a balance of power between the branches—while itself balancing the need for a strong presidency against the risk of abuses of power. The *Steel Seizure* case—and in particular Justice Jackson's concurring opinion—remains the epitome of the balanced government approach. It stresses a dynamic interaction between Congress and the president, which then provides insights into whether the president has strayed into forbidden ground. In other cases involving unilateral presidential actions, the Court has remained faithful to this approach.

All that being said, I would not attempt to fit all the Supreme Court's decisions into one model or the other. Even an individual justice may rely on either model or both in different cases or sometimes even within the same opinion. At most, what I am pointing to involves very general trends with many exceptions.

The most acute issues about presidential power relate to foreign affairs and the use of military force. When individual rights are not involved, the Court has used various procedural and jurisdictional arguments to avoid getting in the middle of issues. Not since the Civil War has the Supreme Court ruled on the legality of a president's decision to use military force. Apart from upholding the legality of executive agreements, the Court has been wary of intervening in disputes about presidential power in foreign affairs. Although the modern Court has not been willing to review the president's decisions to use force, it has been less hands-offish when those decisions impinge on individual rights. The Court's interventions to protect the rights of Guantánamo detainees were a high mark in its oversight of presidential national security powers. Or, from another perspective, it was a judicial low point, gratuitously interfering with core national security decisions that only the president should make.

As with any other institution, the history of the presidency is a rich tapestry. The past is surely a prelude to the future. Yet, to quote an old saying, "Prediction is difficult, especially when it's about the future." I always thought this came from someone like Yogi Berra, but it is generally attributed to the famous physicist Niels Bohr. Taking a look at the broad sweep and at current trends, we may at least get some hints about the future.

What Does the Future Hold?

In the years since George Washington first took the oath of office, the realities of presidential power have changed dramatically. We have gone from a tiny government with a minuscule military to a gigantic federal government with the world's most powerful military. The president's staff has grown into a huge bureaucracy of its own, which sits astride the immense bureaucracy of cabinet officers and public servants. Perhaps originalists are right that the constitutional rules were set in stone before Washington even swore that oath, but the effective scope of the president's powers has changed dramatically.

The biggest change in the modern presidency may be the president's connection with the public. George Washington would no more have addressed a mass partisan rally than walked down the street naked; each would be inconsistent with his sense of decorum and personal dignity. Even in Lincoln's time, it was considered completely inappropriate for a presidential candidate to actively campaign. For much of our history, the State of the Union address was sent to Congress in writing.

The transformation began with Teddy Roosevelt at the start of the twentieth century. He actively worked to rally public opinion and held informal conferences with reporters while he was shaving. Woodrow Wilson held the first formal press conference in 1913. Another major leap took place under Franklin Roosevelt, who used the new medium of radio to talk directly to the public in his famous "fireside chats." Television came along a few years later, followed by social media. Technologies have changed, but the goal is the same: to forge a direct link between the president and the public. At the same time, the process of nominating and electing presidents has become more and more open to the public.

The upshot is that presidents can now present themselves as the voice of the public. It is a commonplace that the president, alone of all public officials, represents the American people. To defy the president is not simply to defy one powerful official, it is to defy "We the People." Congress, in contrast, is seen as representing parochial local interests. This powerful mystique has undoubtedly contributed to the growth of presidential power. Especially during the mid-twentieth century, presidents may well have represented the views of the average American voter.

Changes in American politics have undermined this narrative. The electorate is deeply polarized, making it harder to imagine the president as embodying the views of the voters as a whole. We have had more than one recent president who did not win the popular vote, which weakens the claim to speak for the public as a whole. In the meantime, congressional elections are now much more national in character. Senate Majority Leader Mitch McConnell may have represented the views of the Republican Party as much as Donald Trump has. Thus, presidents have lost some of their claim to represent the nation, and Congress has gained some. There is no direct link between this change in the popular view of the presidency and any specific legal doctrine. But it is not hard to imagine that judges may have been influenced to frame the issues before them a little differently because of these changes in American politics.

The composition of the Court will also change in ways that are hard to predict. Originalism currently seems to be close to the official philosophy for political conservatives, who control the Republican Party. Thus, future Republican successes at the polls are likely to result in growing reliance on originalism by the Supreme Court. Liberals have tended to react to originalism in two ways: either they co-opt it by finding historical support for their own views or they reject it in favor of a living Constitution. Or, as in the recent decisions involving the Trump subpoenas, originalism could mostly serve as a frame on which to hang pragmatic arguments about interbranch conflicts. Depending on future appointments to the Supreme Court, any or all of these approaches could dominate.

At present, conservatives have largely identified themselves with the unitary executive theory. But even among conservative originalists, there are considerable disputes about presidential power. There are different ways of interpreting the historical record, and different originalists may find themselves drawing different conclusions. In particular, there are serious divisions about the scope of presidential power in foreign affairs and military initiatives, as well as disagreements about other matters such as presidential immunity.

Larger political trends may also matter. In an era of political polarization and divided government, the stakes in disputes over presidential power are especially high. The stakes may seem lower if polarization eases or if we enter a long period of united government, with Congress and the White House controlled by the same party. The world may also look different if Congress's current tendency to deadlock comes to an end and it becomes more active and able to take on big issues.

Other trends may also matter. A strong presidency may seem more necessary if the country is faced with serious external threats.

On the other hand, we have recently seen how other democracies have been threatened by the rise of autocratic chief executives. If that trend continues, the courts may become more sensitive to the risks of reinforcing presidential autonomy.

I do not mean to imply that judicial decisions are just a reflection of larger political and societal trends. The *Steel Seizure* case itself is proof that judges' commitments to constitutional principle can override their political orientations. Yet it would be foolish to deny what everyone knows: judicial decisions do not take place in a vacuum. Judges' backgrounds and worldviews determine how they frame issues, and their decisions inevitably are influenced by changes in society. No one would quarrel over judicial appointments if we all believed otherwise.

In the end, the safest prediction is that the Court will continue, as it has in the past, to avoid taking a fixed position in favor of either presidentialism or the balanced government approach. Complete theoretical coherence is hard enough for a scholar to attain but far more difficult for a multimember body continually faced with changing circumstances. Presidentialism may triumph in terms of the president's control of the bureaucracy, but the balanced government model will probably continue to remain strong in other areas. So long as most of the justices are committed to a belief in following precedent, the pace of change will also remain relatively gradual.

A Final Comment

If I had a grand theory of all the issues I have covered, I would have written a different book. My own legal philosophy is more pragmatic and eclectic, incorporating the presidency's history, judicial precedents, practical necessities, and constitutional principle. But it has not been my purpose to persuade you of that philosophy either. Nor have I wanted to persuade you to adopt or reject originalism, or to read the vesting clause as either a rhetorical flourish or a sweeping grant of authority. While my own views have undoubtedly colored the discussion, I have mostly wanted to provide a basis for thinking critically about the issues.

If there is one thing I would hope you would take away from reading this book, it is a simple lesson. The lesson is easy to grasp intellectually but hard to implement. It is simply this: the same rules must apply to the presidents we love and the presidents we hate. In the heat of political debate, it is easy to lose track of this vital principle. But we need to embrace it as fully as we can if we are to have any hope of living under a government of laws rather than rulers.

Afterword

After revising the manuscript for publication, I thought I was done except for proofreading and indexing. Events forced me to reconsider. On January 6, a mob seized the US Capitol, threatening the lives of the vice president and members of Congress. President Donald Trump was impeached on charges of inciting the mob and failing to take steps to end the mob's occupation of the Capitol. Those events raised issues that were too important to ignore in a book about presidential power and too significant to squeeze into an existing chapter.

The Election and the Assault on the Capitol

The 2020 election took place in the middle of the COVID-19 pandemic. To avoid risks posed by large gatherings of voters on election day, many states liberalized their voting procedures by expanding early voting opportunities and the use of absentee voting.

As expected, Democrats made far more use of the newly expanded access to absentee ballots. Ballots cast in person, especially on election day, tilted Republican, but political observers knew that the later counting of absentee ballots would cause a shift. Less sophisticated observers, however, may have been surprised that what seemed like strong Republican margins were mysteriously disappearing as more votes were counted. In the end, Joseph Biden carried enough swing states to provide a comfortable margin of victory in the electoral college. Like Trump's 2016 victory, Biden's electoral college victory in 2020 rested on relatively slim margins in those key states.

Trump vocally maintained that the results of the election were fraudulent. While the polls were still open, he tweeted, "We are up BIG, but they are trying to STEAL the Election." The night after the polls closed, he said, "This is a fraud on the American public. This is an embarrassment to our country." Two days later, he tweeted, ""STOP THE FRAUD!" Just before Thanksgiving, he proclaimed at a news conference, "This was an election that we won easily. . . . This election was rigged, and we can't let that happen." The drumbeat of fraud claims by Trump and his allies continued until the electoral votes were finally counted. Even later, Trump's lawyers would not concede the legitimacy of the election results during his impeachment trial.

After the election, President Trump and his allies launched a swarm of lawsuits to set aside the vote counts in swing states. The suits demanded recounts or sought to set aside the popular vote entirely, either in certain cities or statewide. The primary legal claims were fraud and violations of state statutes regulating elections. Some lawsuits claimed that any deviation by election officials from a state's election statutes was unconstitutional. They argued that such deviations violated Article II's requirement that a state's electoral college representatives be chosen "in such Manner as the Legislature thereof may direct."

The lawsuits were remarkably unsuccessful. Of the more than sixty cases filed by the Trump side, only one earned even a partial victory. Even that partial victory had little significance, since it did not affect the outcome in Pennsylvania, the state in question. Many claims were dismissed for lack of standing, for belatedly raising issues that should have been raised before the election, for misinterpreting state law, or for misrepresenting the procedures the state had actually implemented. In a Philadelphia case, lawyers claimed observers were excluded when votes were counted, only to have to admit that some observers were actually allowed in the room. Because of haste in filing the lawsuits, there were blatant errors, such as initially filing one case in the wrong court entirely. In another case, lawyers had apparently assumed that "MI" stood for Minnesota and used Minnesota data to challenge Michigan election results. Even after states certified their results, lawsuits continued in an effort to set aside the electoral votes in key states, also without success.

Judges who considered claims of fraud or misconduct by election officials uniformly rebuffed them. One federal district judge remarked on the failure of the Trump campaign to justify disenfranchising such a huge number of voters. "One might expect," he wrote, "that when seeking such a startling outcome, a plaintiff would come formidably armed with compelling legal arguments and factual proof of rampant corruption." Quite the contrary, "this Court has been presented with strained legal arguments without merit and speculative accusations, unpled in the operative complaint and unsupported by evidence."

There were other reasons to doubt the fraud claims. Attorney General William Barr directed US attorneys in the relevant jurisdictions to investigate possible vote fraud. After they reported back to him, he informed Trump that there was no evidence of fraud on a scale that could affect the election results. The head of the Department of Homeland Security's Cybersecurity and Infrastructure Security Agency insisted that there had been no tampering with the election. Barr unexpectedly resigned under attack from Trump; Trump fired the cybersecurity expert.

Two of the states in play, Arizona and Georgia, were under Republican control. Their officials staunchly defended the validity of their vote counts. Georgia reaffirmed its results after two separate recounts. Trump had a lengthy phone call with Georgia's Republican secretary of state. He asked the secretary of state to find enough votes to tip the result in the state and hinted that the secretary might face criminal prosecution for failure to do so. The secretary of state held firm and released a tape of the conversation to counter Trump's account. Trump also ran into resistance from Republican legislative leaders in Michigan, whom he had brought to the White House in an effort to persuade them to overturn the state's election results.

Trump repeatedly called on followers to rally in Washington on January 6 when the electoral votes were to be counted by Congress. On December 19, for instance, he tweeted, "Big protest in D.C. on January 6th. Be there, will be wild!" Two of those most vocally echoing his calls for action were Roger Stone and Michael Flynn, political supporters he had recently pardoned for committing felonies.

The "Save America" rally was held on January 6 about a quarter of a mile from the US Capitol. The climax was an hour-long speech by Trump. Much of the speech was given over to a lengthy recitation of allegations of fraud. Trump warned the crowd, "You'll never take back our country with weakness." The speech was filled with exhortations to "fight." Trump told the crowd near the end of the speech, "We fight like hell, and if you don't fight like hell, you're not going to have a country anymore. . . . So we are going to walk down Pennsylvania Avenue— I love Pennsylvania Avenue—and we are going to the Capitol."

Unrest broke out at the Capitol, where proceedings to count the electoral votes were beginning. By 1:30 p.m., Capitol police had ordered the evacuation of nearby congressional office buildings. Within forty minutes, rioters had broken through police lines and scaled the Capitol's walls. Vice President Mike Pence quickly left the Senate, where he had been presiding over the electoral vote count.

Trump chose to attack Pence at almost exactly the same time. He tweeted, "Mike Pence didn't have the courage to do what should have been done to protect our Country and our Constitution, giving States a chance to certify a corrected set of facts, not the fraudulent or inaccurate ones which they were asked to previously certify. USA demands the truth!" This was a reference to a far-fetched theory that in his ceremonial role as presiding officer Pence could overturn state certifications of their electoral votes.

A few minutes later, Trump tweeted again, saying, "Please support our Capitol Police and Law Enforcement. They are truly on the side of our Country. Stay peaceful!" He did not, however, ask the rioters to stand down or leave the building.

Events continued to escalate, with armed rioters nearly catching up with members of Congress who were being taken to safer locations. Over an hour after the rioters entered the Capitol, Trump tweeted again: "I am asking for everyone at the U.S. Capitol to remain peaceful. No violence! Remember, WE are the Party of Law & Order—respect the Law and our great men and women in Blue. Thank you!"

The congressional leadership was evacuated from the building in the late afternoon, hours after the riot began. A few minutes later, Trump released a video in which he expressed sympathy with the rioters: "I know your pain. I know you're hurt. We had an election that was stolen from us. It was a landslide election and everyone knows it, especially the other side." Nevertheless, he told them they had to "go home now." "We love you, you're very special. . . . I know how you feel. But go home and go home in peace." This was the first time Trump had told the rioters to leave.

At 8:00 p.m., Congress reconvened and continued the count of electoral votes, declaring Joseph Biden and Kamala Harris the victors. Apart from the disruption to a critical congressional proceeding, the riot had resulted in five deaths and destruction and damage to congressional offices and public spaces.

The Impeachment and the Constitution

A week after the riot, the House voted to impeach Trump. The Democrats voting for impeachment were joined by ten Republicans, including the third-ranking Republican, Rep. Liz Cheney.

The House adopted a single article of impeachment. It charged that Trump repeatedly made false claims of election fraud; attempted "to subvert and obstruct the certification of the results of the 2020 Presidential election," including his effort to pressure Georgia's secretary of state; and finally "willfully made statements that, in context, encouraged—and foreseeably resulted in" the assault on the Capitol. The House alleged that these actions violated the presidential duty to take care that the laws be faithfully executed and his oath to preserve, protect, and defend the Constitution.

Senate Majority Leader Mitch McConnell indicated that there would be insufficient time to conduct a Senate trial in the week remaining before Trump's term ended, at noon on January 20. After a delay, due in part to discussions between Democrats and McConnell over the process, House Speaker Nancy Pelosi sent the article of impeachment to the Senate on January 25.

On January 26, the Senate voted 56–44 that it had jurisdiction to proceed with the trial even though Trump's term had expired. The Democrats were joined on this vote by six Republican senators. On February 13, the Senate voted on Trump's guilt. The Democrats were joined by seven Republicans, falling short of the two-thirds majority needed for a conviction.

This result, however, was far less than a complete vindication for Trump. Many Republican senators argued that the Senate lost jurisdiction after Trump left office. Mitch McConnell, Republican leader in the Senate, explained his vote on that basis but proceeded to excoriate Trump's role in the riot. He said that the rioters had acted "because they had been fed wild falsehoods by the most powerful man on Earth—because he was angry he'd lost an election." Once the assault took place, McConnell said, it was obvious that only President Trump could end it, but he refused to do so even though "former aides publicly begged him to do so" and "loyal allies frantically called the Administration." In short, according to McConnell, "there is no question that President Trump is practically and morally responsible for provoking the events of that day."

The Trump defense team raised two noteworthy constitutional arguments. The first was that the Senate only had jurisdiction over current officeholders. The argument is supported by language in Article II relating to impeachment, which states that the president and other civil officers shall be removed from office if convicted by the Senate. Language in Article I limits the penalties for impeachment to removal from office and disqualification from holding future office. These two constitutional provisions arguably imply that the targets of impeachment are sitting government officers and that the main purpose is removal.

The text of the Constitution, however, is somewhat ambiguous. The constitutional language cited by Trump's lawyers is suggestive, but it does not expressly speak to the situation of former officials who have committed high crimes and misdemeanors. Moreover, language in Article I governing the procedures for impeachment speak of defendants as "persons" without referring to whether a defendant is currently a government officer.

When the Constitution was adopted, the term "impeachment" clearly swept beyond current officeholders. Some state constitutions did not even allow impeachment until after an official had left office. Moreover, the debates at the Constitutional Convention show that the delegates were well aware of the contemporaneous impeachment trial of Warren Hastings in England. That proceeding took place well after he left office.

Precedents involving federal former officeholders also exist. Soon after the Constitution went into effect, the House impeached a senator. The Senate expelled the senator and then proceeded with an impeachment trial, before finally concluding that members of the Senate were not "civil officers" subject to impeachment. In the 1876 impeachment of Secretary of War William Belknap for bribery, the House and the Senate both concluded after thorough deliberation that he was not immune from impeachment after leaving office.

There are also practical arguments for proceeding with impeachment and trial even after an official has left office. If the Senate's jurisdiction ended when an official left office, the official could resign as soon as a verdict of conviction seemed likely—even the second before the last senator voted—and thereby avoid the risk of being disqualified by the Senate from holding further office. There is another, more important problem. Given that impeachment and conviction take time, an outgoing president would have practical immunity from impeachment for postelection misconduct such as sabotaging the transfer of power to a validly elected successor. It is true that some types of misconduct might still be subject to criminal prosecution, but abuses of power can occur and gravely injure the nation without violating any specific criminal statute.

Thus history and practical considerations support the power to impeach and remove former officials so as to expose their misconduct and disqualify them from future office. The best argument on the other side is the potential for abusing this power. It is not hard to imagine misuse of impeachment by the House to score political points. The two-thirds requirement for Senate conviction, however, provides a powerful safeguard against abuse.

An appealing intermediate position is that only a sitting official can be impeached by the House but that Senate proceedings can continue even after the official has left office. The rationale would largely be a practical one, based on the "January" problem and the need to prevent defendants from short-circuiting the process. Independent of removal from any current office, disqualification from holding future office furnishes an important remedy for grave misconduct by an officeholder.

Trump's lawyers offered another constitutional defense based on the First Amendment. The Supreme Court has narrowly defined "incitement." The First Amendment requires proof that speech is "directed to inciting or producing imminent lawless action and is likely to incite or produce such action." Some lower courts interpret the Court's language to require that a speaker explicitly call for violence. Trump's words could be interpreted to call only for peaceful protest. Other courts allow a broader look at the speaker's intentions and the surrounding context. Under that approach, it's arguable whether Trump crossed the line into incitement. Trump's lawyers contended that he did not intend to incite violence and did not actually cause the violence to occur. Others might disagree.

Even assuming that the First Amendment would protect a private individual who gave the same speech, Trump was not necessarily immune from impeachment. The Supreme Court has recognized that governments have a special interest in controlling the speech of their employees even when employees are "off the clock." The test is whether the speaker posed a significant risk of disrupting the government's functioning. Trump's speech clearly met the test.

Trump's lawyers argued, however, that Trump's speech as a private citizen was entitled to greater constitutional protection than that of other government officials. They relied on two Supreme Court rulings from the Civil Rights era involving speech by elected officials. In a 1962 case, a Georgia sheriff had accused a grand jury investigation into black voting of being racist. He was held to be in contempt of court by the judge overseeing the investigation. The Court said that the sheriff's statements were unlikely to interfere with the investigation or the performance of his duties. In upholding his First Amendment claim, the Court said that "the role that elected officials play in our society makes it all the more imperative that they be allowed freely to express themselves on matters of current public importance."

In another case from Georgia decided three years later, the Court took a similar position. The Georgia state senate had refused to seat a black civil rights advocate who had expressed support for men who resisted the draft during the Vietnam War. The Supreme Court held that his statements were constitutionally protected. According to the Court, "Legislators have an obligation to take positions on controversial political questions so that their constituents can be fully informed by them and . . . so they may be represented in governmental debates by the person they have elected to represent them."

These decisions do contain some good language for Trump, but it seems dangerous to extrapolate them to such a different situation. In neither Supreme Court case was there evidence that the speech in question actually caused a disruption to the functioning of the government. The disruption was much clearer in Trump's case, and it posed a direct threat to the safety of one branch of government and to the functioning of the democratic process.

Moreover, the sheriff and state legislator were both speaking outside the context of their official functions. A sheriff or a state legislator has a relatively defined official role. For a president, the line between public and private conduct is harder to draw. If the president says in his "private" capacity or in a tweet that tariffs should be raised, or a foreign country should be sanctioned, or that an election has been stolen, the effect is exactly the same as if he said the same thing in a more official setting like a White House press conference or a speech to Congress.

The conduct described in the article of impeachment cannot be easily separated from Trump's role as president. His inflammatory tweets came from an account that he also used for official pronouncements like firing subordinates. Certainly, the subject of Trump's speech—massive illegal conduct during a federal election—related to his official responsibilities. The president, unlike a legislator or a private citizen, also has the ability to silence government officials who might contradict his statements, as Trump did more than once.

More important, the First Amendment argument ignores the unique nature of the presidency, which the Supreme Court has cited as the basis for treating the president quite differently from other officials. Presidential misconduct poses a unique threat to the national interest, requiring greater precautions.

Even if Trump's pre-riot speech were discounted as a basis for impeachment, the impeachment resolution contained other important charges. Those charges covered Trump's efforts to pressure the Georgia secretary of state by referring ominously to possible criminal charges and his refusal to intervene promptly once the threat to the Capitol became clear. A reference to possible criminal charges means something different coming from the person who supervises all federal law enforcement rather than from an ordinary citizen. Even more clearly, failure to intervene to protect Congress implicated the president's duty to "take care that the laws be faithfully executed."

Broader Implications

So far in US history, the House has voted four times to impeach a president, none of which resulted in conviction in the Senate. A fifth president (Nixon) resigned rather than face a formal vote and Senate trial. Even an unsuccessful impeachment is damaging to a president's reputation and disruptive of other presidential plans. It would be a mistake to write off impeachment altogether as a remedy for abuse of power as a deterrent, but its limitations are also clear.

Trump's efforts to overturn the 2020 election results were ultimately blocked by his own party: resistance from his attorney general; rejection by Republican as well as Democratic judges of unfounded legal claims; the refusal of Republican legislators and election officials to heed his pleas for assistance; the refusal of a 6–3 Republican Supreme Court to intervene; and finally the refusals of Vice President Pence and a critical block of congressional Republicans to throw out electoral votes. The ability of these Republicans to resist presidential pressure is partly a tribute to personal integrity and partly a tribute to the system of separation of powers and federalism that allowed most of them to act independently.

This book has explored the powers that are rightfully given to the president, as well as the checks and balances on the president. The importance of those structural protections should not be overlooked. Ultimately, however, the onus is on us, We the People, to elect state officials, members of Congress, and presidents who are worthy of our trust.

Sources and Further Reading

For the benefit of those wanting to explore this topic further and for scholars who want to check my sources, some of the main sources that I used are given below. This is not by any means meant to be a comprehensive survey of the many excellent scholarly works on the subject. My focus here is on works that are relatively recent and most likely to be accessible. These days, most law reviews have public access to articles on their websites.

Introduction

Forrest McDonald's book, *The American Presidency: An Intellectual History* (1994), is a good introduction to the evolution of the presidency and debates over presidential power. Steven Calibresi and Christopher Yoo trace the history of presidential governance practices in *The Unitary Executive. Presidential Power from Washington to Bush* (2008); their perspective is indicated by the title. Richard Neustadt, *Presidential Power and the Modern Presidents: The Politics of Leadership from Roosevelt to Reagan* (1991), is an updated version of Neustadt's 1960s classic. In terms of particular presidents, there is an excellent series of books from the University of Kansas Press covering individual presidencies. Good biographies of individual presidents often cover some of the same material.

Chapter 1: Creating the Presidency

At present, the definitive history of the time between the Declaration of Independence and the Constitution seems to be Gordon S. Wood's *The Creation of the American Republic, 1776–1787* (1998).

Equally useful on the post-constitutional period is Gordon S. Wood's *Empire of Liberty: A History of the Early Republic, 1789–1815* (2009). David Currie provides a lively, if opinionated, guide to Congress's struggles to interpret the Constitution in *The Constitution and the Courts: The Federalist Period, 1789–1801* (1997). For a more detailed description of the debates at the Constitutional Convention and during ratification, along with excerpts from Madison's notes and other documents, see Daniel A. Farber and Suzanna Sherry, *A History of the American Constitution*, 3rd ed. (2013), 115–63. Jack Rakove's *Original Meanings: Politics and Ideas in the Making of the Constitution* (1996) provides a concise and perceptive analysis of the convention's proceedings. The full text of the Federalist Papers can be found on the congress.gov website. For an extensive analysis of the Hamilton-Madison dispute over the Neutrality Proclamation, see Martin S. Flaherty, "The Story of the Neutrality Controversy: Struggling over Presidential Power Outside the Courts," in *Presidential Power Stories*, ed. Christopher H. Schroeder and Curtis A. Bradley (2009), 21–52. Finally, on the Washington letter accompanying the Constitution, see my article, "The Constitution's Forgotten Cover Letter: An Essay on the New Federalism and the Original Understanding," 94 *Michigan Law Review* 614 (1995). I continue to think that legal scholars have given too little attention to this document as a public statement of the Framers' collective views.

Chapter 2: Clashing Visions of Presidential Power

The scholarship on originalism is voluminous. For arguments in favor of originalism, see Antonin Scalia and Bryan A. Garner, *Reading Law: The Interpretation of Legal Texts* (2012); Robert H. Bork, *The Tempting of America: The Political Seduction of Law* (1990). Some recent elaborations on originalist theory are offered in Randy E. Barnett and Evan D. Bernick, "The Letter and the Spirit: A Unified Theory of Originalism," 107 *Georgetown Law Journal* 1 (2018); William Baude and Stephen E. Sachs, "Grounding Originalism," 113 *Northwestern University Law Review* 1455 (2019). In his book *Living Originalism* (2011), Jack Balkin offers a rare liberal approach to originalism, though his theory is not terribly far removed from the "living Constitution" approach in some ways. On the critical side, see Frank B. Cross, *The Failed Promise of Originalism* (2013); David A. Strauss, The *Living Constitution* (2010); Mitchell Berman, "Originalism Is Bunk," 84 *NYU Law Review* 1 (2009).

The citations for the cases mentioned in this chapter are Youngstown Steel & Tube Co. v. Sawyer (the *Steel Seizure* case), 343 U.S. 579 (1952); Dames & Moore v. Regan, 453 U.S. (1981). Fascinating background on these cases can be found in two contributions to Christopher H. Schroeder and Curtis A. Bradley, eds., *Presidential Power Stories* (2009): Patricia L. Bellia's "The Story of the Steel Seizure Case" and Harold H. Bruff's "The Story of Dames & Moore: Resolution of an International Crisis by Executive Agreement."

Chapter 3: The President and Foreign Affairs

David P. Currie's *The Constitution in Congress: The Federalist Period, 1789–1801* (1997), details relevant foreign affairs debates in Congress. The vesting clause thesis is ably presented in Saikrishna Prakash, *Imperial from the Beginning: The Constitution of the Original Executive* (2015). The opposing side is argued in Martin Flaherty and Curtis Bradley, "Executive Power Essentialism and Foreign Affairs," 102 *Michigan Law Review* 545 (2004); and Jack N. Rakove, "Taking the Prerogative Out of the Presidency: An Originalist Perspective," 37 *Presidential Studies Quarterly* 85 (2007). On the historical practice regarding treaties, executive agreements, and joint executive-congressional agreements, see Oona A. Hathaway, "Treaties' End: The Past, Present, and Future of International Lawmaking in the United States," 117 *Yale Law Journal* 1236, 1250 (2008). Chapter 5 of Peter M. Shane and Harold D. Bruff, *Separation of Powers Law: Cases and Materials*, 3d ed. (2011), collects a great deal of relevant source material and commentary. Fascinating background on some of the key controversies and cases can be found in Martin Flaherty, "The Story of the Neutrality Controversy: Struggling over Presidential Power Outside the Courts," and H. Jefferson Powell, "The Story of Curtiss-Wright Export Corporation," both in Christopher Schroeder and Curtis A. Bradley, eds., *Presidential Power Stories* (2009).

The citations for the cases discussed in this chapter are United States v. Curtiss-Wright Export Corporation, 299 U.S. 304 (1936); Zivotovsky v. Kerry (*Zivotovsky II*) (the passport case involving the status of Jerusalem); United States v. Belmont, 301 U.S. 324 (1937) (the first of the two cases involving the executive agreement with the Soviet Union); United States v. Pink, 315 U.S. 203 (1942) (the second case); Goldwater v. Carter, 444 U.S. 996 (1979) (the treaty termination case involving Taiwan); Medellín v. Texas, 552 U.S. 491 (2008) (presidential effort to enforce a treaty against state governments).

Chapter 4: Taking the Country to War

The war power has attracted enormous attention from scholars and statesmen alike. On the side of congressional power, two classics are Arthur M. Schlesinger

Jr., *The Imperial Presidency* (1973); and John Hart Ely, *War and Responsibility: Constitutional Lessons of Vietnam and Its Aftermath* (1995). Also important are Louis Fisher, *Presidential War Power,* 3rd ed. (2013); and William Treanor, "Fame, the Founding, and the Power to Declare War," 82 *Cornell Law Review* 771 (1997). John Yoo has become perhaps the most visible academic proponent of the president's power to initiate and control the use of force, subject only to Congress's ability to cut off funding for a war. For his views, see *War by Other Means: An Insider's Account of the War on Terror* (2006); and "Clio at War: the Misuse of History in the War Powers Debate," 70 *University of Colorado Law Review* 1169 (1999). A more balanced approach from a former government lawyer is David J. Barron, *Waging War: The Clash between Presidents and Congress, 1776 to ISIS* (2016). Also calling for shared decision making is Harold Koh, *The National Security Constitution: Sharing Power after the Iran Contra Affair* (1990) (Koh was later a legal adviser in the Obama administration). I discuss Lincoln's use of executive power and related issues such as the use of military tribunals in *Lincoln's Constitution* (2003).

The citation for the War Powers Act is P.L. 93-148, codified at 50 U.S.C. § 1541 et. seq. The cases discussed in this chapter are the *Prize* cases, 67 U.S. 635 (1863); Talbor v. Seeman, 5 U.S. (1 Cranch) 1 (1801); and Little v. Barreme, 6 U.S. (2 Cranch) 170 (1804).

Chapter 5: The Bureaucrat in Chief

The academic literature has focused on the removal power rather than the nuances of the appointments clause. On appointments issues, see Curtis A. Bradley and Neil S. Siegel, "After Recess: Historical Practice, Textual Ambiguity, and Constitutional Adverse Possession," 2014 *Supreme Court Review* 1 (2015). On the removal power, see Lawrence Lessig and Cass R. Sunstein, "The President and the Administration," 94 *Columbia Law Review* 1 (1994); Kevin M. Stack, "The Story of *Morrison v. Olson:* The Independent Counsel and Independent Agencies in Watergate's Wake," in *Presidential Power Stories,* ed. Christopher Schroeder and Curtis Bradley (2009); Martin S. Flaherty, "The Most Dangerous Branch," 105 *Yale Law Journal* 1725 (1996); Saikrishna Prakash, "The Story of *Myers* and Its Wayward Successors: Going Postal on the Removal Power," in Schroeder and Bradley, *Presidential Power Stories.* David Currie, *The Constitution in Congress: The Federalist Period,* 1789–1801 (1997), thoroughly explores congressional deliberations about the executive branch in the founding era. Peter Strauss presents the anti-unitarian case in "Overseer, or 'The Decider'? The President in Administrative Law," 75 *George Washington Law Review* 696 (2007).

Cases discussed in this chapter include Edmond v. United States, 520 U.S. 651 (1997); Morrison v. Olson, 487 U.S. 654 (1988) (constitutionality of the independent counsel law); Free Enterprise Foundation v. Public Company Accounting Oversight Board (PCAOB), 561 U.S. 477 (2020) (appointments/removal powers); Lucia v. Securities & Exchange Commission, 138 S. Ct. 2044 (2018) (appointments power); Buckley v. Valeo, 424 U.S. 1 (1976) (appointments); NLRB v. Noel Canning, 134 S. Ct. 2550 (2014) (recess appointments); Myers v. United States, 272 U.S. 52 (1926) (removal power); Humphrey's Executor v. United States, 295 U.S. 602 (1935) (independent agencies).

Chapter 6: The Domestic Policy Czar

For analysis of the constitutional issues related to DACA and DAPA, see Louis W. Fisher, "Executive Enforcement Discretion and the Separation of Powers: A Case Study on the Constitutionality of DACA and DAPA," 120 *West Virginia Law Review* 131 (2017); Patricia Bellia, "Faithful Execution and Enforcement Discretion," 164 *University of Pennsylvania Law Review* 1753 (2016). Andrew Kent, Ethan Leib, and Jed Shugerman, "Faithful Execution and Article II," 132 *Harvard Law Review* 2111 (2019), takes an in-depth look at the history of the "faithful execution" duty. On the nondelegation debate, much of the writing in favor of reviving the doctrine comes from libertarians and conservatives opposed to government regulation, such as Gary Lawson, "Delegation and Original Meaning," 88 *Virginia Law Review* 327 (2002); Neomi Rao, "Administrative Collusion: How Delegation Diminishes the Collective Congress," 90 *NYU Law Review* 1463 (2015). Arguing that efforts to revive the doctrine lack historical roots are Julian Mortensen and Nicholas Bagley, "Delegation at the Founding" (forthcoming but available at ssrn.com); Nicholas R. Parrillo, "A Critical Assessment of the Originalist Case against Administrative Regulatory Power: New Evidence from the Federal Tax on Private Real Estate in the 1790," 130 *Yale Law Journal* 1288 (2021); Keith Whittington and Jason Juliano, "The Myth of the Nondelegation Doctrine," 165 *University of Pennsylvania Law Review* 379 (2017).

The cases cited in this chapter include United States v. MacDaniel, 32 U.S. 1 (1833) (navy employee); In re Nagle, 135 U.S. 1 (1890) (protection of Supreme Court justice); In re Debs, 158 U.S. 564 (1805) (railroad strike); United States v. Midwest Oil, 236 U.S. 459 (1915) (oil on public lands); Heckler v. Chaney, 470 U.S. 821 (1985) (enforcement discretion); Gundy v. United States, 139 S. Ct. 2116 (2019) (delegation doctrine); Paul v. United States, 140 S. Ct. 342 (2019) (Kavanaugh, J., concurring in denial of certiotrari); Whitman v. American Trucking Associations,

Inc., 531 U.S. 457 (2001) (intelligible principle test); Panama Refining Co. v. Ryan, 293 U.S. 388 (1935) (holding a statute to be an unconstitutional delegation); A.L.A. Schechter Poultry Corp. v. United States, 295 U.S. 495 (1935) (same as above). Jerry Mashaw, *Creating the Administrative Constitution: The Lost One Hundred Years of American Administrative Law* (2012), provides a fascinating look at how power was delegated and exercised before the Civil War.

Chapter 7: Presidential Power versus Individual Rights

Mark E. Neely Jr., *The Fate of Liberty: Abraham Lincoln and Civil Liberties* (1991); Martin S. Lederman, "Of Spies, Saboteurs, and Enemy Accomplices: History's Lessons for the Constitutionality of Wartime Military Tribunals," 105 *Georgetown Law Journal* 1529 (2017); John Yoo, "FDR, Civil Liberties, and the War on Terror," in *Security v. Liberty: Conflicts between Civil Liberties and National Security in American History,* ed. Daniel Farber (2008). Amanda Tyler's *Habeas Corpus in Wartime from the Tower of London to Guantanamo Bay* (2017) provides an examination of the history.

Cases discussed in this chapter include Ex Parte Milligan, 71 U.S. 2 (1866) (Civil War military tribunals); Ex parte Quirin, 317 U.S. 1 (1942) (German saboteurs); Korematsu v. United States, 323 U.S. 214 (1944) (Japanese evacuation); Ex parte Endo, 323 U.S. 283 (1944) (Japanese internment); Johnson v. Eisentrager, 339 U.S. 763 (1950) (post–World War II habeas); Hamdi v. Rumsfeld, 542 U.S. 507 (2004) (post-9/11 detention); Hamdan v. Rumsfeld, 548 U.S. 557 (2006) (post-9/11 hearing procedures); Boumediene v. Bush, 553 U.S. 723 (2008) (post-9/11 habeas power); Trump v. Hawaii, 138 S. Ct. 2392 (2018) (travel ban).

Chapter 8: The President and the Courts

Background on the Watergate tapes case can be found in Christopher H. Schroeder, "The Story of United States v. Nixon: The President and the Tapes," in Christopher H. Schroeder and Curtis A. Bradley, eds., *Presidential Power Stories* (2009). Saikrishna Prakash's book, *Imperial from the Beginning* (2015), ably presents the originalist case against presidential immunity and executive privilege. Burr's flirtation with treason is discussed in Gordon S. Wood, *Empire of Liberty: A History of the Early Republic, 1789–1815* (2009), though it naturally gets more attention from Burr's biographers.

The cases cited in this chapter include Luther v. Borden, 48 U.S. 1 (1849) (political question doctrine); Baker v. Carr, 369 U.S. 186 (1962) (political question doctrine); Zivotofsky v. Clinton, 566 U.S. 189 (2012) (the passport case); United States v. Nixon, 418 U.S. 683 (1974) (the Watergate tapes case); United States v. Burr, 25 F. Cas. 30, 37 (C.C.D. Va. 1807); Nixon v. Fitzgerald, 457 U.S. 731 (1982) (civil liability for personal acts); Clinton v. Jones, 520 U.S. 681 (1997) (civil liability for official acts).

Chapter 9: Congressional Checks and Balances

Heidi Kitrosser, *Reclaiming Accountability: Transparency, Executive Power, and the U.S. Constitution* (2015), thoroughly examines barriers to public accountability through congressional investigations and other disclosure mechanisms. Frank Bowman, *High Crimes and Misdemeanors: A History of Impeachment for the Age of Trump* (2019), provides excellent coverage of the history, although I do not always agree with his conclusions. Two brief but useful discussions are Cass R. Sunstein, "Impeaching the President," 147 *University of Pennsylvania Law Review* 279 (1998); Gary L. McDowell, "High Crimes and Misdemeanors: Recovering the Intentions of the Founders," 67 *George Washington Law Review* 626 (1999). There is also useful material in books relating to the Trump impeachment by leading scholars such as Neal Katyal, Michael Gerhardt, and Larry Tribe, but readers may find the earlier works more helpful simply because they are further away from today's political strife.

The cases discussed in this chapter include Comm. on Judiciary of United States House of Representatives v. McGahn, 968 F.3d 755 (D.C. Cir. 2020); Train v. City of New York, 420 U.S. 35 (1975) (presidential impoundment of funds); Immigration and Naturalization Service v. Chadha, 462 U.S. 919 (1983); Bowsher v. Synar, 478 U.S. 714 (1986); Metropolitan Washington Airports Authority v. Citizens for Abatement of Aircraft Noise, Inc., 501 U.S. 252 (1991); McGrain v. Daugherty, 273 U.S. 135, 161 (1927).

Chapter 10: Concluding Thoughts

The growing identification of the executive branch with the person of the president, and the attendant turn toward populism, has not escaped notice. Susan Hennessey and Benjamin Wittes, *Unmaking the Presidency: Donald Trump's War on the World's Most Powerful Office* (2020), has useful information that can be read apart from the book's discussion of Trump as what the authors view as the culmination of this trend.

Afterword

In addition to the materials on impeachment discussed in chapter 9, discussions of the constitutionality of impeaching past officers can be found in Congressional Research Service, "The Impeachment and Trial of a Former President" (January 15, 2021); Jonathan Turley, "Senate Trials and Factional Disputes: Impeachment as a Madisonian Device," 99 *Duke Law Journal* 1, 48–56 (1999); Harold J. Krent, "Can President Trump Be Impeached as Mr. Trump? Exploring the Temporal Dimension of Impeachments," 95 *Chicago-Kent Law Review* 537 (2021).

McConnell's statement after the impeachment trial can be found at CNN, "Read McConnell's Remarks on the Senate Floor Following Trump's Acquittal" (February 13, 2021) (available on CNN's website). The legal filings in the impeachment case, the evidentiary standards, and the debates have been assembled at www.govinfo.gov/collection/impeachment-related-publications.

The cases discussed in this chapter include Bond v. Floyd, 385 U.S. 116 (1966) (exclusion of a Georgia state legislator); Wood v. Georgia, 370 U.S. 375 (1962) (contempt citation against Georgia sheriff); Brandenburg v. Ohio, 395 U.S. 444 (1969) (defining incitement narrowly for First Amendment purposes); Donald J. Trump for President, Inc. v. Boockvar, No. 4:20-CV-02078, 2020 WL 6821992 (M.D. Pa. Nov. 21, 2020), aff'd sub nom. Donald J. Trump for President, Inc. v. Sec'y of Pennsylvania, 830 F. App'x 377 (3d Cir. 2020) (rejecting lawsuit challenging election results).

Index

Delegation doctrine. *See* Nondelegation doctrine.

Discriminatory presidential actions: based on race, 166–169; based on religion, 173–180

Deutsche Bank subpoena case, 208–211

Early state constitutions: on role of chief executive , 17–18, 20–21; legislative investigations, 207; on military powers of governor, 87–88

Election procedures for president, 9, 21, 24–25, 240–242

Emergency powers, 132–136, 159, 213. *See also* war powers.

Enforcement discretion, 149–154

English monarchy: compared to presidency, 29–30, 33, 36, 70, 73; prerogative powers, 23, 29–30, 59, 73; treaty power, 20–30; war powers, 30

Environmental policy, 109, 131, 136, 138–139, 141–142. *See also* Paris Agreement.

Executive agreements, 78–80

Executive-congressional agreements, 81–82

Executive orders, 129–130, 139

Executive privilege, 185–187, 190–192

Federal bureaucracy. *See* appointments power, nondelegation doctrine, removal power.

Federalist papers: on comparison with monarchy, 29–30; on need for energy and unity, 29, 52; on presidency generally, 28–31; on presidential impeachment, 221;

on removal power of president, 30; on treaty negotiation and Senate role, 39; on war powers, 90–91;

Foreign affairs powers: appointment and reception of ambassadors, 9, 24, 66–67, 69 ; as advocacy, 28; on impeachment, 221; on need for executive energy and unity, 29–30; negotiation of treaties, 12, 30–31, 39; executive and executive-congressional agreements, 59–60, 78–82; extra-constitutional powers, 67–68; judicial review, 82, 64–65, 183–185; revocation of treaties, 82; recognition power, 768–69, 78; treaty enforcement, 70–72. *See also,* vesting clause.

First Congress: "Decision of 1789," 118–119; debate over delegation issues, 147–148; deference to, 18–19; foreign affairs issues, 52–53; removal of officers, 118–119; subpoena issues, 193–194;

Freedom of speech, 161–162, 174–175, 247–248

German Saboteurs case, 164

Ginsburg, Ruth Bader, 177

Gundy v. United States, 143–146

Habeas corpus, 84, 157–159, 164–165

Hamdi v. Rumsfeld, 171–172, 177

Hamilton, Alexander: as Secretary of Treasury, 28; in Federalist Papers, 29–30, 90–91; on impeachment, 211; on need for strong presidency, 29–30; on Neutrality Proclamation, 35–36; 94; on removal power, 30, 116, 127; on vesting clause, 35–36;

on war power,90–91, 93; presidentialism of, 231
High crimes and misdemeanors, 10,
217–225 *See also* Impeachment.
Holmes, Oliver Wendell, 116, 118

Immigration policy, 78, 131, 152–154,
173–180, 213–215
Iranian Hostages case, 51, 59–60,
79–80
*Immigration & Naturalization Service
v. Chadha,* 213–217
Impeachment: and First Amendment,
247–248; constitutional text,
217–218; grounds for, 10; in
American colonies, 219; in English
history, 218–219; judicial review of,
224–225; procedure for, 217–218. *See
also* specific presidents.
Independent agencies, 49, 116, 122,
126
Iraq wars, 102–103

Japanese internment cases, 166–169
Jackson, Andrew, 53–97, 114, 157
Jackson, Robert, see *Steel Seizure* case,
Steel Seizure test.
Jefferson, Thomas, 11, 26, 34–37, 76,
95–96, 194–196
Johnson, Andrew, 117, 184, 222
Judicial review: deference to
President, 173; of agency ac-
tions,137–139, 181; of impeachment,
225; limitations on, 64–65, 69–65,
182–185, 225; political question
doctrine, 64, 182–185, 225
Jerusalem passport case, 6–70, 184

Kagan, Elena, 126, 144, 177
Kennedy, John, 101
Korean War, 55–58, 101

Lincoln, Abraham: accused of
dictatorship, 1; "all the laws but
one," 158; claim of necessity,
158–159; freedom of speech and the
press, 161, 174–175; habeas
suspension by, 156–160; military
trials, 160, 175; response to attack
on Fort Sumter, 57–58, 97–98, 132;
take care clause, 158–159
Locke, John, 23, 29, 51, 74
Luther v. Borden, 161

Madison, James: and Council of
Review, 52; as member of Congress,
34, 38, 119, 147–148; as President,
94, 97; at Constitutional Convention, 21, 35, 220; in Federalist Papers,
26, 31, 90; in ratification debates,
92–93; on Neutrality Proclamation,
37; views on delegation, 31, 147–148;
views on foreign affairs power, 37;
views on impeachment, 220; views
on presidential immunities, 197;
views on removal power, 53, 119–120
views on war power, 36, 38, 233,
88–90, 93–94, 97
Marshall, John, 195–196
Mason, George, 32, 89, 91–93, 119
Mazars subpoena case, 188–190
McGahn subpoena case, 211
Merryman case, 157–158
Mexican-American War, 97, 161
Military trials, 160, 163–165, 172
Militia Act, 132
Mississippi v. Johnson, 185
Montesquieu, Baron de, 23, 51
Morrison v. Olson: as restricted by later
cases, 122–123, 125–147; facts, 123,
124; holding on appointment
power, 113–114; holding on removal
power, 124–126

Unitary executive theory, 65, 116–125, 235. *See also* removal power, vesting clause.

United States v. Nixon, 185–187, 190–192

Vacancies Reform Act,113
Vallandigham controversy, 161–163
Vesting clause: debate regarding, 73–77; foreign affairs powers, 36, 93–94; military powers, 85–86; original understanding of, 36, 74–75; text, 8–9; theories of, 41–42
Vietnam War, *ix*, 2, 161–163, 185, 204–205
Veto power. 13, 23, 20, 30

War on Terror, *ix*, 72, 103–104, 168–173
War powers of president: constitutional text, 84; commander in chief clause, 84; debates at Constitutional Convention, 88–90; early practice, 86–87, 89–90, 94–96; Federalist Papers, 90–91; ratification debates, 91–92; state constitutions, 87–88; summary, 104–105; vesting clause, 85, 93–94. *See also* specific wars.
War Powers Resolution, 102–103, 105–106
Washington, George, 33–34,37, 76, 86–87, 193
Watergate scandal. *See* United States v. Nixon.
Watergate Tapes case. *See* United States v. Nixon.
Wilson, James, 197–198
Wilson, Woodrow, 100, 235
World War I, 100
World War II, 57, 161, 102, 164–165

Founded in 1893,
UNIVERSITY OF CALIFORNIA PRESS
publishes bold, progressive books and journals
on topics in the arts, humanities, social sciences,
and natural sciences—with a focus on social
justice issues—that inspire thought and action
among readers worldwide.

The UC PRESS FOUNDATION
raises funds to uphold the press's vital role
as an independent, nonprofit publisher, and
receives philanthropic support from a wide
range of individuals and institutions—and from
committed readers like you. To learn more, visit
ucpress.edu/supportus.